AFRICAN ISSUES

Series Editors Alex de Waal & Stephen Ellis

Fortress
Conservation
The Preservation of the
Mkomazi Game Reserve
Tanzania

DAN BROCKINGTON

Killing for
Conservation
Wildlife Policy
in Zimbabwe

ROSALEEN DUFFY

Asbestos
Blues
Labour, Capital, Physicians
& the State in South Africa

JOCK McCULLOCH

Angola
From Afro-Stalinism
to Petro-Diamond Capitalism

TONY HODGES

Mozambique
& the
Great Flood
of 2000

FRANCES CHRISTIE & JOSEPH HANLON

Congo-
Paris
Transnational
Traders on the Margins
of the Law

JANET MACGAFFEY & RÉMY BAZENGUISSA-GANGA

Africa
Works
Disorder
as Political Instrument

PATRICK CHABAL & JEAN-PASCAL DALOZ

The Criminalization
of the State
in Africa

JEAN-FRANÇOIS BAYART, STEPHEN ELLIS
& BEATRICE HIBOU

Famine
Crimes
Politics & the
Disaster Relief Industry
in Africa

ALEX DE WAAL

Above titles
Published in the United States & Canada
by Indiana University Press

Peace without Profit How the IMF
Blocks Rebuilding
in Mozambique

JOSEPH HANLON

The Lie of Land Challenging
Received Wisdom on the
African Environment

Edited by

MELISSA LEACH & ROBIN MEARNS

Fighting for the Rainforest War, Youth
& Resources in
Sierra Leone

PAUL RICHARDS

Above titles
Published in the United States & Canada
by Heinemann (N.H.)

AFRICAN ISSUES

Fortress Conservation The Preservation of the Mkomazi Game Reserve Tanzania

AFRICAN ISSUES

Fortress The Preservation of
Conservation the Mkomazi Game
DAN BROCKINGTON Reserve Tanzania

The International
African Institute

in association with

JAMES CURREY
Oxford

MKUKI NA NYOTA
Dar es Salaam

INDIANA UNIVERSITY PRESS
Bloomington & Indianapolis

The International
African Institute
in association with
James Currey
73 Botley Road
Oxford OX2 0BS

Indiana University Press
601 North Morton Street
Bloomington
Indiana 47404
(North America)

Mkuki Na Nyota
P.O. Box 4246
Dar es Salaam
Tanzania

British Library Cataloguing in Publication Data available

Brockington, Dan
  Fortress conservation : the preservation of the Mkomazi
  Game Reserve, Tanzania. – (African issues)
  1. Mkomazi Game Reserve (Tanzania)
  I. Title II. International African Institute
  639.9′5′0967822

ISBN 0-85255-417-6 (James Currey Paper)
ISBN 0-85255-418-4 (James Currey Cloth)

Library of Congress Cataloging-in-Publication Data

Brockington, Dan.
    Fortress conservation : the preservation of the Mkomazi Game Reserve,
Tanzania/Dan Brockington.
        p. cm. – (African issues)
    Includes bibliographical references (p.) and index.
    ISBN 0-253-34079-9 (cloth : alk. paper) – ISBN 0-253-21520-X (paper :
alk. paper) 1. Mkomazi Game Reserve (Tanzania) I. Title. II. Series.

    SK575.T3 B76 2002
    639.9′5′0967822–dc21   2001051529

Typeset by
Saxon Graphics Ltd, Derby
in 9/11 Melior with Optima display
Printed and bound in Great Britain by
Woolnough, Irthlingborough

CONTENTS

LIST OF TABLES

LIST OF MAPS, ILLUSTRATIONS, FIGURES & BOXES

ACKNOWLEDGEMENTS

The book is based on six years of research into the Mkomazi Game Reserve, in northern Tanzania. That is a short time. All mistakes are mine, but that which I understand, owes much to many people.

A post-doctoral research fellowship from the British Academy enabled me to write this book. The data were collected during research sponsored by the Department for International Development. I wish to thank the Royal Anthropological Institute's Emslie Horniman Fund; the Parkes Foundation; the Kathleen and Margery Elliot Trust; the Boise Fund; the Central Research Fund of London University and the Graduate School of University College London for supporting this research. I am also grateful for the help and cooperation of the Ministry of Tourism, Natural Resources and the Environment, especially the Department of Wildlife and the staff of Mkomazi Game Reserve; the Commission for Science and Technology of Tanzania; the Institute of Resource Assessment; the University of Dar es Salaam; the National Archives of Tanzania; the Tanga Regional Archives; the Public Records Office; Rhodes House, Oxford University; the Seeley History Library, Africa Studies Centre, University Library, Department of Geography and New Hall, of Cambridge University; the Colindale National Newspaper Library; the Royal Geographical Society and the Libraries of University College and the School of Oriental and African Studies, London University; and the Anthropology Department of University College London.

Many members of local government of districts, divisions, wards and villages in Tanzania extended their help, cooperation, welcome and warm hospitality. In particular I wish to thank the District Commissioners and District Executive Directors of Same, Lushoto, Mwanga and Muheza, especially Peter Kangwa, Col. Mahawa, Dr Mugoha, Mary Mwangisa, Mr Chewewe and Mr Mwinyimvua.

My special thanks are due to Paul Marenga; Miriam Zachariah; Issa Swai; Mr Mushi; Idris Kikula; Issa Shivji; Alan Rodgers; Nick McWilliam; Mike Packer; Charles Lane; David Anstey for his patience and hospitality; Richard Waller; Sara Randall; Phil Burnham; Barrie Sharpe; Leslie Aiello;

Dawn Hartley; Ellen Messenger Rogers; Beth Pratt; Sven Schade; Joel Freeling; Tim Kelsall; Paul Thwaite; Stuart Wardlaw; Christine Carpenter; Simon Grimble; Martin Walsh; Shane and Emma Doyle; Richard Nixon; Anne-Marie Harsam; an anonymous reviewer of the first manuscript; Dr and Rev. Kiel; Geir Sundet; Chris Conte; Kevin Brown; E.B. O'Malley; Glady Msumanje; Peter and Aafke Zoutewelle; Charles Gazigelle; Christopher and Victor Ndangoya; Bibi Mwanyika; Mneuria Njakuri; Omari Assumani; Masaine Keiya; Kopera Keiya; Daniel Destin; Anna Elee; Anna Abraham; Ramadhani Zuberi; Lekei Milakon; Matei Kairanga and Maziwa Kairanga and their families.

For some thoroughly enjoyable times, both writing and not writing theses, I thank Sian Sullivan, Allan Dangour, Dan Nettle, Pippa Trench, Amar Imandar, Emmanuel de Merode, Kate Hampshire, Tina Coast, Julius Kivelia, Jo Abbott, Solveig Buhl and Adam Biran. Ilfra, David, Charlotte and Geir, Stuart, Dave, Martin, Becky, Mike, Beth, Clare, Paul, Chris, Fiona, Penny, Paul, Andy, Brendon, Stephen and Katie put up with domestic disorders and were faithful correspondents, and the Strange Blue frisbee team taught me the best game in the world.

There are six people to whom I am particularly indebted. Kathy Homewood, my supervisor, has given time and energy far beyond the call of duty, and I am indebted to her for her sense of humour, ideas and guidance without which this work would not exist, and because of which these years have been so enjoyable; Hilda Kiwasila, for communicating some of her passion and understanding of her country; Lobulu Sakita, who worked with me around the Mkomazi Reserve, was tireless, tolerant and sensitive – I could not have worked with a better man; Bill Adams, for being both wise and anarchically radical in his advice; and Jim Igoe and Peter Rogers, who made no impression at all on my naivety but have made it more amusing.

I thank Alice, Grace, Sam and my parents, who have given more than I can record. Finally, I thank my wife, Tekla for her love, support, companionship and good humour. This book is dedicated to her with love and anticipation.

Parts of this book have appeared separately in various journals. My thanks to the publishers of *Azania* for letting me use material from my article 'Pastoralism on the margins', Volume 35, pages 1–19, in Chapter 3; *Africa*, for use of material from the piece jointly published with Kathy Homewood called 'Degradation debates and data deficiencies', Volume 71, pages 449–80, in Chapter 4; *Global Ecology and Biogeography*, for use of material from another piece jointly published with Kathy Homewood called 'Biodiversity, conservation and development', Volume 8, pages 301–13, also in Chapter 4; elements of Chapters 5 and 7 appeared in *Nomadic Peoples* (NS) 3: 74–96. Nick McWilliam generously provided the photographs.

DISCLAIMER

The Department for International Development (DFID) is the British Government department that supports programmes and projects to promote overseas development. It provides funding for economic and social research to inform development policy and practice. DFID funds supported this study and the preparation of the summary of findings. DFID distributes the report to bring the research to the attention of policy-makers and practitioners. However, the views and opinions expressed in the document do not reflect DFID's official policies or practices, but are those of the author alone.

Several caveats are required to explain the terms I use to talk about the people, places and Mkomazi Reserve that are the subject of this book. Naming and identifying groups is fundamental to the history of the Reserve, as we shall see. I shall consider issues of identity in more detail later, but for the sake of clarity the following remarks may be helpful.

The ethnic groups now living near to the Mkomazi Game Reserve are dominated by the Pare, based on the Pare mountains, and the Shambaa, or Sambaa, based on the Usambara mountains (see Map 2). The Kamba, who live on the plains, and the Maasai and closely related Parakuyo, who were also concentrated on the plains, form significant minorities. The Pare people are properly called the Asu, and their language Chasu; I shall use 'Pare' for both. The Parakuyo were once commonly known as the Kwavi, or Kuafi. These terms are not common, or popular, today, but to be consistent with the sources I use 'Kwavi' when discussing early events and 'Parakuyo' for the period after the early 1950s. Some quotations refer to the 'Wakwavi' or 'Wapare'. The prefix 'wa' means 'people'.

The pastures west of the Pare and Usambara mountains are known as the Pangani Valley. Names for the plains east of these mountains are problematic and can cause confusion. Krapf called this area the 'Wakuafi Wilderness' (Krapf, 1860: 222; 1854:5). Maa-speaking pastoralists call it *Alaililai Lemwazuni*, but the antiquity of that name is disputed by the Tanzanian Government (Civil Case no. 33 of 1995, High Court of Tanzania, Moshi). I use two terms. The first was given by Baumann to the plains north of the Usambaras, north and east of the Pares and south of the Taita hills: the Umba Nyika (Baumann, 1891: 167).[1] The second is 'the borderland plains'.

The name 'Mkomazi' is particularly problematic.[2] It was originally, and still is, the name of a village on the banks of a river found in a dry area between the South Pare and Usambara mountains; I refer to this place as 'Mkomazi village'. The conservation area I am writing about is officially split into two game reserves and called the Mkomazi/Umba Game Reserves in government documents. The eastern part, in Lushoto

District and Tanga Region, is called 'Umba', the western part, in Same District and Kilimanjaro Region, is 'Mkomazi'. They are, however, managed as one unit and are commonly known as 'Mkomazi'. I shall therefore use 'Mkomazi' or 'Reserve' with a capital letter for the area covering both reserves.

There have been numerous changes to the administrative boundaries governing the area since the inception of British rule. The present Same and Lushoto Districts were once part of a larger Usambara District (which also included Mwanga District) and was part of Tanga Province. In 1928 Usambara District was split into Lushoto and Pare Districts. In 1962, after independence, provinces became known as regions. In 1963, Pare District became part of the newly created Kilimanjaro Region, and Lushoto District remained part of Tanga Region. In 1978, Pare District was split into Mwanga District and Same District. Mwanga District now borders the Reserve on the north-west side.

The Department of Wildlife was called the Wildlife Division during most of the Reserve's history. I shall refer to it as it is currently known. The mainland of Tanganyika was known as Tanzania before independence.

Notes

1   'The second separate area of steppe of northeastern German East Africa I should like to term Umba Nyika. It stretches between the Pare mountains in the west and the coastal zone in the east, and extends, interrupted by the fertile mountain oases of Taita, far into the British sphere of influence.' Baumann, 1891: 167.

2   It means 'source of water' in Chasu.

TERMS & ABBREVIATIONS

AAME average adult male equivalent
ADO Assistant District Officer
ALDEV African Land Development Board
AWF African Wildlife Foundation
BMR basic metabolic rates
CAWM College of African Wildlife Management
CCM *Chama cha Mapinduzi* (Revolutionary Party of Tanzania): the party founded by Julius Nyerere and in government since independence
CCS Community Conservation Service
CID Criminal Investigation Department
CS Chief Secretary
CUSO Canadian Universities Service Overseas
DC District Commissioner
DFID Department for International Development
DO District Officer
DoW Department of Wildlife
DPO District Political Officer
DVO District Veterinary Officer
DVS Director of Veterinary Services
EBA endemic bird area
FAO Food and Agriculture Organisation
FZS Frankfurt Zoological Society
GAWPT George Adamson Wildlife Preservation Trust
ICDP Integrated Conservation-With-Development
IIED International Institute for Environment and Development
ILCA International Livestock Centre for Africa
IRA Institute of Resource Assessment
IUCN International Union for the Conservation of Nature
KNA Kenya National Archives
Ksh Kenyan shillings
KWLF Kisiwani Ward Livestock File
LU livestock unit
MERP Mkomazi Ecological Research Programme
MGR Mkomazi Game Reserve
MNRT Ministry of Natural Resources and Tourism

NCA Ngorongoro Conservation Area
NGO non-governmental organisation
ODA Overseas Development Administration
PAWM Planning and Assessment for Wildlife Management
PC Provincial Commissioner
PO Political Officer
PRA Participatory Rural Appraisal
PRO Public Records Office
PS Principal Secretary
PVO Provincial Veterinary Officer
RAE reference adult equivalent
RC Regional Commissioner
RCE regional centre of endemism
RGS Royal Geographical Society
RH Rhodes House, Oxford University
SHL Seeley History Library, Cambridge University
SPC Senior Provincial Commissioner
SPSS Statistics Package for Social Sciences
SRF systematic reconnaissance flight
SSU standard stock unit
TANAPA Tanzania National Parks
TF/GAAWPT Tony Fitzjohn/George Adamson African Wildlife Preservation Trust
TLU tropical livestock unit
TNA Tanzania National Archives
TRA Tanga Regional Archives
TWPF Tanzania Wildlife Protection Fund
TWPT Tanzanian Wildlife Preservation Trust
Tzsh Tanzanian shillings
UCL University College London
UNICEF United Nations Fund for Children
UNSO United Nations Sudano-sahelian Office
URT United Republic of Tanzania
VO veterinary officer
WCMD Wildlife Conservation and Management Department
WHO World Health Organisation
WWF The World Wide Fund for Nature

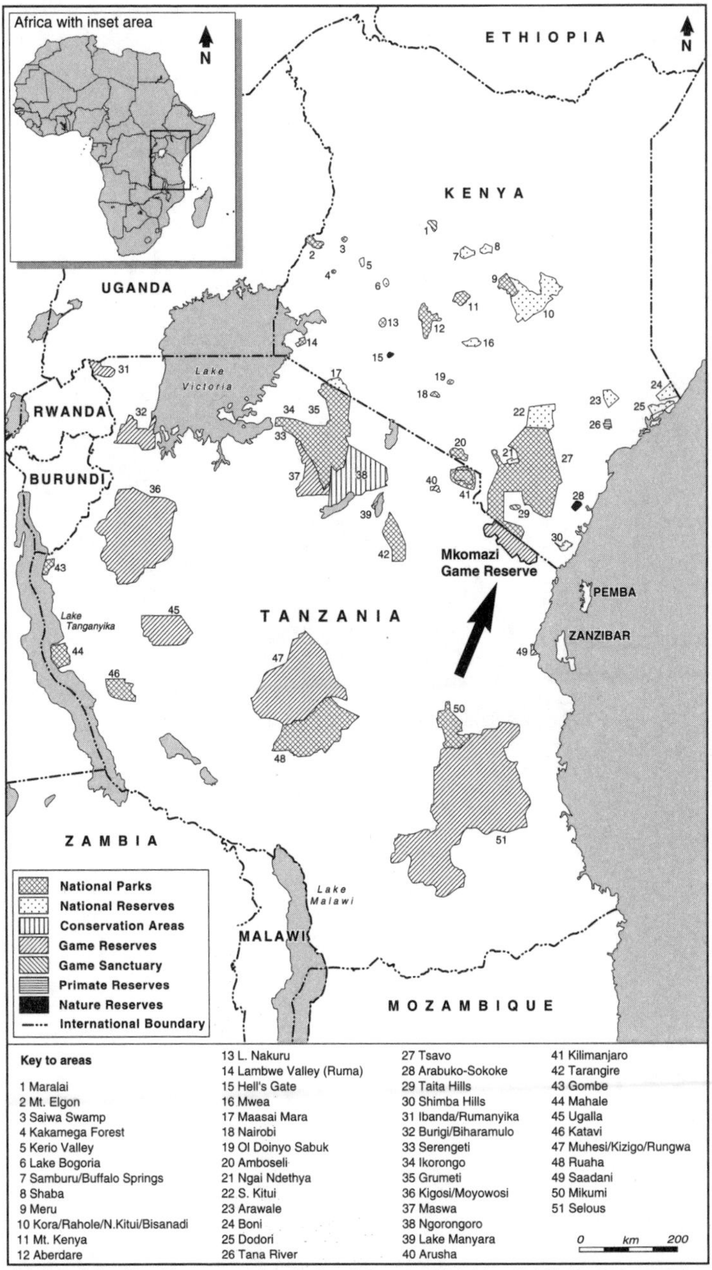
Africa with inset area
N
ETHIOPIA
N
KENYA
UGANDA
RWANDA
BURUNDI
Lake Victoria
Lake Tanganyika
TANZANIA
Mkomazi Game Reserve
PEMBA
ZANZIBAR
ZAMBIA
Lake Malawi
MALAWI
MOZAMBIQUE
National Parks
National Reserves
Conservation Areas
Game Reserves
Game Sanctuary
Primate Reserves
Nature Reserves
International Boundary
Key to areas
1 Maralai
2 Mt. Elgon
3 Saiwa Swamp
4 Kakamega Forest
5 Kerio Valley
6 Lake Bogoria
7 Samburu/Buffalo Springs
8 Shaba
9 Meru
10 Kora/Rahole/N.Kitui/Bisanadi
11 Mt. Kenya
12 Aberdare
13 L. Nakuru
14 Lambwe Valley (Ruma)
15 Hell's Gate
16 Mwea
17 Maasai Mara
18 Nairobi
19 Ol Doinyo Sabuk
20 Amboseli
21 Ngai Ndethya
22 S. Kitui
23 Arawale
24 Boni
25 Dodori
26 Tana River
27 Tsavo
28 Arabuko-Sokoke
29 Taita Hills
30 Shimba Hills
31 Ibanda/Rumanyika
32 Burigi/Biharamulo
33 Serengeti
34 Ikorongo
35 Grumeti
36 Kigosi/Moyowosi
37 Maswa
38 Ngorongoro
39 Lake Manyara
40 Arusha
41 Kilimanjaro
42 Tarangire
43 Gombe
44 Mahale
45 Ugalla
46 Katavi
47 Muhesi/Kizigo/Rungwa
48 Ruaha
49 Saadani
50 Mikumi
51 Selous
0 km 200

Note: Marine Parks and Forest Reserves are not shown. Newly gazetted areas around Katavi also omitted. Together with the protected areas shown, these add up to 27% of Tanzania's land surface area. *Source: Homewood, 1995; Wildlife Section Review, Task Force 1995.*

Map 1 Protected areas in Kenya and Tanzania. The arrow points to Mkomazi Game Reserve

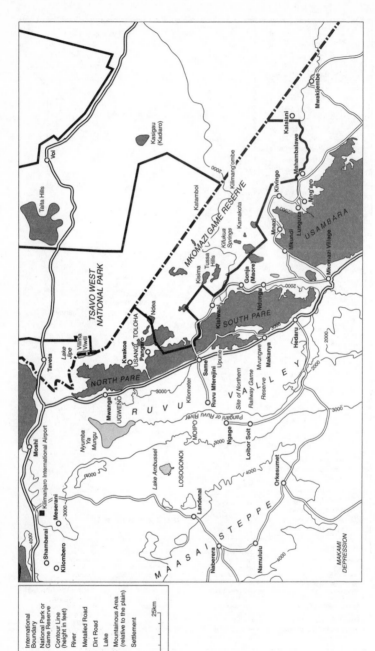

Map 2 The setting of the Mkomazi Game Reserve

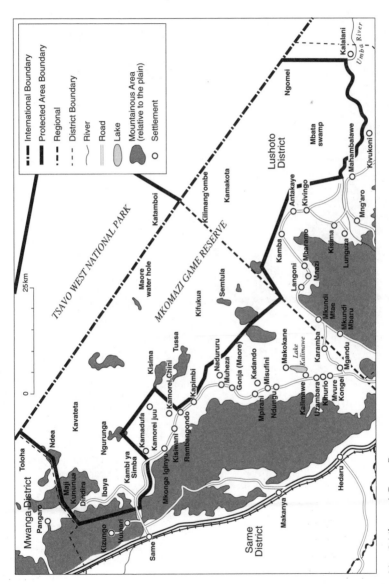

Map 3 Mkomazi Game Reserve

Map 4 Detail from late nineteenth century map for German Anti-slavery Committee by Dr Oscar Baumaun showing German-British border between Tanganyika and Kenya (note that the longitude and latitude lines identify the points of the compass)

Photo 1 Views over western Mkomazi: From Ndea with South Pare mountains in the distance. (Nicholas McWilliam)

Photo 2 Views over western Mkomazi: looking over towards the Tussa Hills. (Nicholas McWilliam)

Photo 3 Lions near Dindera Dam. (Nicholas McWilliam)

1
Introduction

In 1988 the Tanzanian Government completed its operation to evict the occupants of the Mkomazi Game Reserve. The operation had taken years to set up and complete. It was the culmination of a long-running campaign by the Department of Wildlife. Several thousand people and tens of thousands of livestock were moved.[1]

The moves were ordered because of fears for Mkomazi's environment. When the Reserve was gazetted in 1951, a few pastoral families and about five thousand cattle were allowed to continue to live within it. But pastoralists' numbers increased, as did their livestock. Their residence facilitated immigration by other herders. By the mid-1980s, close to 100,000 cattle grazed there. Wildlife officials thought the Reserve ravaged by human habitation. Pastures were overstocked and eroded, poaching rampant, and wildlife numbers were low. It was virtually impossible to administer the Reserve as a wildlife reserve with people resident. The government saw eviction of all occupants as the only way to save Mkomazi and reassert control over its environment. In the words of a Tanzanian zoologist:

> Habitat destruction, as a result of overgrazing, [led] to choking of dams with silt, and change in vegetation composition and structure. No dams ... could now hold water for the entire dry season period. Settlements increased around waterholes denying access by wildlife. These circumstances forced most of the wild animals to move out of Mkomazi into Tsavo National Park. Wildfires, often started by pastoralists, became an annual phenomenon, destroying and opening woodlands and montane forests (Mangubuli, 1991: 12).

In June 1994, a number of evicted herders took their government to court alleging that their constitutional right to live on their customary lands had been denied.[2] The government maintained that former residents had no rights to the Reserve. In March 1999 the High Court of Tanzania ruled that they were only recent immigrants, who therefore did not qualify for ancestral customary rights.

The evictions, then, were undertaken and defended by the Tanzanian state. But evictions alone would have been insufficient for the Reserve to prosper. Herders had been moved from Mkomazi before, with no lasting changes. Additional support was urgently needed to protect Mkomazi and enhance its status. Since the evictions, that support has been provided by international conservation organisations, which have played a key role in maintaining and promoting the Reserve.

The principal organisations supporting Mkomazi are the George Adamson Wildlife Preservation Trust (GAWPT), based in the UK, and the Tony Fitzjohn/George Adamson African Wildlife Preservation Trust (TF/GAAWPT), based in the USA.[3] The Trusts have supported an expensive and prestigious rehabilitation project at Mkomazi involving road building, boundary clearance and the reintroduction of the Black Rhinoceros and Wild Dog. They have sponsored an outreach programme, run by the department of wildlife, whose purpose is to disseminate benefits from the Reserve and encourage local support for it.

Both Trusts are run by people with political influence and connections in the media and film industries. In Britain, the Trustees include senior ecologists, a Member of Parliament, journalists and distinguished conservationists. In America they have strong links to the entertainment industry and the cream of Californian society. Their supporters include wealthy and well-connected individuals in Europe and the USA. Annual celebrations in London are reported in *Hello!* magazine; fund-raising galas in California are held on Rodeo Drive. The work is supported by film stars, such as Clint Eastwood and Sylvester Stallone, while corporate benefactors include Tiffany's, Cartier and British Petroleum. The Hollywood connections extend to a film about the work at Mkomazi called *To Walk with Lions* (which continues the story of *Born Free*).[4] Articles in leading English and American newspapers celebrate the project.

The Trusts' work is driven by a powerful vision of the Reserve's history, environment and neighbours, which is apparent in the image of Mkomazi they promote. Its most prominent element is that Mkomazi's environment was once threatened with destruction, but is now saved:

> Mkomazi is potentially one of the most beautiful and important game reserves on the continent. ... Until 1988, it represented a classic example of ecological decline and degradation, overgrazed, persistently eroded and the subject of indiscriminate and widespread poaching. ... Since 1988 the entire resources of the Trust have been devoted to the project. ... One of the most fragile, threatened and beautiful parts of Africa has been reborn ... The Mkomazi Project has a unique aspect. The rebuilding of Mkomazi Game Reserve, the rehabilitation of its wildlife, the endangered species programmes and the outreach programmes do not simply attempt to 'hold the line' on conservation. They are an endeavour to re-establish a complete ecosystem and thus positively reverse the damage that has been done (GAWPT (UK) fundraising document, *circa* 1994).

A second element of the vision is that the evicted people were 'not indigenous to the area'.[5] The operation to clear the Reserve therefore did not deprive people of their ancestral lands but was a necessary step to restore a pristine wilderness. The third element is a concern to meet human needs around the Reserve by providing educational equipment, and medical supplies, and by investing in schools, clinics and development projects.

These three elements are typical of a broader vision of Africa's environment, history and society that drives conservation throughout the continent. Its premise is a belief that people have harmed the environment. This is buttressed by scientists' interpretations of environmental change. It is powered by the emotive and mystical appeal of wilderness, stunning landscapes and the aura of extraordinary biodiversity. It is grounded in interpretations of the history of protected areas that play down the presence of people before gazettement. It is characterised by concern to provide for peoples' needs around protected areas in order to win local support. It is a powerful, persistent and popular vision. Fortunes are invested in its promotion; multitudes absorb the books, films, television documentaries and glossy magazines that endorse and reproduce it; millions of tourists spend billions of dollars visiting the parks and reserves set up to preserve it.

It is a vision that can be harmful, unjust and unnecessary. There have been numerous challenges to its different elements. Ecologists have expressed doubts about degradation in environments like Mkomazi's; they query the importance of people and livestock in environmental change. The historical validity of 'wilderness', of nature devoid of people in its past or processes, has been questioned. Many people, not least local groups themselves, are voicing increasing concern for the rights and needs of those who live near to, and bear the brunt of, protected areas. The benefits offered from protected areas rarely meet the losses experienced. The costs of eviction and exclusion are not always counted.

I will argue that, at Mkomazi, this vision is flawed either in fact, or in its assertion of certainty, and that the reality it imposes is harmful to a number of the Reserve's neighbours. Many evicted herders were not recent immigrants, they had lived there for generations; there is strong evidence that the Reserve was not degraded, and the social and economic costs of eviction have been severe and not matched by the benefits offered. But I will show that despite these flaws the vision remains strong and successful. Mkomazi's case demonstrates the power of fortress conservation, despite the errors or injustices it may entail. In doing so it illustrates the weaknesses of alternatives proposed by community conservation.

There are two stories here. First, Mkomazi encapsulates the dilemma of African conservation. The Reserve is beautiful; its plant, bird and insect diversity is great; its wildness spectacular. Its conservation is pursued in the name of a good cause – to save biodiversity and beautiful landscapes for humankind. But at the same time its conservation has imposed decisions with little or no consultation and with violent enforcement. It has invented and obliterated history. It has caused impoverishment. The evictions therefore pose a problem. They have come at a time when provision of meaningful benefits and power to local people is being voiced as the answer to Africa's conservation problems. Yet at Mkomazi, fortress conservation is flourishing in the face of so much rhetoric to the contrary, and despite many of the facts on the ground.

Second, the evictions are another incident of land loss to add to the catalogue of changes dealt to pastoral societies in Africa in recent decades. It is commonplace for studies of pastoralism to observe that herding societies have experienced rapid changes in recent decades.[6] Some are internally driven, but many result from imposed projects and development plans. Pastoralists' current predicaments are partly due to development schemes, which have seen, for example, rangelands converted to wheat fields in order to boost national food production.[7] They also reflect particular ways of thinking about and applying development, which have urged that backward irrational herders be transformed into modern progressive stockmen to the detriment of their livelihoods.[8]

These stories are closely related. At Mkomazi, policies to move people in the name of conservation have been seamlessly joined to plans to move them in the name of development. But at a deeper level both conservation and pastoral development are part of a broader desire to induce or impose productive change on society and nature in the name of development in Africa. Alienating pastures for wheat farms or game reserves, establishing national parks and tourist lodges, moving rural people into planned villages, enclosing communally managed resources and importing improved stock breeds are different aspects of the same goal. They are about ordering society and nature, determining how landscapes and resources should best be used, and who should be the most appropriate users and who the beneficiaries.

Both conservation and development are concerned to enhance national well-being. They aim to provide revenue for central government, from tourists' dollars or exported goods, and productive employment for the state's citizens. But both carry costs that are rarely properly counted and cause loss and hardship. Although both desire enhanced well-being, both intimately reorder peoples lives, environments and futures, and have been characterised by authoritarian planning and execution. As Adams has written:

> Development ought to be what human communities do to themselves. In practice, however, it is what is done to them by states and their bankers and 'expert' agents in the name of modernity, national integration, economic growth or a thousand other slogans (Adams, 1990: 199).

But despite their common ground writing about both stories is not straightforward. While the substance of this book concerns environments, livelihoods and histories, the implications I discuss largely concern conservation policy and ethics. The literatures addressing these issues are different. It has not been easy combining both within one structure. I have proceeded on the assumption that if we are to understand conservation then we will need to do so from a thorough knowledge of its consequences to people and nature. Saving wildlife and wilderness entails continuously wrestling with what people do – the energy and resources they consume, the waste they produce, the landscapes they value, where they live and the way they use land. A study of conservation is therefore a study of both nature's dynamics and people, of how they are affected by conservation, cope with it and negotiate with its advocates.

Amartya Sen, the Nobel Prize-winning economist, has observed that when:

> assessing the claims of property rights, or the right not to be hungry, the examination cannot be confined to issues of basic valuation only, and much of the challenge of assessment lies in the empirical analysis of causes and effects. In the world in which we live – full of hunger as well as wealth – these empirical investigations can be both complex and quite extraordinarily important. The big moral questions are frequently also deeply economic, social or political (Sen, 1988: 68).

We could add 'the duty to protect nature', 'freedom from impoverishment' or 'biodiversity rights' to the list of claims Sen mentions. Knowing about conservation dilemmas requires perspectives deeply rooted in the histories and livelihoods of the people involved and the environments conservation has sought to protect.[9]

Land loss and livelihoods

Land loss has been a dominant theme in East Africa over the last century. It has resulted from dispossession by state or private organisations, generally for use in large-scale farms or conservation, and immigration of smallholders (who may themselves have been evicted or excluded from their agricultural areas). Dispossession is sudden, but immigration can be a relatively gradual process, allowing gradual adaptation of livelihoods. The sudden appropriation of large areas can require large numbers of people to move or adapt their livelihoods.

In Kenya the principal cause of land loss has been alienation of land for settler agriculture. By 1963, 18 per cent of good arable land (5.5 per cent of the colony's total) had been taken.[10] A significant proportion of the best agricultural land was alienated during colonial rule. Since independence, land grabs continue through the corruption of local politicians and the failure to make just division of ranches held in common by groups of herders.[11]

In Tanzania alienation for settler interests during colonial times was slight. Only 1.5 per cent of the country's land had been alienated by the time of independence for settlers and government schemes.[12] Instead much of the land loss experienced in rural Tanzania has followed independence. This occurred first in schemes for diverse state enterprises and, since the late 1980s, for private and foreign investors. But to rural dwellers loss of land to private enterprise has much the same feel as alienation by the state. It may serve a higher purpose, such as economic growth or national development, but the rural dwellers experience few immediate benefits and often suffer much inconvenience. The chairman of the Presidential Commission of Inquiry into Land Matters in Tanzania has reported that:

> The Land Commission received overwhelming evidence showing large-scale encroachment of customary individual land and village lands by parastatals, District Development Corporations (and) state organs such as the army, prisons, national service, parks and reserves. The story is varied, details are different but the theme is the same. Village and rural folks holding land under customary tenure have no security. Their lands are under constant threat of alienation by state organs ostensibly for 'national projects' or in the 'public interest' but very often in favour of high and middle echelons of the bureaucracy or well-connected 'outsiders' (Shivji, 1995: 10–11).[13]

Land loss then is a prominent feature of rural life in Tanzania. What might its consequences be for livelihoods? Shaw-Taylor, writing on the effects of parliamentary enclosure in England, distinguishes two processes resulting from land loss.[14] The first is immiseration, the second is proletarianisation – a decrease in self-reliance and increased dependence on wage labour. Shaw-Taylor observes that proletarianisation does not necessarily mean immiseration. It can be a change for the better. But in the absence of alternative sources of income, the consequences of land loss must mean impoverishment. In Tanzania there are few alternative sources of employment for displaced peasants. They will have to remain self-reliant because there is nothing else for them to depend upon.

Immiseration and proletarianisation following land loss need to be understood in the context of other transformations of rural livelihoods. Livelihoods in East and Southern Africa in general are becoming less agricultural, more diverse and more urban.[15] Bryceson has argued that, in Tanzania specifically, the agricultural sector is shrinking owing to declining land availability, decreased returns from falling crop prices, price rises in crucial inputs such as fertilisers, and the attrition of droughts or floods which eat away at people's coping strategies and the buffers they set up against hardship.[16] The result has been a move away from agriculture and a diversification of livelihoods into the 'the rural informal sector'.

It is important to emphasise that Bryceson's descriptions of 'deagrari-anisation' [*sic*] and 'depeasantisation' [*sic*] concern the *relative* impor-tance of agriculture in the economy. In *absolute* terms the amount of farmland is increasing. In northern Tanzania agricultural land is expanding at the cost of pasture. Farming is an important part of the diversification of pastoral livelihoods, and much of the conversion of pasture to agricultural use is undertaken by impoverished pastoralists themselves. In southern Tanzania there is widespread immigration of herders and farmers seeking new livelihoods in relatively unpopulated places.[17] Few families abandon all farming activity, which remains central within diversified livelihoods. Land loss in Tanzania therefore takes place in a context of decreasing land availability.

Diversification is well-documented in pastoral societies. Much writing about pastoralists is dominated by accounts of the way that their livelihoods are diversifying in the face of multiple pressures to change. Historians emphasise that flexibility and change underpinned pastoral livelihoods in the nineteenth century.[18] Accounts of contemporary change identify a number of coping and adaptive mechanisms, which include seeking urban income, milk sales, changing herd structure or earning money from tourists.[19]

However, attention to the specific consequences of sudden dispos-session of land for pastoral livelihoods is not common. Writings on pastoralism concentrate on diversification and the long-term and short-term strategies that rural people use to adapt to and cope with change. They rarely look at the specific impacts of land loss *per se*, but group it among broader concerns of marginalisation, commoditisation, sedentari-sation, development or structural adjustment. These impacts will be reconsidered at the end of the book.

Conservation – by fortress or community?

Land alienation in Tanzania is marked by the prominence of land loss for conservation purposes.[20] Conservation in Tanzania is distinguished by its energetic pursuit of more lands to gazette as protected areas. No less than 27 per cent of Tanzania's land is now national park, game reserve or forest reserve, and so prohibited to human habitation.[21] Since these data were compiled the Katavi National Park has been expanded, and the Usangu, Rukwa and Luafi Game Reserves established, enclosing more than 10,000 km² of land within the protected area network.

However, the wisdom of alienating land and defending the resultant conservation 'fortresses' has been queried as part of a large-scale reap-praisal of conservation ethics practices that has been gathering strength since the early 1980s. Current writing on African conservation questions the appropriateness of its values (because of their western origins and wholesale imposition on different societies and ecologies) and the possibility of sustaining previous practices (because they entail setting up parks and reserves from which local people are kept out by force).[22] Over the last twenty years there has been a growing feeling that this policy is failing.[23] It has failed to protect many elephant and rhino populations. Parks are surrounded by people who do not condone their presence and who actively, in their daily lives, undermine or defy the regulations protecting the parks' wildlife and resources. It is widely suggested that if protected areas are to have a long-term future, they must enlist support from their immediate neighbours. Only if they exist with local approval can they exist at all.

Accordingly, the search has been on for successful means of promoting community conservation policies that are more beneficial to local people and that involve them more in decision-making. The search has generated a voluminous literature.[24] The case studies can be usefully sorted by the nature of power-sharing involved. Hartley distinguishes between 'Conservation with Development', where conservation authorities retain control over the resource but offer handouts of money or services to protected areas, and 'Community-Based Natural Resource Management', which involves more local control of the resources and wildlife in question.[25] Similarly, Murphree differentiates between approaches that decentralise power to local authorities, but where lines of accountability still go back to central government, and devolution of power, where responsibility is to a local electorate.[26]

Amboseli National Park in Kenya is typical of Conservation with Development approaches. Here neighbouring Maasai communities have received funds for water supplies and local government services and cash payments to members of group ranches adjoining the park in an effort to bolster good relations between the park and its neighbours.[27] Similarly, the Tanzania National Parks administration has set up a Community Conservation Service, which funds clinics and schools and organises educational visits to the park for school children in the villages surrounding it.[28] The most celebrated attempt to devolve power to local communities over wildlife is the CAMPFIRE programme in Zimbabwe, where villagers have control over hunting rights on wildlife on their lands and varying degrees of access to the revenues from tourist hunters who shoot there.[29]

Three doubts have been raised about community conservation.[30] First, where handouts are used, are they adequate? If wildlife authorities offer goods or services to neighbouring communities so that they value the park, then it is reasonable to expect that the goods received should at least equal the costs and inconvenience incurred by not using the protected resources. But the cost of conservation is rarely counted. There is rarely a conscious attempt fully to compensate people for the inconveniences the park may have caused to their livelihoods. If people are to become allies of parks then the benefits needed are likely to be considerable.[31]

(Second,) the nature and politics of participation are not straight-forward.[32] Typologies of participation are readily generated that map out varying degrees of local involvement (Table 1.1). But the political processes entailed are often not examined. Too often 'communities' are portrayed as unproblematic homogeneous political entities when they are in fact heterogeneous – divided along economic, ethnic and social lines.[33] To western ideals, participation carries democratic connotations. But rural African societies may be hierarchical, excluding women, the landless and uneducated, ethnic minorities and others. Participation is open to takeover. Power offered to a group will tend to become concentrated into the hands of a few.[34]

The dilemmas of participation reflect a central ambiguity in community conservation: is it concerned primarily with development or conservation? Some authors suggest that it combines conservation and development goals, whose challenges are irrevocably intertwined.[35] Murphree counters that it is vital to distinguish between projects whose aim is to bring the benefits of conservation to local people as an end in itself (a development objective), and those that aim to conserve wildlife and wilderness (a conservation objective).[36] The former are potentially radical. They could entail empowering groups at the local level with real authority over their own resources. But they carry the threat that the people may not prioritise the conservation of biodiversity or scarce wildlife. Some ecologists fear that sustainable use is ecologically problematic. Trophy hunting or market-driven harvesting could work to the detriment of wildlife.[37] On the other hand, local groups may wish to liquidate wildlife resources and use the land for other purposes.[38] It is

Table 1.1 Levels of participation in community conservation.

Kiss, 1990	Wells *et al.*, 1992	Pimbert and Pretty, 1996	Miombo editorial, 1996
Participation in benefits	Information-gathering	Passive participation	Passive
Participation in planning and design	Consultation	Participation by consultation	Interactive (benefit sharing)
Participation in implementation and management	Decision-making	Participation for material incentives	Dynamic (agendas determined by local communities)
	Initiating action	Functional participation	
	Evaluation	Interactive participation	
		Self-mobilisation/ active participation	

Source: Homewood *et al.*, 1997.

not reasonable to assume that local groups will wish simple, low-impact lifestyles to continue.[39] Empowerment could mean that conservation goals are lost, especially in areas ecologically or economically suited to more profitable uses than wildlife.[40] Real empowerment would risk giving rural communities the option to convert wilderness to pasture and farmland.

Third, the nature of the threat from local groups, and the alliance sought with them to counter it, may be ill thought through. Community conservation risks suggesting that the poor are central to the operation of African states, that without their support nothing long-lasting can be achieved. But the rural poor in Africa tend to be weak and marginal to their countries' affairs.[41] They can be, and often are, ignored by their rulers. It may be true that unsupported parks will decline, but it is not necessarily true that they can only be saved by participatory democratic empowerment of local groups.[42]

However it meets these challenges, community conservation is likely to evolve in institutional frameworks that have previously been geared towards fortress conservation models since colonial times.[43] Independent African governments have strongly supported the continued existence of protected areas. 'Alien' values and policies have taken root. The patronage and resources they provide are political assets.[44] Knowles and Collett argue, *contra* Turton, that the value of tourist revenues are such that African governments cannot afford *not* to set aside wilderness areas.[45] Indeed, the conservation programme in some African countries is more ambitious than under colonial rule. When Major Hingston proposed the establishment of national parks in Tanzania in 1931 he suggested three parks – the Serengeti, the Selous and Kilimanjaro.[46] The current protected area network in Tanzania is much larger, with more protected areas gazetted since independence (1961) than before (see Table 1.2 and Map 1).

The weaknesses and inefficiencies of many African states have meant that numerous protected areas have existed in name only, but support from international organisations has strengthened conservation capabilities on the ground. Conservation receives continual and valuable support from a number of non-governmental organisations (NGOs),[47] which lobby and raise money for conservation causes. They provide valuable funds to African governments without the means to endorse ambitious conservation schemes. Many have actively promoted community conservation practices and reform of the institutional environments.[48] However, from a political perspective their support may make it unnecessary for state officials to seek legitimation for protected areas from local groups. The resources provided by conservation interests, as well as the powerful rhetoric of providing for future generations, may serve to justify the existence of protected areas to government officials.

Table 1.2 Game reserves and national parks in Tanzania.

Reserve	Gazetted as a reserve	Gazetted as a park	Area/km²
Selous	1922	–	50,000
Ngorongoro	1928	1959*	8,292
Serengeti	1929	1951	14,763
Gombe streams	1943	1968	52
Mkomazi	1951	–	3,234
Rungwa	1951	–	9,000
Ruaha	1951	1964	10,380
Arusha	1953	1960	137
Kilimanjaro	1956	1973	756
Lake Manyara	1957	1960	330
Biharamulo	1959	–	1,300
Maswa	1962	–	2,200
Mikumi	–	1964	3,230
Ugalla	1965	–	5,000
Rubundo Is.	1965	1977	450
Saadani	1968	–	300
Tarangire	1967	1970	2,600
Uwanda	1971	–	5,000
Katavi	1971	1974	2,253
Burigi	1972	–	2,200
Ibanda	1974	–	200
Rumanyika	1974	–	800
Mahale Mountains	–	1980	1,577
Moyowosi	1981	–	6,000
Kizigo	1982/70	–	4,000
Kigosi	1983	–	7,000
Udzungwa	–	1992	1,900
Saa Nane	1994	–	0.5
Grumeti	1994	–	2,000
Ikorongo	1994	–	3,000
Kijereshi	1994	–	300
Muhesi	1994	–	2,000
Pande Forest	1994	–	12

*Conservation area, not a national park.
Source: Wildlife Sector Review Task Force, 1995.
Note: since these data were compiled more protected areas have been gazetted.

None of this is to argue that empowerment is impossible or that community conservation cannot work. There are several cases across Africa that testify to progress.[49] But in writings about community conservation the failures of fortress conservation have been sometimes overstated and its strengths overlooked. The goal of this book is to look at the nature of these strengths by exploring the histories, environments and societies that have been altered by conservation policies at Mkomazi and what conservationists have been able to say about these changes.

Outline of the book

Chapter 2 introduces Mkomazi, the diverse peoples found near the Reserve, and the methods and focus of this study.

Chapter 3 considers the history of the Reserve. Mkomazi's problems predate its creation. They become comprehensible if we view them as but one part of a series of state interventions in response to long-term trends in population growth and dispersal. The operation to clear the Reserve, and the court case brought by evictees, were the latest in a long series of contests and negotiations between state representatives and local groups, and between local groups themselves, over ethnic identity and access to range resources. Current contests are different because they take place in an international arena.

Chapter 4 examines competing explanations of the dynamics of Mkomazi's semi-arid environment. The history of contests between herders and the state has been dominated by concerns for the environment that were crucial for the evictions policy. But opinion is sharply divided over the effect of cattle on Mkomazi's environment. Using various data I examine the contention that people degrade the environment, and I evaluate recent research that has recorded high levels of biodiversity within the Reserve. I argue that there are no data to support the idea that the Reserve's environment was degraded and that ill-advised claims about the Reserve's biodiversity have been used to support exclusion policies.

In Chapter 5 I discuss the impact of exclusion on people and particularly livestock owners. I show that livelihoods have been adversely affected, and the wealth of the regional livestock economy has declined. The Reserve's tourist revenues and outreach activities have not compensated for the losses that some groups have experienced. I argue that this is manifest in the resistance to the Reserve demonstrated by local people. The failure of this resistance underlines the marginality of the losers in Mkomazi's conservation. It also points to weaknesses in the organisations that have championed the evictees' cause.

There are two concluding chapters. Chapter 6 examines the nature of the power of fortress conservation and the implications of the Mkomazi case for community conservation. Finally, in Chapter 7, I consider the current prospects and lives of the evicted herders.

Notes

1 Estimates range from 5,000 to 8,000. Fosbrooke papers: URT G.10/4/111/123; Neumann, 1995a: 367; Johnston, 1997. From the attendance records of the minutes of displaced people, I calculated that more than 8,000 Maa-speakers were evicted. This was derived from listing the adult men present at the various

meetings around Mkomazi and multiplying the total by the average family size recorded during a 1992 census of pastoralists at Kisiwani (source: Fosbrooke papers). There are no good estimates of the cattle numbers involved, but most observers thought that numbers had declined by about 75 per cent. In the 1984 census 88,210 cattle were counted in or around the Reserve.

2 Tenga, 1999.

3 Hereafter referred to as 'the Trusts'. There are also branches in Holland and Germany. They were originally set up to support the work of the late George Adamson in Kenya. They channel funds for work on Mkomazi to the Tanzanian Wildlife Preservation Trust (TWPT), which is based in Tanzania.

4 *Born Free* was a film that celebrated the work of George and Joy Adamson with lions and wildlife in Kenya.

5 GAWPT, TF/GAWPT fundraising material. The full text in both documents reads: 'In 1989, when the restoration of Mkomazi was declared a National Priority Project, the Tanzanian Government was faced with a tough decision. Over the years, people and livestock had moved into the reserve, causing serious overgrazing. However the resident tribes and their livestock were not indigenous to the area, and in order to save the remaining wildlife and reverse the years of deterioration, they were relocated outside the reserve.'

6 Anderson and Broch-Due, 1999; Galaty *et al.*, 1994.

7 Lane, 1996.

8 Fratkin, 1991.

9 Smith, 2000.

10 Zwanenberg and King, 1975: 30.

11 Rutten, 1992; Galaty, 1994.

12 United Republic of Tanzania (URT), 1991.

13 Hereafter 'Land Commission'. It was set up following disorder and concern with respect to land claims.

14 Shaw-Taylor, forthcoming.

15 Bryceson and Jamal, 1997.

16 Bryceson, 1999.

17 Igoe and Brockington, 1999 for northern Tanzania; Charnley, 1994 and Brockington, 2001a for southern Tanzania.

18 Anderson and Johnson, 1988; Spear and Waller, 1993.

19 Anderson and Broch-Due, 1999; Dahl, 1979; Talle, 1988; Baxter and Hogg, 1990; Ensiminger, 1992; Igoe and Brockington, 1999.

20 McCabe *et al.*, 1992: 354.

21 Wildlife Sector Review Task Force, 1995: 20.

22 Kjekshus, 1977; Marks, 1984; Anderson and Grove, 1987; MacKenzie, 1988; West and Brechin, 1991; Neumann, 1995b, 1997, 1998; Ghimire and Pimbert, 1997.

23 Marks heralded a paradigm shift in thinking about conservation in his book *The Imperial Lion* (Marks, 1984).

24 The commonly cited works that discuss the search for alternatives to traditional conservation practice are Western and Wright, 1994; IIED, 1994; Kiss, 1990; Wells *et al.*, 1992 and Marks, 1984. Gibson and Marks (1995) also mention a number of works in the 1980s, Martin (1999) earlier sources. Hulme and Murphree (1999; 2001a) offer the most recent assessment of the debate and its innovations. Adams and Hulme (2001a) give a detailed history of the idea.

25 Hartley, 1997.
26 Murphree, 2001.
27 Western, 1994.
28 Igoe and Brockington, 1999; Kipuri and Nangoro, 1996.
29 Duffy, 2000; Murphree, 1996; B. Child, 1996; G. Child, 1996. The extent to which CAMPFIRE has devolved authority to local groups or decentralised authority to local governments is debatable (Murphree, 2001; Murombedzi, 1999).
30 Cf. Adams and Hulme, 2001b.
31 Emerton, 2001; Emerton, 1999a, 1999b; Emerton and Mfunda, 1999; Duffy, 2000: 105; Norton-Griffiths, 1996: 1574–5.
32 Little, 1994; Songorwa, 1999.
33 Brosius *et al.*, 1998: 165; IIED, 1994; Noss, 1997.
34 Wells *et al.*, 1992: 43; Kiss, 1990: 9; Strum, 1994; Gibson and Marks, 1995: 946–7; Korten, 1980.
35 Barrett and Arcese, 1995.
36 Murphree, 1996.
37 Newmark and Hough, 2000; Hackel, 1999; Spinage, 1998; Noss, 1997; Oates, 1995.
38 Norton-Griffiths, 1996; Alexander and McGregor, 2000; Hackel, 1999.
39 Spinage, 1998, 1999; Colchester, 1998; Murombedzi, 1999.
40 Marks, 1984: 102; Murphree, 1996: 166; Adams and Hulme, 2001a: 20; Noss, 1997; Struhsaker, 1998; Kramer *et al.*, 1997.
41 Bayart, 1993; Chabal and Daloz, 1999.
42 Gibson, 1999.
43 Hulme and Murphree, 2001b: 5.
44 Duffy, 2000; Gibson, 1999.
45 Knowles and Collett, 1989; Turton, 1984.
46 Hingston, 1931: 410.
47 They are diverse, ranging greatly in size, scope and orientation. A brief list might include the Frankfurt Zoological Society (FZS), the World Wide Fund for Nature (WWF), the African Wildlife Foundation (AWF), Flora and Fauna International (FFI), Conservation International (CI) and the Wildlife Conservation Society (WCS) as well as international organisations such as the International Union for the Conservation of Nature (IUCN) and the United Nations Environment Programme (UNEP), not to mention myriad diverse smaller organisations such as Tusk Force, the Environmental Investigation Agency and the Born Free Foundation (cf. Bonner, 1993; Duffy, 2000: 114).
48 Hulme and Murphree, 2001c: 284.
49 Hulme and Murphree, 2001b; IIED, 1994.

2
Mkomazi

First and foremost the area provides a sanctuary for game without in any way interfering with the legitimate present or future needs of the local population.

Bates, DC of Same, 25 April 1949, commenting on
the proposal to establish the Mkomazi Game Reserve

The north-east borderlands of Tanzania are characterised by fertile, well-watered mountains rising amid relatively dry rangelands. The Pare and Usambara mountains climb abruptly from the plains, their fault lines forming steep escarpments, to over 2,000 m above sea level. The highlands support dense forests, intensive irrigated agriculture and many people. The rivers that drain them – the Pangani (Ruvu) and the Umba – provide water for the plains. Numerous small streams coming down from the hills form the focus for other dwellings.

In pre-colonial times this geography gave rise to several types of settlement. On the Pare and Usambara mountains were the villages of the Pare and the Sambaa cultivators and the Mbugu pastoralists, secure from malaria but not quite out of reach of raiding parties from the plains. At the base of the hills, where there is water, were other villages dependent on irrigated agriculture and trade with coastal caravans, and between plains dwellers and the hills. These villages then, as now, were eclectic collections of numerous ethnic groups. The Pare and Sambaa people place great store on retaining a foothold in the highlands, and look down on friends or relatives who live in the plains. Nonetheless many have come down seeking farmland and pasture, mingling with the Zigua, Kamba, Kwavi (Parakuyo) and Maasai. The rangelands themselves are often too dry to be suitable for cultivation.[1] They mainly supported hunting and herding by Kamba hunters, and Kwavi and Maasai pastoralists and agropastoralists.

When the British and German governments agreed the boundary here between Kenya and Tanganyika, they drew an arbitrary line from the coast to Kilimanjaro. In doing so they enclosed a triangle of land between the border and the mountains to the south. It is relatively isolated from present-day Tanzania, the mountains forming a barrier between it and the

15

rest of the country. The old caravan routes north of the mountains are largely forgotten. The new main road and the railway pass to the south. Within this triangle lies the Mkomazi Game Reserve (Map 2).

Ecologically, the international boundary is irrelevant. Mkomazi forms a wet season dispersal area for the Tsavo ecosystem; elephants and ungulates migrate across the border with the rains. The Reserve is quite large, 3,200 km² in size, and together with Tsavo is part of one of the larger protected areas on the continent. Mkomazi itself contains diverse habitats. Its main vegetation is a mosaic of grassland and Acacia–Commiphora woodland, and in the west it contains high hills that support montane forest. With its mountains and continuity with Tsavo, Mkomazi is beautiful and wild, with a high diversity of life.

But the villages around the base of the mountains that ring this backwater have grown in size since the Reserve was first created. Wealthy businessmen have built smart houses in their centres. Their markets are a focus for much economic activity, linking the plains and the hills and providing people with a regular flow of money to meet everyday needs. Villagers here largely depend on the resources of the surrounding plains and mountain edges for their livelihoods. The cultivators require land, water and protection from wild animals. Hunters and honey gatherers set traps and hives in the bush. Herders concentrate in small hamlets a few kilometres from the village centres where their herds are less likely to graze crops and are nearer to pastures. All require firewood or charcoal for cooking and warmth.

The proximity of the Reserve to these villages, and its obstruction to resource use, is a central aspect of life here. Standing in the villages south of Mkomazi and looking north, the plains stretch out into the distance to Kenya and beyond. The blue haze of Teita and Kasigau rise beyond the horizon. There is a sense of immense space and openness. But working there, what struck me most was that the expanse was prohibited. The plains before me were separated by a thin, cut line, the borders of the Reserve, which skirted close to the mountains, leaving scant room for people. Beyond this line one cannot travel except by paying the entrance fee, and within it all use of resources is forbidden. Standing without this perimeter and looking in, the impression is of a vast land that lies unused, denying the pressing needs of thousands of people.

One of the central problems that Mkomazi faces is the sheer number of people who live close to it. In 1988, 48,000 were counted in the census (Table 2.1). These people live close enough to be potential daily users of it. There are more people in the wider region above the Pare and Usambara mountains (Table 2.2).[2] Another problem is that the geography of the Reserve and its environs means that many people live sandwiched between the Reserve's borders and the mountains to the south and west. Many evictees live in this corridor. A central complaint of residents here

Table 2.1 Population around Mkomazi Game Reserve, 1978–1988.

District	Area	1978	District	Area	1988	Annual growth rate
Same	Toloha	830	Mwanga	Toloha	1,573	9%
	Vumari/		Same	Vumari/		
	Kizungo	1,975		Kizungo	3,949	10%
	Kisiwani	9,568		Kisiwani	6,314	–3.4%
	Maore	10,480		Maore	9,703	–0.7%
Lushoto	Mng'aro	1,724	Lushoto	Mng'aro	4,053	13.5%
	Mbaramo	5,325		Mbaramo	7,027	3.2%
	Lunguza	5,643		Lunguza	6,891	2.2%
	Mnazi	7,195		Mnazi	8,861	2.3%
Reserve Total		**42,740**	**Reserve Total**		**48,371**	1.3%

Source: Tanzanian Government census data.
Note: the areas defined for collection of population data sometimes changed between censuses, owing to administrative changes. To adjust for this the table pools ward and village data into areas that remain more or less constant between censuses, despite administrative (and enumeration area) changes.
The table shows that the populations closest to the Reserve grew at 1.3 per cent per annum between 1978 and 1988, and can be expected to have grown further since. The 1988 count of something over 48,000 is therefore a minimum estimate of the Reserve-adjacent population.

Table 2.2 Population in the wider region, 1978–1988.

District	Area	1978	District	Area	1988	Intra-censal growth rate per annum
Same	Kwakoa	2,070	Mwanga	Kwakoa	2,668	2.9%
	Toloha	830		Toloha	1,573	9%
	Kigonigoni	980		Kigonigoni	1,632	6.7%
	Vumari/		Same	Vumari/		
	Kizungo	1,975		Kizungo	3,949	10%
	Kisiwani	9,568		Kisiwani	6,314	–3.4%
	Maore	10,480		Maore	9,703	–0.7%
	Ndungu	10,368		Ndungu	10,430	0.1%
	Bendera	6,238		Bendera	11,421	8.3%
Lushoto	Mng'aro	1,724	Lushoto	Mng'aro	4,053	13.5%
	Mbaramo	5,325		Mbaramo	7,027	3.2%
	Lunguza	5,643		Lunguza	6,891	2.2%
	Mnazi	7,195		Mnazi	8,861	2.3%
Total		**60,326**	**Total**		**71,854**	1.9%

is that there is insufficient space for their livestock. This is a Reserve with no room for a buffer zone (Map 3). The mountain barrier that cuts the Reserve off from its country, and which is the source of so much of its water, serves also to concentrate its neighbours around it.

The pre-eminence of the Reserve in local affairs is apparent in the Participatory Rural Appraisals (PRA) undertaken in villages close or adjacent to Mkomazi by Hilda Kiwasila between May and October 1995.[3]

She found that in some villages the pressure on land and water resources sparked ethnic conflicts. These were exacerbated by conservation restrictions and local development projects. Access to land and water were seen as problems common to farmers and herders. Shortage of land for grazing and lack of support from the Reserve have fomented dissatisfaction and discontent with Mkomazi's extent and their relations with it. Several villages among the 11 surveyed are currently seeking alterations to the Reserve boundary.

It also became apparent that these villages are not united by their needs. They are ethnically heterogeneous, housing individuals with different livelihoods and resource needs, different histories and different ambitions. The restrictions of the Reserve affect them all, but in diverse ways. They are 'communities' only in the geographical sense that they all live in the same place. Politically, socially, ethnically and economically they are divided.

The needs of the cultivators and pastoralists are different.[4] Kiwasila has shown that cultivators, the largest group numerically, are sometimes also mixed farmers, with livestock as well as irrigated and/or rainfed crops.[5] They include several ethnic groups. The largest are the Pare and Sambaa, who dominate in Same and Lushoto District, respectively. These groups have a long association with Mkomazi.[6] Their main concerns are access to cultivable land, water for irrigation, and grazing for cattle and smallstock. They may also use the Reserve for placing beehives, gathering fuelwood, wild foods and medicines, mining gemstones, ritual use of sacred groves and other ceremonial sites, and hunting.[7] Of the interaction between Pare cultivators, agropastoralists and the Reserve, Kiwasila writes:

> Since eviction they have incurred crop losses to wildlife (particularly buffaloes and elephants), loss of grazing due to the proximity of Reserve boundaries, and water shortages because of the need to supply dams far from the village to keep wildlife away from farms. Losses to birds (perceived [to nest] in the Reserve) limit cultivation of drought resistant crops such as sorghum, or cash crops like sunflowers. Villagers feel they subsidize the Reserve more than they benefit from it. Some farmers have challenged Reserve boundaries over grazing, livestock watering facilities and/or farms which have been enclosed inside Mkomazi Game Reserve boundaries (Homewood *et al.*, 1997: 30).

Kiwasila also highlights the importance of traditional communal systems of land and water distribution. These have long been important for local production systems and for dealing with wildlife (Box 2.1) She argues that, although weakened and altered, water and land management systems persist in many villages and are vital to any future resource management planning.

The pastoralists include Pare, Sambaa, Maasai, Kamba and Parakuyo people. They have a strong interest in the grazing and water resources inside Mkomazi. Eviction affected pastoralists most, as they had gained

---

Box 2.1 Provision of water for wildlife in Kisiwani's past

'I have the honour to inform you that my attention has been drawn to the serious struggle that is ensuing between the natives and the game in the Kisiwani area by the following circumstances.

'When examining the Native Court Register at the end of the month I found one case in the Kisiwani Court where a man had been fined for irrigating his *shamba* (farm) from the river out of his turn. This is not a particularly uncommon type of case, for water is desperately short this year, and has to be shared out most carefully. The feature of this case that was striking was that the man was not fined for taking water that rightly belonged to someone else, but for taking it at night when, to paraphrase the actual words: 'the water is left in the river for the benefit of wild animals who, when there is no water, come into the *shambas* and destroy them'.

'I consider that this case is more illustrative and more convincing of the actual struggle for existence that is going on between the people and the game than any ordinary complaints or outcry could be. The situation at Kisiwani and elsewhere on that side of the hill is very serious indeed. The water in all the rivers is very low and there is barely sufficient to irrigate the rice fields and food *shambas* during this hot dry period. The fate of the rice crop, the staple product of the District, is hanging in the balance these few months.

'In these circumstances the people cannot possibly afford to sacrifice their right of taking water during the night – that is, in effect, to sacrifice one half of their available water supply for the benefit of wild beasts. On the other hand they dare not risk an invasion of their *shambas* by their hereditary enemy.'

Acting District Officer to the Game Warden at Arusha, 2 February 1935
TNA, 451/III/vol 1. Game Vermin and Marauding Game

---

most from the Reserve's resources and were most reliant upon it for their livelihood. Pastoralists, among the most vocal and vehement in opposing eviction and state regulation, have been most active in trying to regain access to the resources inside Mkomazi Game Reserve.

But even the pastoralists are a diverse group: Pare, Sambaa and Kamba are more settled, and have tended to combine agriculture with pastoralism through cooperative herding arrangements called *ndisha* by the Pare.[8] The Parakuyo and Maasai, who are closely related and both speak the Maa language, have tended to be more mobile, moving many kilometres from the mountains to watering points on the plains and commonly crossing international boundaries. The different groups are not united in their opposition to the evictions. Maasai and Parakuyo pastoralists legally challenged the right of the government to evict them. They were represented by lawyers from the Legal Aid Committee of Dar es Salaam University and 'Indigenous Peoples' non-governmental organisations. But the organisations fighting the cases conduct their meetings in

Maa; non-Maa speakers are not members of these groups. Pare, Sambaa and Kamba herders are not among the plaintiffs named in the legal cases. Indeed, some Pare agropastoralists, particularly towards the west of the Reserve, do not relish the prospect of large Maasai populations inside the Reserve, fearing an increase in cattle theft. For many decades Pare herders have resisted Maasai incursions on to their pastures. Pare elders are even said to have used magic to dry up a water source in the west of Mkomazi before the colonial period to discourage these visits. Rather than permitting permanent access to grazing inside the whole Reserve, some would prefer to see the borders moved, to allow more room for grazing and special provision to use the Reserve during drought.

The 'communities' around Mkomazi, then, are numerous, diverse and divided. Their politics are complicated. It would be easy for this text to become embroiled in the separate demands, alliances and conflicts that are the stuff of Mkomazi's local politics. But that is not my goal. My aim is to consider the dominant conservationist vision of Mkomazi, and its implications for community conservation. For this purpose I will focus on the groups whose histories are the most contested, who are held mainly responsible for the alleged environmental degradation, and who have been most affected by the loss of rangelands. These are the pastoralists, especially the Parakuyo and Maasai. The starkness of their case illuminates the contrasts and contradictions of the conservation vision.

Methods and sources

This book is based on two years' research around Mkomazi between 1994 and 1996. It was part of a project examining 'conservation with development' on East African rangelands, conducted by the Institute of Resource Assessment (IRA) of the University of Dar es Salaam and the Anthropology Department of University College London (UCL). It was funded by the Overseas Development Administration (ODA), now the Department for International Development (DFID), which is the British Government's department for administering international development aid.

Our brief was to look at the resource use and needs of people living around the Reserve, and to assess the possibilities of practising some form of conservation with development there. My colleague from IRA, Hilda Kiwasila, worked principally with agriculturalists around Mkomazi, mainly at Kisiwani. I worked with evicted herders, mainly Maasai and Parakuyo, at Kisiwani and Mng'aro. I spent the time interviewing people, collecting oral histories, observing their livelihood practices, collecting survey data from 52 households, talking to government officers and reading archives in Tanga and Dar es Salaam. Outside Tanzania I consulted documents kept at the Public Records Office (London), Rhodes House (Oxford) and the Kenyan National Archives (Nairobi).

The work was loosely associated with a parallel three-year research project organised by the Royal Geographical Society (RGS) and led by Dr Malcolm Coe of Oxford University. Their brief was to find out about the ecology and biodiversity of the Reserve. Their findings are discussed in Chapter 4, which examines the Reserve's environment.

The details of my methods are explained in Appendix 1, but a word is necessary about the political context of this research. Field work is normally politically charged but because our work was conducted in the shadow of the legal claims brought by pastoralists, work at Mkomazi was more than normally difficult.[9] Some evicted pastoralists could remember youthful white men making enquiries about their history and material circumstances when David Anstey and Henry Fosbrooke worked there in the 1950s. In 1994 Fosbrooke returned and alerted the Legal Aid Commission to the herders' plight. Expectations were high that my work would endorse their case for compensation, and their claims to have customary rights derived from decades of residence. My research was continually lobbied by herders bringing my attention to the hardship they suffered as a result of eviction and the strength of their historical associations with Mkomazi.

This meant that, when we talked about their lives, virtually every elder claimed to have been born inside the Reserve and their fathers before them. But the archival records and contemporary observers' accounts showed that the longest records of occupation were in the east of the Reserve. This casts doubt on the statements of a large number of people who claimed to be born in the west of the Reserve in the 1950s. The situation was too politically charged to rely heavily on oral histories. This account draws primarily on the archival record.

The complaints of impoverishment, however, rang true. As I analysed the data, it became clear that there had been substantial decreases in herd size and the livestock economy. I was disturbed that these problems were absent from the conservation literature about Mkomazi and that much of it was silent about the conflicts besetting the Reserve. I have tried to draw attention to these omissions.

With this in mind, let us consider the history of the area in which Mkomazi came to be gazetted.

Notes

1 Rainfall in Same averages 566 mm a year and in Voi 556 mm. There is more rain near higher ground: Kisiwani 734 mm/yr; Mnazi 782 mm/yr. See Harris, 1972; McWilliam and Packer, 1999.

2 Table 2.2 sets out the population changes in the wider area and includes all people north and east of the Pare and Usambara mountains. This shows a total population of 71,854, with an annual population increase of 1.9 per cent.

3 Homewood *et al.*, 1997.

4 Although many people hunt and gather wild resources, hunter-gatherers *per se* did not emerge during our survey as a significant separate group.

5 Kiwasila and Homewood, 1999.

6 Appendix F, Homewood *et al.*, 1997.

7 Kiwasila and Homewood, 1999.

8 Maghimbi, 1994; TNA 723/III, H.A. Fosbrooke, 'The development of the lower areas, North Pare,' 1951; interview, IM, 4/7/96.

9 Hobart, 1996.

3
Histories

Even the landscapes that we suppose to be most free of our culture may turn out, on closer inspection, to be its product.

Simon Schama, *Landscape and Memory*

At a lawyer's office in Tanga, on 9 November 1953, a Maasai man named Lobitara ole Saris received the final instalment of a 97,098 shilling compensation payment from the government. The event was unusual for three reasons. First, Lobitara was Tanganyikan, and the money was paid by the Kenyan government. Second, in 1953, 97,000 shillings were worth about US$ 50,000 in today's money. Third, at the claimant's insistence, the final instalment was the bulk of the payment. Lobitara walked out of the office with 82,098 shillings (more than US$ 40,000) in his bag.[1]

The compensation was paid because Lobitara was judged to have been unjustly fined after his compound was raided while he was illegally grazing his animals at the Katamboi waterholes, near Kasigau, in Kenya. Lengthy and painstaking negotiations between the governments in Dar es Salaam and Nairobi, and repeated appeals in the Kenyan courts, were required to resolve the issue. The raid on Lobitara's camp, and its repercussions, took much government time and effort, and caused some bitterness. Chandler, the District Officer who confiscated the cattle, was initially triumphant after the raid. He was amusedly exasperated when herders offered to swap milch cows for other stock lest their calves die.[2] His humour soon turned to anger when the Kenyan government had to make amends for confiscating too many animals. Memory of the compensation lives on locally; elders still talk of the incident with some wonder.

The conflicts, confusion, debates and negotiation that surrounded that particular event have been the very stuff of life in the borderland plains, then and now. Lobitara's case is an unusual example, the result of an overzealous new official misinterpreting his orders. More important are the broader forces and policies that gave rise to that incident.

Three perspectives are useful to understand the history of these plains and Mkomazi's current problems. First it is necessary to see them in the

23

context of political alliances and authority, of population movements and dispersal.[3] The history of the Reserve is part of a larger picture of migration, expansion and integration.

Second, at the government level, we should look beyond debates about conservation and consider the broader priorities of development and environmental management. Current conflicts began before the Reserve was established. Mkomazi should be seen in the context of the political and administrative goals of the colonial and independent governments.

Third, migration and government policy should be viewed from the point of view of the farmers and herders whose daily lives are deeply affected by both. Their perspective brings out the continuity of the plains' history which pre-colonial, colonial and independence periods only appear to divide. It also makes clear the close ties between conservation policy and development plans. Mkomazi's creation should be seen as the latest stage, an added complication, in a long series of disputes between the state and locals. From a resident's perspective, the establishment of the Reserve just added another layer of regulations to those already restricting the movement of people and livestock.

The contest for control of the plains is the persistent theme. In the nineteenth century conflicts between ethnic groups led to the evacuation of the Umba Nyika. In the twentieth century there were conflicts between ethnic groups and the state, and disputes between ethnic groups in which the state became involved. Of these, the disputes between ethnic groups have possibly been the more important. Governments had little control over the arrangements that herders made to gain access to pastures, and were rarely able to control herders' movements. They could, however, respond when residents brought their attention to the activities of troublesome neighbours. Local reaction to pastoral movements is therefore a vital consideration in the history of the plains.

From the nineteenth century to the Great War

In the nineteenth century the Umba Nyika was labelled the 'Wakwafi wilderness', and often portrayed as an empty and desolate land. For a long time these plains were on the margins of pastoral occupation and control. But their emptiness was in reality intermittent and partial. It has a history. Herding has been disrupted by war and interrupted by outbreaks of disease.

The plains are dry and were probably most used by herders and hunters. Although the story I relate is therefore a pastoral one, it should be put in its broader social context. Historians of East African societies emphasise how relations between different livelihoods are the key to understanding pre-colonial economy and society. Pastoralism is best seen as part of a continuum of livelihoods involving varying degrees of dependence on livestock, which were interlinked in a regional system by ties of trade, marriage and stock friendship. Livelihoods were dynamic. Families, individuals and larger groups could expect to move up and down the continuum of reliance upon livestock according to their fortunes.[4]

Society in East Africa was composed of complex congeries of different livelihoods mutually dependent upon each other. The varied environments of plains, hills, mountains, forests, lakes and valleys were each conducive to different modes of life, but each had limitations that necessitated dependence or predation on other places and groups. Pastoral livelihoods thrived in conjunction with agricultural societies and made sense only in a wider, less pastoral context.

Ties of trade, exchange and kinship provided for immediate needs and long-term security. The uncertainties of the environment and society meant that people lived with the continual spectre of hunger from drought, diseases or conflict. Families had to deal with these risks as well as pursue prosperity. The ties were also the product of specialisation. Those who spent less of their time tilling soil still needed agricultural produce, and those with fewer animals wished to acquire stock and their produce. Pastoral patterns of transhumance or nomadism not only meant moving livestock to the remaining water and grazing but also moving closer to agriculturalists with whom trade for foodstuffs was possible. Provision of meals was the responsibility of women, and they traded with their neighbours to make best provision for their households. They were safe to do so even if there was armed conflict going on at the time.

The economic connections operated in a context of variable and flexible ethnicity. Intermarriage and changing livelihoods meant that it was possible for people to join other societies. Ethnic identity was debated, interpreted and mutable.[5]

A survey of accounts of the Umba Nyika and its environs underlines the importance of ties between agriculturalists and pastoralists on the hills and plains. Trade provided strong connections. In Uzigua, south of the Usambaras, trade between herders, locals and mountain groups was a central part of the economy.[6] Kimambo records that Maa-speaking pastoralists exchanged livestock for iron and food with the Pare. Håkansson has argued that the development of intensive agriculture on the Pare hills was driven by trade between plains pastoralists and hillside farmers.[7] There were several large markets below the Pare mountains, at Kihurio, Gonja, Kisiwani, and near the Usambara mountains, at Dongo Kundu, Kitivo and Mbaramu. These served a diversely populated hinterland and became increasingly important as trade with the coast grew. Johnston noted that the main traders in Gonja spoke the Pare, Zigua, Maa and Swahili languages.[8]

Alliances, protection and cooperation formed another link. There were communities of stockless Maa-speakers who formed alliances with neighbouring agriculturalists. Baumann and Johnston observed Kwavi farmers living close to other agricultural peoples. Baumann reported one case of close links between Maa-speaking Ndorobo hunters and the Pare, noting that a band of Ndorobo had settled near Kisiwani and had adopted Pare customs and an agricultural livelihood. Pare and Sambaa leaders formed pacts with Maasai herders for protection and to attack others. Baumann found that a large number of people in north and central Pare had some command of Maa.[9]

However, the most prominent form of contact for many observers in the nineteenth century was raiding. Accounts are replete with the agropastoralists' fear of, and measures to prevent, cattle raids by the Maasai. Baumann noted that only the most inaccessible or well-protected mountain pastures were safe from Maasai raids in the second half of the nineteenth century. Feierman reported that the Shambaa were only prepared to risk trading with the Kwavi if they had a 'Kwavi blood partner'. Maghimbi suggested that Pare herding on the plains only began in the twentieth century, having been restricted to the mountains for fear of raids by Maa-speaking pastoralists.[10] The Maasai did not always win these encounters. Johnston noted that the Maasai kept away from Kisiwani because they had suffered previous defeats there.[11] The Taita raided the Maasai for cattle.[12]

The presence of trade cannot be taken to mean thriving exchange between vigorous populations. Cattle and their herders on the Umba Nyika in the nineteenth century were often sparse. Its aridity proscribed intensive use; droughts would disperse those frequenting the plains. The earliest account of the Umba Nyika, from the late 1840s, described it as frequented by elephant hunters but otherwise 'unoccupied and without rivers or streams'.[13] But its emptiness then was the result of internecine strife; it had been used much earlier. It is possible that the intensive agriculture Håkansson describes was a product of exchange much earlier on in the century.[14]

There is evidence of extensive use of the Umba Nyika by a number of Maa-speaking groups collectively called the Kwavi, or *Iloikop*, in the early years of the nineteenth century. In the late 1840s Krapf named the plains 'the Wakuafi wilderness' and noted that the Kwavi 'infested the countries adjacent to the sea coast'. He recorded that they had resolved to occupy the Kadiaro hill (also known as Kasigau) shortly before he travelled there. Guillain labelled a similar hinterland as 'Oua-Kouavi', and reported that the same group had formerly occupied 'Bomboui' and 'Kidangga-dangga', dry places two and three days' journey behind Vanga respectively (see Map 4). Similarly, Thornton noted that a place called Sogoroto two days' journey from Vanga had 'formerly been a station of the Wakuafi'.[15]

The main area of Kwavi occupation was probably in the western part of the coastal hinterland. Krapf recorded their homeland was called Kaptei, or Kaputei, found north of Kilimanjaro.[16] Thompson wrote that in the first decades of the 1800s the Kwavi occupied 'the large district lying between Kilimanjaro, Ugono (Ugweno) and Pare, the hills of Taita and Usambara' (Young, 1962: 128). New noted that:

> The Wakuavi formerly occupied the whole of the plains around the base of Mount Kilima Njaro, also the extensive tracts lying between Taveta and Jipe, on the one hand and the Taita mountains, on the other (New, 1873: 355).

But who were 'the Kwavi'? 'Kwavi' was, and is, a pejorative term, used to describe stock-poor and defeated Maa speakers' neighbours. 'Kwavi' people, however, would refer to themselves as Maasai.[17] It seems to have been used as a general name to covering numerous peoples who were displaced and dispossessed by wars fought in the first decades of the nineteenth century.[18]

In the early years of that century both the *Iloikop*/Kwavi and the Maasai were predominantly pastoral peoples. They shared a common history, and had closely related language and cultures.[19] The wars that divided them – known as the *Iloikop* wars – were fought in several stages. In the 1820s and 1830s, herders were pushed out of the Kwavi wilderness and fled westwards to Taveta or south to the plains west of the Pangani.[20] Then residents and refugees were driven to the south and east of the Maasai steppe between 1830 and 1850. They took refuge with cultivators along the southern edge of the Usambara mountains and the Nguru mountains.[21] New gave an account of the process for the Kwavi of the Umba Nyika, which illustrates the flexible nature of ethnicity and the close connections between agricultural and pastoral peoples:

> In the course of time the Masai, emerging from the west, swept over the open plains, smote the Wakuavi and scattered them to the winds, leaving, however, the Wataveta in their forest fastnesses in perfect security. The Wakuavi, robbed of all and completely broken up, some wandered this way and some that, while many turning to their friends the Wataveta, asked and found refuge with them. Ever since the two peoples have lived together, assimilating more and more to each other's habits and modes of life. The Wataveta, however, seem to have been far more influenced by the Wakuavi than vice versa; for they have become Kikuaviized in almost everything but the giving up of agricultural pursuits, whereas the Wakuavi remain Wakuavi still, except that from necessity they have turned to the cultivation of the soil (New, 1873: 355–6).

The disturbances of the wars resulted in the evacuation of the Umba Nyika by the end of the 1830s. The portrayals of an empty wilderness come from accounts written after the devastation of the wars. The plains in 1850 were depopulated, not unpopulated.

After the wars use of the plains remained slight for some time. They were on the borders of the main area of Maasai pastoralism. Wakefield marked these plains as 'Uninhabited Wilderness subject to raids of the WaMasai and WaKwavi'. Farler called the areas around Mbaramu (near Mnazi), between the Pare and Usambara mountains and at Lake Jipe, 'uninhabited'.[22] But both were writing second-hand versions based on caravans' reports. First-hand accounts reported more activity, but still never recorded the volume of cattle or numbers of people seen in the 'densely populated Masai district(s)' in the late 1880s.[23] Only much later in the century were larger numbers of livestock and herders found here, and then only in the southern margins of the plains, near the Pare and Usambara mountains.

There appears to have been a slow increase in herding in the plains surrounding the mountains up to the end of the 1880s. Johnston recorded meeting around a thousand Maasai at Ngurunga, at what seems like a large meat feast, in 1884. Willoughby noted that Maasai raiding parties and herds could be found north-east of Lake Jipe in the late 1880s. Meyer met a group of Maasai warriors with a troop of donkeys close to the south-west corner of the Usambaras, and reported good relations between the Maasai and Kamba residents of a village called Mkumbara. In 1887 Count Teleki met a large number of Maasai in the Ruvu (Pangani) valley, west of the northern end of the South Pare mountains. Frontera reported that Taveta herding increased from the 1880s onwards.[24]

Baumann gave a comprehensive account of Maasai grazing patterns in 1890. He stated that the Umba Nyika used to be the domain of the Kwavi, but that these people were displaced by the Maasai. The main users were the Sogonoi Maasai, whose main camps were in the Sogonoi mountains on the western side of the Pangani but who maintained large camps at Mwembe, near Same, and at the south end of the North Pare mountains. He noted:

> they range over the whole of the Umba Nyika and consider as their main area for plunder the eastern Pare mountains, Usambara, the foreland and the Coast (Baumann, 1891: 168).

He also noted that they exploited the wetter places on the top of the Tussa hills and the mountains of central Pare, which more readily afforded water and grazing than the plains.[25]

The only reference to any quantity of cattle on the plains comes from Le Roy, who reported seeing thousands of Maasai cattle on the plains between Mnazi and Gonja and visited a Maasai compound one hour's walk from Gonja in the second half of 1890.[26] This is the one account to resemble Von Hohnel's description of the densely populated Maasai lands between Mounts Meru and Kilimanjaro. But the gains were temporary and vulnerable to misfortune. At the end of the nineteenth century a disaster struck livestock whose effects are especially visible here.

Between July and December 1892, Smith travelled along the same route as Le Roy, surveying the Anglo-German boundary. He described the Umba Steppe as:

> Nearly level country with gently rolling surface; thorn scrub; no paths. No water. No inhabitants (PRO, FO 925/228/A).

Similarly, the area north-east of Lake Jipe is labelled on his map as '[r]olling plains covered with thorns, apparently wilderness'. In contrast to Le Roy, Johnston and Meyer, he met no pastoralists. He observed that game populations were small and much less than Thompson, Johnston and Meyer had reported; there was no sight or sign of buffalo. Smith speculated that absences were due to the ravages of the recent cattle disease. He reported that the Maasai were nearly exterminated by famine.[27]

Between Le Roy's visit and Smith's, the cattle disease rinderpest had struck. The first clear record of the disease in East Africa comes from a German campaign up the Upper Pangani, west of the Pare Mountains, in early 1891. Troops passing north in February noted healthy herds, and returning south in the same month 'found the disease raging'.[28] The difference between Le Roy's and Smith's accounts is almost certainly due to rinderpest, which killed the cattle and forced pastoralists to flee. Elsewhere in East Africa the effect was devastating. Millions of animals, wild and domestic, are thought to have died. The rapid spread of the disease brought catastrophe to thousands of people and disrupted people's homes and livelihoods.[29] It is likely that rinderpest forced pastoralists on the Umba Nyika to flee south to friends or relatives in Handeni or Bagamoyo, or to disperse into adjacent agricultural communities.[30] Disease undid the gains made by pastoralism since the *Iloikop* wars.

But rinderpest was not the only force keeping pastoralists out of the Umba Nyika. Their absence in the early 1890s also reflected the impact of German military action. The expedition that first observed rinderpest also fought the Maasai. In 1891, following Maasai harassment of trading caravans, and a declaration of war on the Germans at Masinde, German troops attacked camps on the east of the Ruvu river and expelled them all to the west bank. They undertook further expeditions to clear the Maasai from what Ekemode terms 'the Pare plains' after caravans were again harassed in 1892 and 1894, and after Arusha and Maasai raids on the North Pare mountains. The Germans maintained their garrisons in settlements on both sides of the mountains.[31]

The Germans attempted to keep the Maasai west of the Pangani river, but it was evidently possible to evade the controls. Fosbrooke suggested that Maasai were resident in the Toloha area until 1916, throughout the

German occupation. Oral histories from Kitivo, near Mnazi, dated the arrival of Kwavi north of the mountains as early as 1907. A history noted in 1952 recorded one man's arrival at Gonja before the First World War. In 1964 a number of Parakuyo elders estimated that they had arrived approximately fifty years earlier. Hodgson argues that the Germans had 'little success confining the Maasai to the Reserve'.[32]

The final disturbance of the time was the First World War. Military accounts carry few details of local presence or activity, and one can only speculate as to their impact. There were patrols, skirmishes and military movements throughout the area in the first months of the war, as the Germans repeatedly sent raiding parties through the Umba Nyika to sabotage the railway line. This would not have been conducive to local use of the plains.[33]

'We just left it' – herders' migrations up to 1953

After the war Britain ruled Tanganyika. A significant consequence of British rule following the disturbances of the previous twenty-five years was stability. Livestock herds began to recover; indeed, the dominant trend of pastoralism in this part of East Africa in the twentieth century, recent reversals notwithstanding, was expansion. British rule also saw state attempts to control, change and earn revenue from its subjects. There were four policies of particular relevance to livestock keepers. These concerned relations between ethnic groups; land alienation; pastoral development; and game preservation. All these policies involved increasing degrees of territorial categorisation and boundary creation – in Collett's phrase a 'packaging of the land' – which set in motion the contests that comprise Mkomazi's history.[34]

The colonial administrations tended to perceive ethnic groups and their territory as distinct. The flexibility that had characterised earlier times was now restricted. In Kenya disputes over the proper path of Maasai development were typified by ethnic reifications by those who sought to have the Maasai included in broader Kenyan progress and those who sought to preserve the Maasai from being swamped by immigrants. In Tanganyika the British continued to restrict the Maasai to the west bank of the Pangani. Maasai families found outside Maasailand were moved into it, and emigration beyond the borders was controlled. The Kwavi east of the Pangani were not included in the moves. State attempts to fix ethnicity did not prevent people from changing identities, but meant that the state became included in their negotiation. This conception of ethnicity was adapted by African subjects to their own ends, as they sought to exclude or allow people into certain areas. The history of Mkomazi is infused with disputes between local groups and between them and the state, about who was who, and who should have access to where.[35]

Land alienation in Tanganyika was generally slight, especially if contrasted with Kenya.[36] But events north of the border had a direct influence on herding patterns on the Umba Nyika. Colonel Grogan, one of the colony's more aggressive settlers, expanded his sisal estates at Taveta towards Lake Jipe and encouraged the exclusion of the Maasai who watered there. Kenyan desires to promote different forms of development variously in the 'native reserves' of Taveta, Taita and Kasigau, the new national park of Tsavo and on settler farms combined to restrict herders' movements.

But it was the government's attitudes to pastoral livelihoods and land use that are most important for understanding developments in the twentieth century. Maasai pastoralists have variously been seen as irresponsible, unproductive citizens who need to be modernised; as people needing protection from forces for change; or as potential collaborators in their own development. The first characterised attitudes in Kenya at the turn of the twentieth century and helped to justify the large-scale land alienations of the Maasai moves.[37] The second came to the fore in Kenyan Maasailand during the interwar years and was closely tied to conceptions of Maasai ethnicity. Waller describes an administration split between those who sought to include the Maasai in the regional economy by encouraging alien settlement and agriculture and those who sought to defend the Reserve from immigration, which might impede future Maasai development.[38] The third was an optimistic assessment from Tanganyikan Maasailand in the late 1940s. It was associated with the Maasai Development Plan, which was to assist the Maasai to breed and produce better cattle.[39] The point is that there was no consistent opinion in one 'official mind'. Since independence, governments in Kenya and Tanzania have generally encouraged commercial beef production among pastoralists. Attempts have rarely been successful.[40]

Despite the diversity in opinions about how, and in what way, the Maasai should change, there was general agreement that their form of land use was dangerously destructive. Collett notes that these fears deepened in Kenya in the 1930s and 1940s, fuelled by the theory that the Maasai suffered from a 'cattle complex', keeping as many animals as possible instead of few of good quality.[41] Hodgson notes that overstocking replaced water conservation as the main problem in Tanganyikan Maasailand in 1930. In the five years before the Mkomazi Game Reserve was established, overgrazing was an overriding environmental concern, associated everywhere with the presence of cattle. The creation and early status of the Reserve hinged upon colonial views about what people, and particularly cattle keepers, would do to its environment.[42]

Attitudes to wildlife changed markedly in the twentieth century. Initially game was abundant, a nuisance to be eliminated from settlers' farms.[43] Pastoralism was not seen to be an immediate threat to wildlife. However, fears grew that the tendency of the Maasai to accumulate cattle would lead to the degradation of the environment, the displacement of wildlife and loss of tourist income. This strengthened calls to have them removed from areas that could be usefully given over to wildlife.[44]

These views were reinforced in the 1930s and 1940s by the growing national park movement, which advocated the preservation of landscapes without a human presence. This period ushered in the policies of fortress conservation that so dominate African conservation.[45] A mixture of European and American values, that sought natural landscapes unspoiled by people, motivated the desire to set up protected areas. It was, at this time, allied to pressure to set aside land that guaranteed good sport for hunters.

The 1945 National Parks Ordinance of Kenya allowed land to be alienated for conservation purposes. Nairobi National Park was created first in 1946. The second, of most significance to this area, was the Tsavo National Park, which was established in 1947. It took several years before the park could be cleared and marked as the warden desired, but, in the 1950s, concerns to protect the park's environment appeared in local government records.[46] In Tanganyika, the National Park Ordinance was passed in 1948, and the Faunal Conservation Ordinance, under whose provisions Mkomazi was gazetted, became law in 1951.

I do not wish to explore these policies in detail. Rather, it is important to focus on what herders made of them at the time. The key concern, around which interactions between the government and pastoralists revolved, was their contrasting goals of livestock keeping. Waller and Homewood succinctly capture the difference between colonial livestock officers and pastoralists whom they were attempting to develop, with this story:

> A meeting supposedly once occurred between a group of Maasai elders and a colonial veterinary officer who was attempting to explain the benefits of stock improvement schemes. After listening in silence the Maasai countered with a generous offer: 'Send some of your young men to live with us and we will teach them to keep cattle properly' (Waller and Homewood, 1997: 69[47]).

The tale may be apocryphal, but it illustrates the gulf between the respective goals and ambitions. Pastoralists in this area were subsistence dairy producers, whose stocking rates maximised productivity per acre and whose herd structure facilitated long-term survival and recovery from drought. They preferred animals that were more likely to withstand the rigours of the dry season and the continual disease threat. Moreover, animals had more than economic value, for they cemented social relations within families and with their neighbours.[48]

From the local point of view, state control in the interest of pastoral development often imposed obstacles that had to be avoided. The advice to destock, to practise certain grazing rotations, not to move between districts, provinces or states was based on reasoning with which herders did not sympathise. It involved boundaries that herders did not recognise, and that were often not clear on the ground. This meant that the separate purposes behind the outlawing of trespass on private ground, foreign territory or a neighbouring district blurred into one. The establishment of Mkomazi in 1951 just added another administrative boundary to existing controls.

If the dominant theme in government during the first half of the twentieth century was increasing state control, that of pastoralism was continued growth and prosperity, as livestock populations recovered from the ravages of the turn of the century. The resurgence involved three groups. First there were Pare, Sambaa and Kamba agropastoralists who grazed their stock around the base of the Pare and Usambara mountains. Second there were Kwavi herders – who it is now more appropriate to call Parakuyo – north of the Usambaras; they spent the dry season close to the mountains and the Umba river and spread out on to the plains as far as Katamboi (in Kenya) in the wet season.[49] Finally, there was a collection of Maasai, Parakuyo and other groups who based their transhumance around Lake Jipe; this group was known to government officials as the 'Toloha Maasai'.

As the century progressed the competing interests of the three different groups of pastoralists clashed with each other, and to various degrees with the agendas of political officers, conservationists and the veterinary department of the Tanganyikan and Kenyan states. Issues came to a head in 1951 quite independently of the gazettement of Mkomazi. Understanding this is crucial to understanding the Reserve's history.

In the 1920s the Tanganyikan government resolved to place all Maasai families in the Maasai Reserve, west of the Ruvu river. Although officials later made temporary concessions to allow grazing east of the river, they firmly believed that Maasailand was where the Maasai ought to be. Officials were frequently concerned that the Maasai were leaving 'their' land and encroaching on other people's.[50] In 1934, the District Commissioner of Pare complained that the Maasai had overrun the grazing east of the Ruvu river and west of the railway line. In the 1940s there were reports of families moving with their stock from Losogonoi, Naberera, Nyumba Ya Mungu and other places west of the Ruvu river into the Toloha area and the Parakuyo grazing grounds east of the river. There are also reports of Maasai families leaving stock with Parakuyo residents east of the river. In 1955, the Provisional Veterinary Officer of Tanga complained that there was an annual invasion of 30,000 head of cattle, and as many smallstock, into Lushoto and Pare Districts from Maasai District.[51]

Government officials were particularly concerned about the growth of pastoralism at Toloha for several reasons. Officials faced pressure from local Pare leaders, who lobbied to control and limit the Maasai presence.[52] A number of Pare leaders wrote to the District Commissioner of Pare to complain of cattle theft by the Maasai and Parakuyo:

> In this country we Pare stay with Maasai, Kwavi, Nyamwezi and Arusha but always the Maasai and the Kwavi are stealing our cattle from the pastures – for they graze together at the same time – but we have never seen stock of the Maasai or Kwavi stolen. ... We citizens ask our glorious government that the Maasai who stay here be returned yonder from whence they came in Monduli District and that they stay there. If a Maasai comes into Pare country he should do so only with certified permission. (TNA, 11/5, vol II, 7/11/44, letter from Pare elders to diverse District Authorities.)

There was also government pressure from officials north of the Kenyan border. The annual transhumance of the Toloha herders crossed the international boundary because the only access point to Lake Jipe was on the Kenyan side, at a place called Vilima Viwili. Reeds and mud on the lake shore made it impossible to water stock elsewhere. Herders took this opportunity to make extensive use of Kenyan grazing. In the wet season they would move east, watering in temporary pools along the border with Kenya and in areas that were to become Tsavo National Park and the Mkomazi Game Reserve. Some went as far north as the Taita Reserve.

Officials found the presence of the 'Toloha Maasai' increasingly troublesome after the Second World War.[53] There was some concern that the stock would bring livestock diseases out of the Maasai steppe.[54] There was also the problem of what they were doing to the colony's resources. Kenyan officials frequently complained that the Toloha Maasai really wanted grazing, not just water, and would be found miles to the north of the lake, encroaching on Kenyan soil. To their chagrin they found that Maasai and Chagga herders were moving as far north as Bura in the Taita Reserve, where they established links with resident herders and gained access to grazing.[55] The herders were using, and in the government's view damaging, lands for which the government had other plans. The government wanted to preserve the land for Kenyan subjects, Africans and settlers, and prevent encroachment on the newly formed Tsavo National Park. To this end they resolved to withdraw permission for Tanganyikan herders to use Lake Jipe.[56]

The number of stock in Toloha at this time was large. Various estimates of 13,000 to 21,000 cattle were offered between 1945 and 1949.[57] Tanganyikan officials had to devise a plan to provide water for some of these herds and resolved to provide for some and move others. New sources were planned for the Pare pastoralists at Toloha, but Maa speakers were to be moved. The Parakuyo pastoralists would go to the Pangani valley, where they would occupy the Northern Railway Game Reserve, which was to be degazetted. Maasai herders would be sent back across the Pangani river, where they would be part of the Maasai Development Plan.[58]

Tanganyikan plans moved slowly, and for a while an uneasy status quo continued. However, pressure mounted within Kenya to put the land to productive use. Colonel Grogan, owner of Ziwani Sisal Estates at Taveta, applied for an extension to his lands in the late 1940s that would include the Vilima Viwili watering point. This was granted in 1951. It was a boost to the Kenyan cause as he had already demonstrated a willingness to keep out pastoralists with his own hands, and was determined to stop Toloha livestock keepers from using his land. The rest of the crown land south of Grogan's land was added to the National Park, and the game rangers' help in patrolling the border was enlisted.[59]

The closure of the Kenyan border put paid to government plans for an orderly removal of Maasai and Parakuyo to separate destinations. Herders coped with the change without state oversight. Facing continued pressure on their grazing, a number of them sought pastures and water elsewhere. In early 1951 one group of Toloha herders travelled down to the Katamboi waterholes, found just across the border in Kenya, and just inside a recently gazetted extension to the Tsavo National Park (Map 2).[60]

The Katamboi waterholes were hitherto virtually unknown to the government on either side of the border, but they had long been used as watering points for wet season grazing by Parakuyo pastoralists based at Mnazi.[61] Although Toloha herders had mixed with the Parakuyo here before, this migration caused tension.[62] Lack of rain in 1952 led to drought, and veterinary staff recorded the death of hundreds of Maasai and Parakuyo animals. Parakuyo leaders lobbied the Lushoto District government to have Maasai herders expelled. The Lushoto District Council readily agreed to this request and decided to send the Maasai back to the Maasai steppe.[63]

The desire to remove the Maasai was reinforced by the establishment of the Mkomazi Game Reserve in 1951. The first game warden of Mkomazi, David Anstey, resolved to allow some Parakuyo families access, because it was their normal home and because their impact on the environment was slight. He was particularly determined to exclude the Maasai on the grounds that this was not their normal place of residence.[64]

In other government departments, the desire to move the Maasai was accompanied by a desire that the Parakuyo should stay in the new Reserve and continue to use the waterholes in Tsavo. The Lushoto District Commissioner wrote in 1953:

The legitimate occupants of the Reserve, with their stock, (e.g. Wakwavi, Wakamba and Wasambaa but excluding Masai) should be allowed to remain. (TNA, G1/7, 7/7/1953, DC Lushoto to PC Tanga) (parentheses in the original).

In 1953 he prepared a formal request to the Kenyan Government for grazing rights at Katamboi to be granted to the Parakuyo.[65]

The Provincial Commissioner of Tanga took the matter up with the Royal Commission on Land and Population. He wrote:

Grazing and watering concessions across the border in the Kenya Tsavo National Park are essential for correct management of stock on the plains on the eastern side of the Usambara–Pare range: such concessions would be no more than a recognition of traditional rights of the Kwavi and Maasai in this area (PRO, CO/892/12/3, 19/5/1953[66]).

In any event, both the District and Provincial Commissioners' requests were refused.[67] Access to the Katamboi waterholes was denied to the Parakuyo because the water was inside the National Park. Some of the Parakuyo could still use the Reserve, but the Maasai were to be returned to Maasailand.

Moving the Toloha herders from Mnazi and Katamboi proved extremely difficult as they tried varied means of resistance between 1952 and 1954. They pleaded to be allowed to remain, hired lawyers, tried to bribe officials, and fled the attentions of the veterinary guards sent to supervise the moves.[68] The Tanganyikan efforts were not helped by Kenyan officials who seized and sold Lobitara's cattle at Katamboi without sufficient warning or due process, necessitating he stay until his compensation was cleared, as we saw at the beginning of the chapter.

In 1954 the Lushoto District Commissioner reported that the 'Toloha Maasai' had been moved out, but noted a return of Maasai into the area.[69] This time, however, the Parakuyo did not complain about Maasai infiltration. One Parakuyo leader of the time described the events in these terms:

Well, when they started coming here in large numbers, it's just human nature. We talked to each other; we understood each other. We understood each other, we married into each other's families, we exchanged cattle ... We kept quiet, we did not raise the alarm any more, we did not complain to the government. We just left it. We all lived here together (Interview, KK, 5/10/1996[70]).

Parakuyo support for Maasai immigrants made it harder for the government to keep them out, but it was in any case a demanding task to sort people into their 'correct' ethnic groups. When the government came to move the Toloha 'Maasai', they discovered that they included families from the Arusha people (from near Mount Meru), and the Kahe (just south of Kilimanjaro). It was not thought appropriate to move these people 'back' to the Maasai Reserve.[71]

A further complication arose when officials tried to separate the Parakuyo and Maasai. Lushoto District officials found that the lines between them were blurred. The Maasai sought Parakuyo identity, or set up links with the Parakuyo to avoid eviction. In early 1954 government officers found themselves dealing with some Maasai families who refused to leave the area; others who had left, but whose stock remained in Parakuyo compounds; some who were allowed to stay on the condition that they had no more than 10 cattle and took up cultivation, and a fourth group, which the officials termed 'pseudo-Kwavi', who had been accepted as Parakuyo by the Parakuyo leaders. The Game Department later realised that the Maasai were also buying the right to use the names of deceased Parakuyo pastoralists from the dead men's families in order to be allowed to use the Reserve.[72]

The events at Mkomazi are reminiscent of Waller's account of Kikuyu immigration into the Kenyan Maasai Reserve in the 1930s and 1940s.[73] He reports Kikuyu petitioning the government to be allowed to stay, offering to pay higher Maasai taxes and seeking out Maasai sponsors who could give them a place to stay, or vouchsafe their Maasai credentials or history. Waller writes:

> None of these claims and pasts were inherently implausible; nor were they necessarily false – though some probably were. But this is to miss the point. They were not intended as 'real' life histories. They represented attempts on the part of the immigrants to accommodate themselves to what they under-stood to be the dominant concern of the colonial administration, to speak the prescribed language of ethnicity and tradition upon which their interrogators insisted and to make themselves acceptable to their prospective neighbours (Waller, 1993: 236).

The context of that analysis was the attempt of agriculturalists to be and to become Maasai. At Mkomazi, ironically, Maasai pastoralists were lobbying to become Parakuyo.

Thus the plan to allow controlled use of the Reserve by a few Parakuyo families foundered from the outset. The requirement of ethnic separation and limited access ran against the very nature of pastoral society. The pastoral practice of creating networks and links and expanding options for grazing, meant that this period saw the initiation of increasingly close links between the Parakuyo of Mnazi and the Maasai from the Ruvu valley, Toloha and the Maasai steppe. The arrangement also ignored the presence of numerous Kamba, Sambaa and Pare pastoralists who were present in Lushoto District and who were accustomed to use the Reserve's resources. The focus on Maa-speakers was to cause dissension early on in the history of the Reserve, and has coloured developments ever since.

The history of the Reserve

Mkomazi was established against a background of continual concern to shepherd pastoralists to different parts of north-east Tanzania. Herders continually resisted control of their movements. The history of the Reserve was set to follow the same pattern. Its main events can be summarised very briefly. Cattle numbers rose dramatically and persistently. For twenty years stock numbers grew in the eastern portion of the Reserve. After 1969, the western part of the Reserve was opened up to herders and stock numbers rose rapidly there too (Table 3.1). In the late 1980s, in response to continual state concern about the environment, herders and other residents were evicted. They dispersed to villages bordering Mkomazi and other sites nearer the coast and on the Maasai steppe, west of the Pangani river.

I wish to highlight three aspects of the history of the Reserve. First, official concern for the welfare of local inhabitants was pre-eminent in the minds of the officials who gazetted Mkomazi. They were anxious that the Reserve should not impede the development of these inhabitants.[74] This was expressed from the outset in a comment by Bates, the District Commissioner of Pare, on a proposal from the Senior Game Ranger at Lyamungu, in 1949:

> First and foremost the area provides a sanctuary for game without in any way interfering with the legitimate present and future needs of the local population (TNA, 451/IV, 25/4/1949, DC Pare to PC Tanga).

'Legitimate' meant needs that were not environmentally damaging, and that were voiced by the appropriate ethnic group. Colonial officers went to considerable lengths to ensure that Bates's priorities were observed. Anstey emphasises that careful consideration was taken of

Table 3.1 Cattle numbers around Mkomazi.

Year	East (Lushoto District)	West (Same District)	Total
1960	21,984	no data, probably not more than 15,000*	21,984 + ?
1965	38,561	19,031	57,592
1967	45,245	no data	45,245 + ?
1978	28,219	39,539	67,758
1984	48,233	39,977	88,210

Sources: 1960, 1967 data Lushoto District Office wall chart; 1965 data Anderson, (1967); 1978, 1984 data from census printouts held in District Offices.
*Evidence suggests that cattle numbers in Same District had been low for some time prior to 1960. Local residents recall that when a Maasai herder came to Kisiwani in the late 1940s he was forced to leave because of the losses he experienced from trypanosomiasis (PRA, Mkonga Ijinyu, 4/7/95). The threat of the disease kept herders away for some time. There was a sudden increase of stock in the west in the 1970s. Harris mounted intensive ground-based observations of the west of the Reserve but recorded only 1,350 – 1,650 cattle inside the Reserve, all in its eastern half (Harris, 1972: 113). Parker and Archer mapped the approximate extent of cattle in the Reserve in 1970 and placed cattle only in the top north-west corner of the Reserve near Toloha (Parker and Archer, 1970: 48).
1978 and 1984 livestock census data for Same District are taken from two wards alone, Gonja and Kisiwani, whose lands were included in the Reserve for the purposes of the cattle census. These wards are remarkable for their low ratio of smallstock to cattle (Table 3.2). However, these totals therefore exclude a number of potential Reserve-using stock, which were found in wards adjacent to the Reserve. Some 8,000 head of cattle were found in Usangi (equivalent to the Toloha area) in 1978 and 1984. There were also nearly 30,000 cattle on the western side of the mountains (Ruvu, Same and Same-Njoro), which might have made temporary seasonal moves into the Reserve.

local needs before the Reserve was created. He recalls that the African District Councils were consulted for two years prior to the Reserve's creation, and asked to confirm that there were no taxpayers living within it.[75] Anstey then searched the Reserve to check that there were no occupants. He drew attention to several groups that the consultation process had missed. These included a large group of Pare herders east of Gonja with about 30,000 cattle, and the Parakuyo herders who lived north of Mnazi.

Nonetheless there were a number of local protests against the establishment of the Reserve (Box 3.1), from herders, hunters and honey gatherers who lived near to the Reserve and whose access to its resources was now denied. Some of the protests were successful. The Gonja herders' complaints released a large section of land from the Reserve, between the Pare and Usambara mountains. It was redesignated the Kalimawe Game Controlled Area, with no controls on pastoral access. Others gained no concessions. Such complaints did arouse sympathy in higher circles of government, reflected in a debate over whether or not to maintain the Reserve at all. Although all were concerned to control what were perceived to be bad environmental practices, some felt that the Reserve placed too great a constraint on people's resource use.

At an early stage the District Commissioner of Lushoto made it clear that:

> There is no objection to the continued existence of the Reserve if it is felt to be worthwhile, provided that the existing human interests within the Reserve (except the Masai) are not prejudiced. (TNA, File 962, Lushoto District Annual Report, 1953) (parenthesis in the original).

In 1953 the Provincial Commissioner of Tanga made a cautious proposal that the Reserve be used for controlled grazing schemes:

> Animal husbandry [is] to be encouraged by permission to ranch on an economic basis within Game Reserves, including seasonal use of grazing and water across the Kenya border. ... The conflicting claims of the Game and Veterinary Departments in respect of the Mkomazi Game Reserve require to be examined, possibly with a view to arranging an easily controlled use by stock of suitable areas within the Reserve (PRO, CO/892/12/3).

The concerns caused the very existence of the Reserve to be questioned. In 1953, a team of district officials from Pare debated the question, but were unable to agree on the merits of Mkomazi. The Reserve was large, occupying a third of Same District, and three members of the team thought it would make good grazing land, while the other three believed it would make a valuable contribution to wildlife conservation.[76] Trotman, the Secretariat Member for Agriculture and Natural Resources, decided the issue in favour of the Game Department in 1955. He declared that proper use was not being made of the area outside the Reserve, where

Box 3.1 Local protests against Mkomazi after its establishment

'... when the government came to put Game Reserve borders here there's not one citizen who was asked or informed where the borders would go; now several citizens have received severe fines ... We bring our request that the borders be placed far away ... so that there will not occur again other complaints which cause disagreements between the government and the citizens. But this request is disregarded by the Game Ranger. Now what is your decision now that the dry season has come?'

The Gonja branch of the Tanganyika African National Union writing to the DC of Same on behalf of Pare pastoralists. The Kalimawe Game Controlled Area was subsequently excised east and south of Gonja to provide room for these pastoralists, 1 July 1956, TNA, G1/7

'We are residents of Kizungo; we are not businessmen or office workers but we get our food and tax for the government from our herds, our farms and our beehives since a long time ago ... All these lands have been the dwelling places of people ... since 300 years ago. ... People have been moved suddenly and left their farms or been evicted from their watering places and houses have been burnt. This was done by armed game guards who evicted people like animals. People moved to areas which for a long time have not sufficed for living, much loss is incurred from the death of goats and sheep and from the lack of water. Moreover the beehives which were hung the Game Ranger decided should be cut down and split, and they were cut down and split and all the honey was eaten by the vandals. ... Since the tribulation we face is great we have no other purpose except this need: that we want help quickly to get our rights which have been lost and to be given our freedom as are the other citizens of the realms of this kingdom.'

The Pare people of Kizungo to the District Commissioner of Same, 24 January 1957, G1/7

'Under instructions from Huseini Mane, Musa Kirewasha and 25 Africans of Baramu in Usambara District I have to address you the following: 1. My clients are African herdsmen and have their cattle *bomas* [compounds] in Mnazi – Kamba near Kivingo. 2. Until recently they were grazing in the Mkomazi area but owing to the said area being declared a game reserve, my clients have been prohibited to enter this area and they have been ordered to graze only in the Bambo near Kamba area. 3. The area allocated near Bambo is a small piece of land infested with tsetse flies and the grass appears poisonous. This area has no water supply as the river dries up in the hot season and the insufficiency of pasturage has put my clients who own about [a] few thousand cattle, sheep and goats into a very awkward situation. 4. The pasturage in the Bambo area has taken a heavy toll of my clients' cattle in that they have lost about 150 heads of cattle recently and they are convinced that the reason is because of the poisonous grass. 5. My clients desire to petition the government for excising a sufficient land from the Mkomazi Game Reserve for their cattle and at which place in the past they ... had acquired grazing rights.'

Barrister writing to the District Commissioner of Lushoto on behalf of Pare and Sambaa herders following the clearing of Reserve boundaries in the late 1950s, 4 February 1960, TNA, G1/7

From Homewood *et al.*, 1997: opposite 22.

overgrazing had not been curtailed. He felt that degazettement was pointless if wanton misuse of resources outside Mkomazi induced a need for the resources inside it.[77]

Trotman's decision introduces the second aspect of Mkomazi's history. Debates over the existence and proper use of the Reserve became dominated by a hegemonic concern in government circles that pastoralists degraded the environment, and that their method of stock keeping was irrational. It was necessary to reduce livestock numbers and increase offtake if pastoralists were to become productive beef farmers and protect the environment.[78] Every time alternative uses for the Reserve have been suggested, they were discounted because of the environmental problems that people were perceived to cause. It is arguable that Mkomazi owes its continued existence largely to perceptions of degradation.

The strength of this view was apparent in the late 1960s, when the issue of Mkomazi's validity and worth again surfaced. In 1967 the Principal Secretary to the Ministry of Agriculture and Co-operatives asked a senior research officer, Dr Anderson, to carry out a land use survey of the Reserve. He informed Dr Anderson that the minister was under pressure to degazette the Game Reserve, but could only do that if he was satisfied that the land was best used for agriculture or pastoral use.[79]

Anderson identified the central questions as:

> (a) whether or not the wildlife resources of the area are sufficient to justify the existence of the Reserve;
> (b) whether the existence of the Reserve is compatible with, or of equal or greater value to the nation than the other human interests in the area (Anderson, 1967: 2).

Anderson found that the Reserve had potential for game viewing but poor arable potential, and that herders were destroying their habitat and causing large-scale erosion. He argued that their use of the Reserve was precluded by the damage they inflicted outside its boundaries. As a consequence of that degradation, access to Mkomazi's resources must be denied, and moreover, the government must take steps to control cattle numbers and land use outside the Reserve. Anderson recommended that the Reserve should not be opened up for pastoralism.[80]

There are no more records of further plans to degazette the Reserve after 1967. But the Game Department was unable to promote the type of land use outside the Reserve that would ensure the sanctity of the environment within its borders. In early 1968 the Game Warden of Same and Tanga pressed for the removal of all Maasai and Parakuyo stock back to Maasailand. There are patchy records of an attempt to move the Parakuyo back to their 'original' dwelling place in Handeni. David Anstey recalls that he deposited in Arusha £16,000 (approximately US$ 32,000) raised from the culling of elephants within Mkomazi, in order to pay for the move.[81] Ultimately local government officials seem to have been reluctant to endorse any large-scale movement of people. They seemed to prefer the status quo, allowing limited access to some, combined with frequent and inevitable illegal use by others.

The ineffectiveness of the Department of Wildlife underlines the third aspect: pastoralists have been able to circumvent official concerns and restrictions with apparent ease, at least until recently. Paradoxically, the history of Mkomazi is largely one of rising cattle numbers and ever-growing pastoral and bovine prosperity. This is apparent in the rising livestock numbers in and around the Reserve. Initially some 3,000 cattle were allowed inside the eastern half of the Reserve in 1951, although many more were present in the area, especially around the borders (see Table 4.4). After a series of showdowns in the 1960s that number was increased to 21,000.[82] By 1984 there were nearly 90,000 cattle inside the Reserve, with 33,000 sheep and goats; 48,000 smallstock had been counted in Mkomazi in 1978. More animals were found nearby (Table 3.2).

Pressure on Reserve resources was initially strong in the east of the Reserve (Lushoto District). Here the pastoral networks built up between the Maasai and the Parakuyo grew and intensified. The expansion of pastoralism that had dominated the period before 1950 was continuing.[83] In 1960, Paul Moreto, a leader of the Kwavi and resident at Hedaru in Same, wrote to the Minister of Natural Resources to complain that there was not enough grazing, and no opportunity to visit friends inside the Game Reserve because of the entry prohibitions.[84] In addition to the continual pressure from plains pastoralists south of Mkomazi, there was also pressure from Sambaa herders based in the Usambara mountains. The Usambara Development Scheme encouraged the movement of stock from the highlands to the plains. In 1959 the Game Ranger refused to allow dry season grazing inside the Reserve for herders living around its boundaries because, he alleged, cattle had been brought down from the hills by the Sambaa deliberately to put pressure on the Reserve.[85]

Table 3.2 Cattle numbers and smallstock: cattle ratios around Mkomazi.*

Ward	1978 cattle	1978 smallstock:cattle	1984 cattle	1984 smallstock:cattle
Usangi	8,443	1:2	8,490	1:3
Same-Njoro	11,202	2:2	12,372	1:4
Ruvu	12,919	2:3	10,576	1:1
Same	6,896	2:2	6,761	1:5
Kisiwani	22,788	0:6	13,856	0:5
Maore	16,751	0:9	26,121	0:4
Ndungu	3,893	1:4	7,075	1:1
Kihurio	6,693	2:2	3,278	4:3
Umba (Division)	28,219	0:7	48,233	0:4

*Reserve livestock populations are found in Kisiwani, Maore and Umba (see notes to Table 3.1).

But it was also clear that the pastoralists had strong allies within local government, who were either not competent to handle herders' requests or, actively promoted them. At one point herders took district officials on a tour of their grazing areas, leading them a considerable distance into Kenya – much to the consternation of the more senior officials when they tried to work out where exactly their junior staff had gone.[86] In the mid-1960s a meeting of people from a number of different ethnic groups with the Lushoto Development Committee condemned the discrimination that allowed only the Parakuyo to use the Reserve. It resolved that either all herders should be given grazing rights, or the borders of the Reserve should be moved back to allow more room for grazing.[87] The Regional Commissioner of Tanga twice refused to move Maasai and Parakuyo herders from around the edge of the Reserve, despite pressure from the Game Department.[88]

The refusal to destock was accompanied by increasing conflict between the Lushoto District officials and the Game Reserve staff. The District Commissioner of Lushoto instructed game scouts to stop harassing Maasai in the area, and was angry when people arrested for illegal entry were sent outside his District to Same. At one point the Regional CID officer instructed that a serious crime file be opened under the heading of Arson, following allegations that the Game Warden had burnt down houses inside the Reserve.[89]

At the end of the 1960s the eastern half of the Reserve was extensively used by livestock. Thereafter pressure mounted on the western half, in Same District. Herders were attracted by improved water supplies, after the Department of Wildlife had built three dams – at Ngurunga, Kavateta and Dindira – in the 1950s and 1960s.[90] They were also attracted by the success of Pare agropastoralists, living in the southern borders of the Reserve, in defeating the tsetse fly challenge. Three Pare families came to Kisiwani to herd in the early 1950s. They engaged in a systematic programme of bush clearance and burning to clear out the tsetse fly.[91] The result was a more favourable environment for cattle. One of the families reported that they had arrived with just 34 cattle and managed to build up a herd of 1,500.[92]

The other factor that stimulated attempts to use the Reserve were the dry times experienced at the end of the 1960s and early 1970s. Residents of Kisiwani recall that they petitioned to use the Reserve in order to cope with the drought. In Mnazi, Pare herders went to Dar es Salaam to ask for permission from the Ministry of Natural Resources and the Environment to herd their cattle inside the Reserve.[93] After that, permits were available from the Game Reserve Manager in Same.

When permission was given to use the west of the Reserve after 1970, it was only intended to be temporary. In the early 1970s the Game Department resolved several times to stop giving permits. Nothing, however, appears to have been done.[94] Maasai and Parakuyo pastoralists went on to establish settlements at Kisima and Kavateta within the Reserve.[95]

The resultant growth of cattle in the area, evident in censuses, had a considerable effect on the local economy. In the mid-1970s a cattle market opened east of the Pare mountains, first at Gonja, then at Kisiwani. It rapidly grew to become the most prominent market in the area, exceeding even Makanya, situated west of the mountains, which had the advantage of a good road connection (see Table 3.3, and Chapter 5 for more consideration of livestock markets). Indeed, immigration in the western half of the Reserve caused some problems to the resource management practised by resident pastoralists. Its consequences are illustrated by the letters written in protest at the arrival of these immigrants by herders themselves. These are discussed in the next chapter.

Eviction and internationalisation
By the early 1980s, pastoral presence at Mkomazi was at its zenith. The Reserve was regularly used by a large number of permanent residents and seasonal immigrants, and it was well incorporated into pastoral economy and society. A number of attempts to evict herders in the 1970s and early 1980s failed.[96] What happened to make the evictions possible in the late 1980s?

This, unfortunately, is an unanswered question about the history of the Reserve.[97] Mangubuli suggests that it has been difficult to move the pastoralists because they had strong allies in local government. Evictions became possible when the Department of Wildlife built up the alliances necessary to carry out the evictions.[98] Others suggested that the persistent presence of the pastoralists in the Reserve was related to the power of Mr Sokoine, the Maasai Prime Minister of Tanzania; when he died in 1984 it became politically possible to order the clearance.[99] Watson mentions the contribution of dedicated staff, whose determination may have made it possible to push through awkward decisions.[100] The Regional Wildlife Officer of Kilimanjaro, Mr Mungure, may well have been important here.

Table 3.3 Cattle sold in Kisiwani and Makanya markets.

Period	Kisiwani	Makanya
Apr 1977 – Jun 1977	139	266
Jul 1977 – Jul 1978	no data	no data
Aug 1978 – Jan 1979	433	567
Feb 1979 – Jul 1979	279	183
Aug 1979 – Jan 1980	763	886
Feb 1980 – Jul 1980	602	1,064
Aug 1980 – Jan 1981	1,025	957
Feb 1981 – Jul 1981	852	1,054
Aug 1981 – Jan 1982	424	980
Feb 1982 – Jul 1982	448	811

Source: District livestock records.

He later became the first Project Director of Mkomazi after the evictions were complete and was renowned for his determination, energy, uprightness and refusal to countenance local opposition. Overall this suggests a pattern of shifting allegiances at higher levels of the state, and a gradual reconfiguration of local support. The data, however, are thin, and the reasons behind the change still obscure.

Once agreed, the removal of herders was relatively rapid. In 1986 all permits for residence and grazing issued after the gazettement of the Reserve were revoked. Local residents reported that the evictions were a gradual process. First to go were those who were illegally present without any form of permit. Then those with false and forged permits were moved out. Finally, in December 1987, the decision to evict permit holders and those named on the lists of 1950 and 1968 was announced. This decision took a while to be confirmed and enforced. In early 1988 the Wildlife Division and local authorities agreed that the Reserve's inhabitants should be moved to the Ruvu valley and Kiteto District (on the Maasai Steppe). In April 1988, the Principal Secretary of the Ministry of the Environment, Natural Resources and Tourism confirmed the revocation of all permission to live inside the Reserve. By July 1988 the Reserve had been cleared. Mkomazi was declared a national project, with its manager reporting directly to head offices in Dar es Salaam.[101]

The evictions were final. There has been continued illegal use of the area, but most estimates suggest that 75 per cent of the livestock numbers present in Mkomazi in the 1980s have gone.[102] Those which remain are confined to the narrow band of land between the Reserve boundary and the mountains to the south and east. Illegal grazing is common, and cattle are still to be found in the Reserve, but aerial counts suggest that their presence is greatly reduced, compared to previous ground counts (Table 3.4).

Since the evictions Mkomazi has been subject to international attention from conservation organisations and human rights activists. This attention has ensured that issues previously contested locally and nationally are now disputed in sites around the world. Six months after the evictions were complete the Department of Wildlife agreed that the Field Officer of the GAWPT, Tony Fitzjohn, should assist the rehabilitation of the Reserve.[103] Since then the Trusts have supported the restoration of the Reserve's infrastructure, an outreach programme and an endangered species reintroduction programme.

The other aspect of international influence is the growth of human rights organisations' interest in Mkomazi. A number of Tanzanian 'Indigenous Peoples' non-governmental organisations have formed links with evicted Parakuyo and Maasai pastoralists and have sought to represent their case within Tanzania. These organisations in turn obtained their funding from international charities and donors, who have

Table 3.4 Aerial survey counts of livestock in and around the Reserve after eviction.

Date	Livestock	Count	Standard error
February 1988[a]	Cattle	14,275*	no data
June 1991[b]	Cattle	11,305	5,626
	Small stock	6,426	1,920
October 1991[b]	Cattle	30,811	11,422
	Small stock	1,792	986
April 1994[c]	Cattle	23,557	12,530
	Small stock	4,739	2,356

a) Wildlife Conservation Monitoring Department, 1988.
b) Huish *et al.*, 1993.
c) Inamdar, 1995.
*Inside the Reserve only.
All data are derived from systematic reconnaissance flights (SRF).
The higher counts in 1991 correspond to a relatively dry time, when a large number of cattle sought access to
water near the Reserve's perimeter. This period was also associated with renewed efforts to keep herders out of the
Reserve, and subsequent distress sales at local livestock markets.

been pressing for pastoralists' rights and development needs. One of the
results of this alliance was the court cases brought by the Maasai and
Parakuyo seeking compensation and renewed access to the Reserve. We
will consider the implications of the internationalisation of the Reserve in
chapters 5 and 6.

Conclusion

There are three themes in this history that I wish to emphasise. First, the
demands made of Mkomazi result from long-term population growth and
movement, and much of the business of the expansion has centred on
inter-ethnic contact, contest and cooperation. But the story told here is
thin. The chapter has traced only the outline of these interactions, the
negative space within which events unfolded. Much of the archival
records on which it is based consist of state reactions to these local initiatives. They miss the colour and detail. As Willis says:

> ... it is impossible to know completely the circumstances of all the micro-
> processes of ethnic change; the thousands of events and discussions through
> which identity is redefined and negotiated in everyday life and discourse
> (Willis, 1992: 192).

Yet these micro-processes are the substance of the history of the occupation of the plains. A local perspective requires more interviews and
discussion than this research could provide.

The importance of local politics serves to highlight the second theme,
the weakness of the state before the 1980s. This version of the story is
one of officials', and particularly colonial officials', reactions to events

of which they were only partially, if at all, in control. Trying to prevent the spread of pastoralism was like keeping the sea out of a sinking boat. Pastoralists and herds kept springing up everywhere. The weakness of the state is also apparent in the marginality of wildlife interests for much of the Reserve's history. Pastoral expansion was often overlooked, even sanctioned, by different interests within the state. During colonial times a number of officials feared the restrictions that the Reserve would impose. After independence, pastoralists within the Reserve found allies in government. When faced with the prospect of evictions, some officials could not stomach the thought of moving so many people. The Wildlife Department has become politically strong only in the past sixteen years.

If the state could not control social relations, it could still exert coercive control over the use of land, and in doing so spur more conflicts. At the same time as pastoralism was expanding, its frontiers were being closed. This is the third theme. Kenyan authorities marked and guarded the international boundary and set aside some of their most useful land for settlers, game preservation and local development. The Tanganyikan authorities set about developing rangelands and expanding protected areas. The Mkomazi Game Reserve was the last in a series of land alienations that closed access to the rangelands of the Umba Nyika. Viewed from below it was but another line on the map, but the map was filling up. The result was intensified conflict between the state and pastoralists, and between different pastoral groups over who was to use the land.

Schama reminded us at the beginning of the chapter that landscapes are cultural products, either by virtue of the meaning invested in them or because of the direct influence of human activity. Mkomazi's wilderness status has been promoted by omitting histories of residents or by labelling their activities as inappropriate and damaging. The history written above shows that it is inaccurate to label these lands as 'primeval' or 'pristine'. Herders used the Umba Nyika for much, possibly all, of the twentieth century, until the evictions. They had used the plains at various times in the nineteenth century. It is quite possible they were there before that. The land here 'wears man's smudge and shares man's smell'.[104] If meaning is invested in the wildness (i.e. 'human-lessness') of Mkomazi, it is being invested in an historical invention. Of course, if wildness is a cultural construct then all meaning therein is an invention of sorts. The point here is that this is a particularly inappropriate application of that invention. The irony is that while herders' activity has been deemed out of place in Mkomazi, in fact conservation's labelling of the land is more problematic.

But if the land was shaped by people, what did they do to it? A central element of conservation's image of Mkomazi is that it was degraded by people. The marked continuity before and after independence in officials' views on herders, regardless of their views about game reserves, is that they were all anxious about the degradation livestock are believed to cause. Fear of degradation has always justified excluding people. The history recorded above tells us nothing about how right or wrong these fears have been. It is to the allegations of degradation that we now turn.

Notes

1 TNA, 723/III, 9/11/1953, W.P. Holder & Co. to PC Tanga. $50,000 and $40,000 are respectively equivalent to £33,000 and £26,000. The calculations made for these figures were crude. The 97,018 shillings was in compensation for 500 cattle that were confiscated and sold and for the loss of calves that died in the absence of their dams. To arrive at present-day values I have estimated the average price of cattle today be 80,000 Tanzanian shillings and the exchange rate of the dollar to be US$ 1: Tzsh 800. Extra compensation for the lost calves amounted to a few thousand shillings in 1953 and is not included in the calculations.

2 'Incidentally,' he wrote to his District Commisioner, 'some Kasigau Masai came to this office this morning. They wanted to exchange the cattle which had been confiscated! I make no comment!' DO Taveta to the DC, Voi, 4 April 1952, KNA DO/Tav/1/26/13.

3 cf. Monson, 1998: 119.

4 Sources are legion. Key references are: Waller, 1979, 1985a, b, 1988; Berntsen, 1976, 1979a, 1979b; Anderson & Johnson, 1988; Anderson, 1988; Sobania, 1993; Galaty, 1993; Lonsdale, 1992; Waller and Sobania, 1994; Bonté and Galaty, 1991.

5 Bravman, 1998.

6 Giblin, 1992: 22–8.

7 Håkansson, 1995.

8 Feierman, 1974: 124–5; Johnston, 1886: 307.

9 Lemenye, 1955: 37; Kimambo, 1969: 22, 177; 1991: 3; 1996: 81–5; Feierman, 1974: 178; Thornton, diary entries, 16 and 18 July 1861; Baumann, 1890: 90; 1891: 136–8, 143, 170–1; Johnston, 1886.

10 Baumann, 1891: 131; Feierman, 1974: 131; Maghimbi, 1994: 10.

11 Johnston, 1886: 306.

12 Bravman, 1998: 57.

13 'Le pays est inhabité et sans cours d'eau.' Guillain, no date, vol II: 290. The hunters are likely to be Kamba people who are thought to have come into these parts since at least the early years of the 1800s and probably a century before that (Feierman, 1974: 125–7).

14 Brockington, 2000.

15 Krapf, 1854: 5; 1860: 222, 362; Guillain, no date: vol II, 289; Thornton, diary entry, 4/10/1861.

16 Krapf, 1860: 236, 361.

17 Waller (1985b: 115–16) cited Johnston, who travelled here in the mid-1880s, as follows: 'If you ask the "Wakwavi" of Mazindi what they are they will reply

at once, "Masai". And if you only ask a nomad Masai … what he calls his congeners of Mazindi who perhaps a generation ago were fighting in the same clan he will answer contemptuously "Embarawuio".' (Johnston, 1886: 213).

18 Waller, 1979: 152–6; Rigby, 1985: 7. See Berntsen, 1980; Beidelman, 1960: 245–51; Waller, 1985: 114–19; Hodgson, 1995: 30–1 and Brockington, 2000 for a more complete discussion of the terms and their origins.

19 Sommer and Vossen, 1993: 34–6; Berntsen, 1980.

20 Waller, 1979: 152–3; 1985: 117; Krapf, 1854: 4–5; Galaty, 1993: 74–5.

21 Waller, 1979: 312; Jacobs, 1965: 82; Hurskainen, 1984: 71–82; Beidelman, 1960: 247–8; Baumann, 1891: 276–7; Fosbrooke, 1948: 4, 11. Berntsen, 1979b: 132–9.

22 Wakefield, 1870: map; Farler, 1882: 741–2. Farler did mention a 'large Maasai town' called 'Mkomazi', where caravans could trade for livestock. This was probably at the site of the present Mkomazi village (see Map 1).

23 Von Hohnel, 1894: 129. Lemenye's account of the massing of stock south-west of Kilimanjaro prior to rinderpest provides a similar contrast (Lemenye, 1955: 41).

24 Johnston, 1886: 302–5; Willoughby, 1889: 73; Baumann, 1890: 94–5; Von Hohnel, 1894: 83–5; Frontera, 1978: 23.

25 Baumann: 119, 139.

26 Le Roy, no date: 120–1.

27 The lack of people and animals is unlikely to reflect the influence of aridity. Although Smith was travelling in the dry season he reported that the Ngurunga and Baya (Ibaya?) waterholes held water; he was also in the area for several months. Smith, 1894: 427–9, 431.

28 See Waller, 1988: 76–7 and footnote 11 for references to rinderpest in the Pangani.

29 See Waller, 1988 for a detailed account; also Lemenye, 1955: 41–2; Berntsen, 1979b: 283 and Hodgson, 1995: 33–4.

30 Lemenye, 1955.

31 Berntsen, 1979b: 302–3; Ekemode, 1973: 103–4, 136, 157–60.

32 Spear, 1997; Iliffe, 1969; TNA, 11/5, vol III, October 1951, report entitled 'The Masai in Same District with particular reference to the Toloha Masai': 3-4; interview, VC, 26/11/95; TNA, 723, vol III, November 1952; TNA, G1/7, 30/1/64; Hodgson, 1995: 36. Other sources give later dates – 1926 – for the arrival of the Kwavi north of the mountains (Anstey, pers. comm., 23/7/1998). This suggests that there were several migrations involved.

33 See Brockington, 2000 for more details and Giblin, 1990a: 76–77 for an account of the disruption of the war in Uzigua.

34 Collett, 1987: 139.

35 Sobania, 1988b: 227; 1990: 11–12; Iliffe, 1979: 324; Waller, 1984: 243; 1993: 236, 240; Waller and Sobania, 1994: 59. Ethnic shifting remains a current reality. At Mkomazi there are many cases of intermarriage and people, especially immigrants, adopting their neighbours' dress, custom and identities (Kiwasila, pers. comm. 1998).

36 Chidzero, 1961; Iliffe, 1979. Locally there were some significant incidents of land alienation of herders' pastures to the west and north of the Mkomazi area (Hodgson, 2000: 68). These did not have a direct influence on events on the borderland plains.

37 Collett, 1987: 141.

38 Waller, 1993: 240–1; Rutten, 1992: 189.

39 Hodgson, 1995: 180–3; Hodgson, 2000: 58. The plan involved opening up new grazing grounds by adding new water points and eradicating tsetse, controlling seasonal movements and encouraging stock sales through taxation and offering goods and services.

40 Raikes, 1981; Rutten, 1992: 223; Hodgson, 1995: 79–80; 1999; Collett, 1987: 138–9; Behnke, 1985; Behnke and Scoones, 1993; Scoones, 1995.

41 Collett, 1987: 142; Herskovits, 1926.

42 Anderson, 1984; Hodgson, 1995: 130, 136–7; Rutten, 1992: 228, 233. Mackenzie, 1998 has a detailed discussion of how soil conservation schemes and fears of erosion become instrumental in imposing colonial will on subjects. Waller cautions against calling overgrazing orthodoxies 'hegemonic', finding more variation in the records than the term suggests (pers. comm., 2000). The relatively few files consulted here are dominated by overgrazing concerns, with a few isolated exceptions. The term is useful for describing thinking about Mkomazi from the earliest stages of the Reserve's history. But this is not necessarily representative of thinking in the rest of Tanganyika or Kenya or in other government circles.

43 Steinhart, 1989: 257.

44 Lindsay, 1987: 152; Collett, 1987: 145.

45 Anderson and Grove, 1987; Collett, 1987; Neumann, 1998; Hulme and Adams, 2001a; Steinhart, 1989.

46 Cobb, 1980: 12; KNA, KW/23/30.

47 Compare with Huxley's recollection of this exchange with Delamere: "'Delamere,' they said, 'how long will you stay here?' 'I shall stay for ever,' he replied. 'Then,' they said, 'we will look after your sheep. You do not understand the pastures. You do not understand sheep. We will help you.'" Huxley, 1935: 152. Cited in Knowles and Collett, 1989: 445.

48 Sandford, 1983; Behnke, 1985; Meadows and White, 1979; Mace and Houston, 1989; Behnke and Scoones, 1993; Dahl and Hjort, 1976.

49 Beidelman, 1960, discusses the rights and wrongs of various names. It is possible that the families allowed to live in Mkomazi were related to the refugee communities of Parakuyo who lived close to agricultural neighbours and patrons around the Usambara and Pare hills following destitution from war and disease. The patriarch of the herders allowed to live in Mkomazi, Kamunyu, was the brother of Matei, the Parakuyo *Laibon* who lived at Hedaru in the 1920s (Fosbrooke's papers, 1/1/1967; Hurskainen, 1984: 185–6). Their descendants dominated the households I worked with around the edge of the Reserve in 1995 and 1996.

50 TNA, 35/3, 9/9/1922, Senior Commissioner Arusha to DPO Usambara.

51 TNA, 723, vol I, 15/5/1934, DO Pare to PC Tanga; TNA, 11/5, vol II, 7/2/1944, Veterinary Officer Usangi to DC Pare; TNA 11/5, vol II, 13/4/1944, DC Pare to Veterinary Guard; TNA, 11/5, vol II, 23/1/1946, DC Pare to VO Tanga; TNA, 11/5, vol II, 3/7/1946, complaint from the Usangi court that Maasai from Arusha Chini are 'finishing' their grazing; TNA, 11/5, vol II, 21/10/1946, request for grazing on the east bank of the Ruvu for Maasai families at Losogonoi and Makweni; TNA, 11/5, vol II, 23/12/1947, report from the Hedaru native court; TNA, 962/15, 16/12/1955, annual report of the PVO Tanga to the Director of Veterinary Services Mpwapwa.

52 TNA, 723, vol I, 9/5/1933, DO Pare to DO Moshi.

53 An earlier attempt to move pastoralists from near Toloha had been made in the late 1930s. A number of Maasai families resident on crown land in Kenya, and using Lake Jipe for their dry season watering, were identified as having come from Tanganyika in 1924. They were moved across to the Pangani valley in 1938 and despite opposition west over the Pangani river in 1939 (see correspondence in TNA, 723, vol I). Many returned east of the Pangani during the war years TNA, 723, vol II, 25/7/1951, PC Tanga to SPC Arusha.

54 TNA, 11/5, vol II, 1/7/1946, DVS Mpwapwa to PVO Tanga.

55 TNA, 11/5, vol II, 18/8/1948, PC Coast to PC Tanga; KNA, DC/TTA/1/1/3, 1951 Annual Report: 3–4; KNA, KW/23/30, Warden's report, April/May 1950: 2; KNA, DO/Tav/1/1/22, 10/11/1952, CS Nairobi to CS Dar es Salaam.

56 TNA, 723, vol II, 30/12/1950, Deputy CS Nairobi to CS Dar es Salaam.

57 TNA, 11/5, vol II, PVO Tanga to the DVS Mpwapwa; TNA, 11/5, vol II, PVO Tanga to PC Tanga.

58 TNA, 11/5, vol II, 26/10/50, Member for Agriculture and Natural Resources to PC Tanga; TNA, 11/5, vol II, November 1950, notes for a meeting about the Toloha Maasai. The Northern Railway Game Reserve is known in some sources as the Pare Game Reserve.

59 KNA, DC/TTA/3/8/37, 29/3/1951, Chief Native Commissioner Nairobi to CS Nairobi; KNA, DO/Tav/1/1/22, 20/11/1953, DC Taita to the Warden of Tsavo Royal National Park. Residents of Usangi still recall the time when Grogan shot cattle that had entered his land. The archives record this, and a number of other incidents when he took an active part in controlling cattle movement. These include demarcating roads and boundaries to limit movement and bull-dozing a temporary compound for impounded cattle (interview, MN, 21/9/96; TNA, 11/5, vol II, 24/11/1946; TNA, 723, vol II, 19/5/1951; TNA, 11/5, vol II, 16/5/1945; TNA, 11/5, vol III, 11/7/1951, DC Pare to PC Tanga; TNA, 11/5, vol II, ?June 1945, Veterinary Guard Usangi to VO Tanga; TNA, 11/5, vol II, 24/10/46, Veterinary Guard Usangi to DC Pare.)

60 TNA, 11/5, vol III, 15/1/1951, DC Pare to PC Tanga; TNA, 11/5, vol III, 18/1/1951, telegram from 'Husbandry' Dar es Salaam to PC Tanga; TNA, 11/5, vol III, 9/2/1951, Member for Agriculture and Natural Resources to PC Tanga; TNA, 11/5, vol III, 22/3/1951, leader of the Kisiwani-Mbaga native court to DC Pare.

61 TNA, 723, vol III. Notes on the impounding of cattle at Katamboi by DC Voi, March 1952.

62 Colonial officers later discovered that the 1951 migration of the Toloha Maasai had been preceded by an earlier move of Toloha pastoralists to Mahambalawe in Lushoto District and that these 'Maasai' had been allowed by the Kwavi to stay with them (TNA, 723, vol III, 3/5/1954, DC Lushoto to PC Tanga). Local elders also recalled that the Maasai had begun to come into the area in 1948 or 1949 (interviews, VC, 26/11/1995; KK, 10/5/96).

63 TNA, 962/15, 11/11/1952, DVO Lushoto to PVO Tanga; TNA, 723, vol III, 26/2/52, DC Lushoto to PVO Tanga; TNA, 11/5, vol III, 3/7/1952, minutes of a meeting of Tanzanian and Kenyan officials to discuss the Katamboi affair; TNA, 11/5, vol III, 6/6/1953, DC Masai to DC Pare.

64 TNA, 6/1, 1952 Annual Report by David Anstey, Game Ranger of Pare; Anstey, pers. comm., 25/2/96; TNA, 723, vol III, 23/6/1952, DC Lushoto to

PC Tanga; TNA, G1/7, 24/1/67, Principal Game Warden Arusha to the Director of Game Dar es Salaam. The ordinance made provision for people whose ordinary place of residence was within a game reserve to be allowed to continue to live there without further written authority. It was in accordance with these rules that the Parakuyo were allowed to carry on living in Mkomazi by the first game warden (Juma and Mchome, 1994: 7; Anstey, pers. comm., 25/2/1996.)

65 TNA, 723, vol III, Aug 1952, Tanganyikan government's request for grazing in Kenya.

66 PRO, CO/892/12/3, 19/5/1953. Given all the statements of his colleagues to the effect that the Maasai did not belong there, his inclusion of their rights with the Parakuyo is obscure.

67 TNA, 723, vol III, 23/12/1952, CS Nairobi to CS Dar es Salaam.

68 TNA, 723, vol III, 17/11/55, Political Lushoto to Provincer Tanga.

69 TNA, 962/1953, annual report of DC Lushoto for 1953.

70 '*Basi walipoingia kwa wingi; sasa ni ubinadamu tu. Tukaongea, tukapatana. Tukapatana, tukaoana, tukapeana ngombe ... Sisi tukanyamasa, hatukupiga kilele tena, hatukulalamikia serikali tena. Tukaacha tu, tukakaa wote.*' Interview, KK, 5/10/1996.

71 TNA, 11/5, vol III, 15/1/1951, DC Pare to DC Masai; TNA, 723, vol /III, 16/11/1955, Political Lushoto to Provincer Tanga.

72 TNA, 723, vol III, 29/11/1954, DC Lushoto to the Game Ranger Pare; TNA, G1/7, 17/4/1968, meeting of pastoralists and Game Department staff. Referred to in other publications as TA/GD/D10/16/22/193.

73 Waller, 1993.

74 TNA, G1/7, 7/7/53, DC Lushoto to PC Tanga; TNA, 723, vol III, Aug. 1952, DC Lushoto's request for grazing in Kenya; PRO, CO/892/12/3, 19/5/53.

75 These are probably the Pare Tribal Councils, a meeting of the nine chiefs of Upare with the District Commissioner, which had jurisdication over local affairs and were part of the mechanism of indirect rule (Kimambo, 1990: 82–6, 119). Anstey states that the Pare and Usambara African District Councils requested the degazettement of the Northern Railway Reserve and suggested the gazettement of Mkomazi as compensation. Although the proposal may have come from African District Council meetings, it is not clear whether Pare leaders pressed the idea on Bates, or whether Bates suggested it to them in their meetings (Anstey, pers. comm., 25/2/1996; 28/9/1998).

76 TNA, G1/7, 9/10/53, extract from the minutes of the District Team; TNA, G1/7, 15/11/55, Le Maitre to Member for Agriculture and Natural Resources, the Secretariat.

77 TNA, G1/7, 21/12/55, Member for Agriculture and Natural Resources to the PC Tanga.

78 A fuller discussion of the record of environmental concern follows in the next chapter.

79 TNA, G1/7, 16/8/67, PS of the Ministry of Agriculture and Cooperatives to the Senior Research Officer Northern Research Centre.

80 Anderson, 1967. His conclusions are discussed in more detail in the following chapter.

soit—

81 TNA, G1/7, 24/8/68, Principal Game Warden Arusha to the RC Tanga; David Anstey, pers. comm., 25/2/95; Anstey to Mrs Fitzjohn, 14/6/97.

82 TNA, G1/7, 17/4/68, meeting of pastoralists and Game Department staff. Referred to in other publications as TA/GD/D10/16/22/193. Anstey recalls that this agreement was not accepted by higher officials in the department (pers. comm., 23/7/98). It appears to have acquired official status later, for when the evictions took place the permission given during that meeting was officially withdrawn.

83 TNA, G1/7, 17/4/68, report by the Umba Game Officer on the new list of residents of Mkomazi Game Reserve; interviews, VC, 26/11/95; MM, 26/11/95; KK, 10/5/96.

84 TNA, G1/7, 27/12/60. Moreto was the son of Matei, who was the Parakuyo *Laibon* in 1922, cf. note 49.

85 TNA, 4/962/17/XIX, annual report for Lushoto District, 1951; TNA, 723, vol III, 26/2/52, DC Lushoto to the PC Tanga; TNA, G1/7, 2/12/65, Regional Game Warden Arusha to the Game Warden Tanga; TRA, V10/10, 22/8/59, Game Ranger to Political Lushoto.

86 TRA, V10/10, August 1959.

87 TNA, G1/7, 30/1/64, minutes of a meeting of pastoralists with the Lushoto District Development Committee.

88 TNA, G1/7, 16/7/64, Regional Administrative Secretary Tanga to Regional Game Warden Tanga; TNA, G1/7, 23/3/66, RC Tanga to the PS of Agriculture, Forest and Wildlife.

89 TNA, G1/7, 27/10/66, DC Lushoto to Divisional Executive Officer Mbaramu; TNA, G1/7, 30/1/67, DC Lushoto to PC Tanga; TNA, G1/7, 1/12/66, Regional CID Tanga to District CID Lushoto.

90 Mangubuli, 1991: 12.

91 PRA, Mkonga Ijinyu, 4/7/95; interview, IRM, 4/7/96.

92 Interview, IRM, 4/7/96; KWLF, 11/10/1983.

93 PRA, Mkonga Ijinyu, 4/7/95; interview, JM, 22/5/96.

94 Management of the Reserve was severely weakened in the 1970s when the decentralisation policy passed authority from Dar es Salaam to the districts and regions. Responsibility for the west and east of the Reserve was divided between Same and Lushoto Districts, respectively. The two halves were renamed Mkomazi (in Same District) and Umba (in Lushoto). See Mangubuli, 1991: 12.

95 Interview, IRM, 4/7/96.

96 Mustaffa, 1994; Brockington, 1998.

97 The failure is a consequence of the research design. Multi-site studies of development projects have successfully combined insights into livelihoods, history and policy process – Ferguson's *Anti-Politics Machine* is probably the best-known example. Recent studies of conservation politics in Zimbabwe and Zambia show what can be achieved (Duffy, 2000; Gibson, 1999). The political history of conservation in Tanzania in the 1980s, which would reveal how Mkomazi came to be cleared, is yet to be written.

98 Mangubuli, 1991: 12

99 Swai, pers. comm., 1996.

100 Watson, 1991: 14.

101 Mangubuli, 1991: 12–13; Fosbrooke papers: URT/G/C/MGR/77/91 and URT GD/18/R/8/226; Mangubuli, 1991: 13; URT GD/18/R/8/246, Director of Wildlife to the George Adamson Wildlife Preservation Trust, 10/10/88. Kiteto is now divided into two districts named 'Simanjiro' and 'Kiteto'.
102 This was the most common estimate I heard around the Reserve.
103 URT GD/18/R/8/246, Director of Wildlife to the GAWPT, 10/10/88.
104 The phrase is from Gerard Manley Hopkins. Turton used it describe the Mursi's domain in Ethiopia (1987).

4
Environments

Captain Wilson:	If your cattle go on increasing and the grass gets finished, what will you do?
Nibilei Olkopen:	I would still keep my cattle. I do not want them to die. I want to look after them. They are our life. As the Government likes shillings, so we Samburu like cattle.
Captain Wilson:	Would you rather have three hundred cattle or five hundred starving ones?
Nibilei Olkopen:	I would rather have a thousand starving ones until God gives us grass, because if a man has a lot of cattle, and some die, he still has some left, but if a man has a few cattle and they die, he has none left.

Kenyan Land Commission, Evidence, 1933: 1602,
cited in Spencer, 1973: 180

Two schools of thought dominate thinking about Mkomazi's environment. The most powerful view is that pastoralism causes overgrazing, soil erosion, deforestation, burning and depletes biodiversity. This justified eviction of pastoralists, buttressed decisions to maintain the Reserve and still infuses publicity about Mkomazi. These ideas have been called the 'received wisdom' of pastoral ecology.[1]

Ecologically they emphasise the role of stocking rates in vegetation dynamics. Interactions between grazers and vegetation determine vegetation cover and composition.[2] Wildlife numbers are naturally regulated, but livestock are not; they are protected by people, and may exceed the natural limits and induce unnatural change. The sociological assumptions are that communally owned pastures will inevitably be degraded, and herders' stocking rates are irrationally high. People's greed and preoccupation with cattle result in too many animals.[3]

The idea that pastoralism is not destructive has been less influential in Mkomazi's history. It is popular, however, in some circles and guides interpretations of environmental change.[4] This view holds that pastoral stocking rates are rational responses to environmental constraints.[5] The effects of livestock are complex, but do not correspond to 'environmental degradation'. In a semi-arid savanna, the disturbance caused by grazing and burning does not necessarily cause damage; it is more likely to result in disturbances that foster biodiversity.[6] Livestock do not necessarily exclude wildlife, rather the greatest concentrations of wildlife in East Africa depend on pastures grazed with livestock.[7]

The ecological basis for this challenge is the theory that holds that vegetation dynamics in drylands are not driven primarily by grazing pressure. Vegetation change is stochastic, non-linear and primarily dependent upon precipitation and the physical environment, not grazing, browsing or trampling.[8] The stress of a prolonged dry season and frequent droughts checks herd numbers so that they rarely approach the concentrations necessary for herbivory to affect vegetation.[9]

Economists' theories of communal property suggest that communal use will not inevitably lead to abuse of the resource.[10] The general conditions for successful and sustainable long-term communal resource management are becoming increasingly clear.[11] Anthropologists and economists have shown that herd sizes enhance long-term survival of household production systems during drought, and optimise long-term offtake in variable environments.[12]

Two different concepts of nature are implied by these competing ideas. One suggests a delicate balance between vegetation, soils and animals. Dryland ecosystems are seen as 'fragile' and threatened by clumsy, careless and short-sighted human action, upsetting the equilibrium between the number of stock and the ecosystem's long-term ability to sustain them. The second sees drylands ecosystems as resilient, shifting between multiple alternative states depending on circumstances and thus able to recover from disturbance and stress. Equilibrium is neither a goal nor an indication of ecosystem health. Change is stochastic, uncontrollable. Nature is independent of people, ungoverned by their actions.

Incorporated into each view are ideas about the changes in vegetation, wildlife and soils caused by the presence of various stocking densities. These beliefs can be set out as hypotheses and tested. When we began to work at Mkomazi, Homewood and I argued that claims about environmental change should be taken as alternative hypothetical explanations for the environmental dynamics of the Reserve. These are reproduced in Table 4.1.[13] In this chapter I will consider what evidence can be brought to bear on these opposing ideas. The chapter falls into two parts. The first looks at evidence for change and degradation in the soils and vegetation of the Reserve, the second examines biodiversity.

Degradation

There are two bodies of evidence. The first is a series of statements about changes to, and the state of, Mkomazi's environment made by adminis-

Table 4.1 Contrasting perceptions of Mkomazi.

	Received wisdom	**Alternative view**
Environmental Change	1. Pastoralists damage the ecosystem by overstocking: – Soil erosion increases. – Rangelands vegetation becomes less palatable. – Bush invades pasture.	1. Pastoralists do not damage the environment by overstocking: – Soil erosion does not increase to dangerous levels. – Vegetation dynamics are not driven by stocking rates. – Pastoralists make a positive impact upon the spatial nutrient concentrations of the area, leaving nutritious grazing on old compounds.
Wildlife	2. Pastoralists compete for resources with wildlife to the exclusion of the latter: – Pastoralists physically exclude wildlife from water sources and use up water, not leaving enough for wildlife. – Pastoralists exclude wildlife from good pastures and use up grazing.	2. Pastoralists and wildlife do not compete to the exclusion of the latter: – Competition over water and grazing is not sufficient to threaten wildlife. – Pastoralists are excluded from some sites by the threat of diseases held or transmitted by wildlife.
Burning	3. Local burning turns woodland into grassland and decreases the Reserve's biodiversity.	3. Changes in vegetation are due to changing intensity and timing of burns: – Exclusion of pastoralists' cattle has left more vegetation to burn, causing hotter fires.
Elephants	4. Exclusion of pastoralists is responsible for the present increase in elephant numbers in Mkomazi.	4. Increases in the elephant population in Mkomazi reflect improved poaching controls in Tsavo National Park.
Hunting	5. The local population's hunting threatens wildlife populations.	5. Local hunting is not endangering wild ungulate populations.
Resource Management	6. Local communities' resource use is not well organised: – Either: they are unable to act collectively to prevent degradation. – Or: attempts which they do organise are ineffective.	6. Local communities organise their resource use: – Levels and extent of use are agreed and negotiated. – Sanctions are available to punish those who ignore these agreements.
Land Tenure	7. The land tenure arrangements inevitably encourage unsustainable use: – Land tenure arrangements should change from communal to private wherever possible.	7. Use of communal land can be controlled: – Changing the form of tenure will not prevent degradation.

Table 4.1 Continued

	Received wisdom	Alternative view
Environmental Awareness	8. The health of the environment does not feature highly in local people's consciousness. Degradation does not concern them sufficiently to provoke preventive action.	8. Local people are aware of environmental problems: – They act to alleviate them.

Source: Brockington and Homewood, 1996.

trators, cattle keepers – both pastoralists and agropastoralists – and conservationists. Administrators have been concerned with the environmental, economic, social and political problems of the location of herders and their stock. Pastoralists wrote to their local government officers and each other in response to overstocking and mismanagement of herds and pastures. Conservationists have left us with a valuable record of what happened to the environment in the absence of people.

The second are more specific data about the environment – rainfall, cattle numbers and vegetation change. Allegations of environmental degradation tend to conflate changes to soil, vegetation composition, vegetation structure and livestock numbers. But the allegations explicitly or implicitly imply specific types of environmental change, and their causes. Correspondingly specific data are necessary to look for these changes.

The administrators
The attention administrators have paid to the use of the plains over the past 60 years has provided a rich collection of records in which environmental concerns feature prominently. A small collection of the many environmental statements about Mkomazi and its environs is shown in Table 4.2. It is derived from archival records of disputes about the location of cattle and herders first at Toloha, and subsequently inside and around Mkomazi.

The record mixes 'simple' environmental concern (about what is happening to soil and grass) with more overtly political goals (about where particular groups should be located, and how they should be contributing to development). Nevertheless there is remarkable consistency about the negative environmental impact of pastoralism in official circles before and after independence. The significant exception was the pro-Maasai view of a prominent government sociologist (Henry Fosbrooke), who was keen that the Toloha Maasai should not be moved and maintained that they were better stock keepers than the Pare.

Table 4.2 Environmental statements about the borderland plains.

Date	Context	Statement	Source
Dec. '38	Annual report of the Pare District Commissioner	'Upare covers about 3,000 square miles. One half is mountainous, fertile and thickly populated: in the other half conditions prevail that are little different from desert conditions. Extensive denudation has taken place as the result of extensive grazing and uncontrolled and unskilful methods of agriculture.'	TNA, 6/1
6/8/48	Assistant DO Same to the DC Same, reporting on a visit to Toloha	'The area is grossly overgrazed and, aggravated by the lack of rain this year, appears likely to become a semi-desert, fit only for goats and camels within a few years. It is essential to find alternative grazing for a large proportion of the stock to allow the area to recover.'	KNA, DO/Tav/1/26/13
8/1/51	DC Voi to PC Coast, urging that action be taken to evict Maasai trespassers.	'… destruction of land and pasture continue on the largest scale to the East of Lake Jipe as a result of the trespassers' cattle. I feel bound to place on record, the fact that one can only view with the greatest concern, Government's continued acquiescence in this fantastic situation; resulting as it will in the ultimate complete destruction of a vast area of land within the boundaries of this district.'	KNA/DC/TTA/3/8/37
26/3/57	Game Warden Arusha to PC, noting that there has been an influx of stock into the degazetted area at Kalimawe.	'… you will note that in the [Same Game Ranger's] opinion overgrazing is still rife in the Pare District and that no remedial measures have yet been taken. As the future of this Game Reserve is closely bound up with the state of the country surrounding it, I will be grateful if you will inform me what steps are being taken to overcome the overgrazing outside the Reserve.'	TNA, G1/7
14/11/66	Game Warden Lushoto to RC Tanga, concerning pressure on the Mkomazi Game Reserve.	'To tell the truth these Wakwavi are causing many problems. Their cows have increased and the area set aside for them has been destroyed and now they are using every means to be given other areas which is just not possible because these additional places would also be destroyed.'	TNA, G1/7

Table 4.2 Continued

Date	Context	Statement	Source
Jun. '76	J.S. Ibeun, dissertation written for Diploma in Wildlife Management at the College of African Wildlife Management, Mweka.	'In most of the Eastern sector of the game reserve soil degradation due to overgrazing and trampling by cattle '(leading to soil erosion) is quite evident. Other major resultsof human pressure are manifest in the occurrences of unplanned fires set by cattle herders and poachers.	Ibeun, 1976

Both pro-pastoral and anti-pastoral views are based on flimsy data. Before 1966 there were no studies of the impact of livestock on vegetation, and all remarks seem to be based on brief observation alone. We have no idea how well-qualified these observers were, or how carefully they made their observations, and what norms or previous conditions they were comparing them to. It is difficult to know what these observers were seeing, and what therefore the environment was doing. Although two studies were completed in 1966 and 1967 (see vegetation change section below), it is hard to tell to what extent these studies were known as the findings were cited only once.

Anderson has shown that fears of erosion in Kenya reflected events abroad (the US Dust Bowl), and that the resulting concern was exploited for political ends.[14] It is easy to see parallels between the convenient coincidence of the government desire to move pastoralists out of the Mkomazi or Toloha area and their agitation about soil erosion. Degradation proved a convenient platform on which to lobby for other agendas. However, that would not *per se* refute the notion that livestock were causing soil erosion. The political utility of an argument does not necessarily invalidate its conclusions.

In some other situations, a long record of perceived degradation has been used to discredit the existence of degradation. If doom-laden predictions have been made and proved false, this discredits the depiction of the environment upon which they were based. If people have long been scared that the environment is about to lose its productivity, and it has not done so over 50 years, then does that mean that the fears were groundless? This argument was employed at Machakos, in Kenya, where experts predicted irrevocable loss of soil in the 1930s, but where the environment subsequently sustained a five-fold increase in the population alongside improving environmental indices.[15] It has also repeatedly been observed that the geomorphologically unstable parts of Baringo (Kenya) were suffering severe erosion, in spite of which the region has repeatedly showed rapid recovery of livestock populations after drought.[16]

We appear to have a similar situation. Dire prophecies have been made about the consequences of pastoralism in and around Mkomazi. Does their reiteration over 60 years alongside the increasing livestock numbers invalidate them? Not in this case, because they do not all refer to the same situation. The claims in the records refer to a variety of different contexts, ranging from whole districts to specific places. Concern in the 1960s was restricted to the eastern half of the Reserve. In the 1970s and 1980s concern was much more general, referring to the Reserve as a whole. We do not have a sufficiently constant record of concern about one place to conclude that the predictions are invalidated because their persistent pessimism has not been fulfilled. Indeed, the predictions of environmental misfortune are not really precise enough to be tested. All we can say is that a consistently gloomy view of the environmental consequences of pastoralism has been taken in the absence of any cited evidence to support it, and despite the presence of thriving cattle populations.

Herders

One of the more interesting records of environmental change and degradation is afforded by livestock keepers themselves (some shown below, others given in Box 4.1). It consists of letters written by local herders to their village governments. Most are complaints about excessive grazing on pastures they had set aside for their herds. Some complain of visitors who have 'finished up' the grazing leaving little for the residents' herds:

> I have received news from Mlao Rashidi that Maasai from Arusha Chini/Moshi have brought their herds to graze at Kinuru-Usangi and that they are finishing all the grass and the cows of Kinuru are lacking grass and when (the Maasai) herds finish all the grass they go back whence they came and the Pare beasts are not able to go to Arusha Chini. Please intervene to resolve this problem so that they do not finish all the grass.
>
> President of the Native Court Usangi to the DC Pare.
> TNA, 11/5, vol II, 3/7/46

> Our problem is our places for herds ... we ask we be given help, for our herds do not have grazing because thousands of other animals are brought by other herders from outside this village. And if they finish the grazing they leave and go back to their place; they await the monsoon and other rains that bring grass, they return and thus they have their benefits and our herds are very sick. Comrade, until now we are looking for your best help.
>
> The Pare people of Igoma sub-village to the Ward Secretary of Gonja Ward.
> Kisiwani Livestock File, 8/6/1977

Others complain that the intruders have used reserved pastures out of season:

> Troubles have resulted in this time of the short dry season which were caused by various cows from outside the Reserve. I have therefore called a meeting to

Box 4.1 Problems with pastures

'Now [the Maasai] are going beyond [the Jipe watering point] where they see much grazing, because on this side of Vilima Viwili there is not even one blade of grass, which is why they try and steal grazing.'

Veterinary Guard Toloha to the District Commissioner Pare,
1/9/46, TNA, 11/5, vol II

'I have received a complaint from these comrades who herd their animals in the Game Reserve of Mkomazi and who live at Njiro and Takita, that there are Maasai who have entered this Reserve and are outsiders from Gujuka and Makanga and Pare from Makanye and many other places. Therefore these citizens have asked me to give help to expel these herders.'

The Ward Secretary of Kisiwani to the District Commissioner of Same,
following a complaint from Parakuyo herders living inside the
Game Reserve about outsiders' incursions.
Kisiwani Livestock File, 6/1/1976

'Since this reserve was gazetted by the government, Kwavi have lived in the areas of Mnazi, Kamba, Mabili, Mnyandege [places north of the Usambara mountains] and others stayed at Muheza, Gonja, Makongoanzege [near Gonja] etc. ... In 1963 here in this Reserve there began serious problems between the Kwavi and employees of the Game department. People were arrested night and day. This dispute carried on until 1967 when the government decided to return these people and to write a new list of names ... But in the years 1968–9 herds from Ngajuka [in the Pangani valley] began to come and gather at Mkundi, Mangara Mbili outside the borders and, after a few months, we saw these cows had entered that Reserve which had been forbidden ... Straight away the Reserve began to be damaged/disturbed and to fill up with people from outside with permits from cash ... In the meeting of the 20th we heard the Game Warden say that the list of people allowed to stay will not be used; what will be used is a Mkomazi Game Reserve card. Here the leaders ... do not refuse to comply but the matter to be heard is why have we not been given these cards? ... Comrade Secretary there are strangers here but I cannot name them.'

Local leader of Parakuyo and Maasai pastoralists to the Ward Secretary
of Kisiwani, following proposed changes in the procedure of
gaining permission to use the Reserve.
Kisiwani Livestock File, 18/7/1977

debate this question from which we reached the conclusion that all the section west of the Korongo la Msara should be a reserved grazing area. All this area which we are setting aside is a store area for the future need of dry season grasses or all people with difficulties. Respected comrade in the meeting we agreed that from the beginning of 1/1/1981 the reserved grazing area will be closed until 25/8/1981 each year until another law is enacted.

Local leader of the Maasai and Parakuyo pastoralists.
Kisiwani Livestock File, 20/12/1980

The last letter refers to a form of grazing management that involves reserving 'calf pastures' close to water in the dry season. These are designated for use by young or sick animals that are unable to travel far to graze and water.[17] Around Mkomazi, these calf pastures were called *olalilii* or *ololopoli* in Maa, *mlimbiko* by the Pare and Sambaa and *kilwa* by the Kamba. They are still used in a limited way. In the Pangani valley fodder trees are also set aside, their seed pods falling to the ground behind dead branch fences, and only made available towards the end of the dry season.

Are these arrangements an indication that herders effectively control their use of the environment? Unfortunately, we cannot tell whether the complaints are testimony to an efficient system (showing that people did something when things went wrong) or a weak system (things went wrong because the controls lacked authority). Nor can we tell how effective people's complaints were. This was something that was hard to investigate using oral histories. In over 50 interviews I received almost entirely normative accounts of how local controls tended to work, not the nuts and bolts of their dynamics.[18]

It was hard retrospectively to investigate the dynamics of a continually contested resource use. All these records show is that people tried to manage their environment through regulation, sanctions and negotiation, and that in some cases the management was contested.[19] This makes them less anarchic than some of the hypotheses of Table 4.1 suggested, but not necessarily effective at stopping environmental degradation.

Was the consequence of these incursions degradation? It would appear that, if people were talking about the 'finishing' of their grazing and the destruction of their pastures, there were at least temporary problems with the vegetation. There is some resonance between the official accounts of degradation around the borders of the Reserve, or at Toloha, and these local complaints. However, they may be talking about different things. The pastoralists may be talking about the loss of one year's biomass, not of long-term damage to the productive capacity of the ecosystem. Only the latter is degradation. There is no indication from these letters that the environment was becoming degraded.

There is a further problem that residents might claim that their grazing was being destroyed in order to encourage official sanctions against immigration. There were clearly long running recurrent disputes between residents and immigrants about the use of grazing. These letters could be seen as an attempt to invoke the power of the state against unwelcome arrivals, and to legitimise the writers' own presence, as much as a complaint about the condition of the environment. This is not to say that there was no 'overgrazing', or no degradation, just that an ulterior motive exists that could exaggerate reporting of the problem. The evidence from these accounts is inconclusive.

The conservationists' record

There is a wealth of assessments of the destruction of Mkomazi's environment under pastoralism, made by conservationists associated with the Reserve (Table 6.6). Mangubuli's claim, quoted at the start of the book, is worth repeating:

> Habitat destruction, as a result of overgrazing, led to choking of dams with silt, and change in vegetation composition and structure. No dams ... could now hold water for the entire dry season period. Settlements increased around waterholes denying access by wildlife. These circumstances forced most of the wild animals to move out of Mkomazi into Tsavo National Park. Wildfires, often started by pastoralists, became an annual phenomenon, destroying and opening woodlands and montane forests (Mangubuli, 1992: 12).

The threat to the environment was made explicit in the eviction orders:

> By this letter I would like to tell you that all those who were permitted to live inside Mkomazi/Umba Game Reserve ... are now required to leave ... This decision was arrived at with the intention of saving this wilderness ...
>
> Principal Secretary, Ministry of Lands, Natural Resources and Tourism,
> 13 April 1988

Right or wrong, the statements cite no data, and refer to no studies of environmental change.

Much more interesting, however, are the observations and comments made after the Reserve was cleared. They tend to conflate changes to game populations with vegetation and soil erosion but in general they speak of an environment that is healthy and well, and which has recovered from the previous ravages.[20] For example, Watson, writing in Swara in 1991, said that Mkomazi had been 'brought from the brink of collapse and restored to its former glory' (Watson, 1991: 14).

One Trustee of the GAWPT wrote:

> I first visited Mkomazi in 1989. The only resources in plentiful supply were hope and expectation. Years of uncontrolled poaching, burning and illegal overgrazing had left most species of game scattered and scarce. ... The progress that has been made in three years is, literally, spectacular. As we visited in the dry season game was not abundant but it was all there.
>
> Robert Marshall-Andrews, QC, MP,
> Report on the first Friends' visit to Mkomazi, August 1992

It is curious that these assessments were made such a short time after the original predictions of doom and assessments of disaster. One has to ask whether the situation was really that bad if game populations recovered so quickly. The degradation of the Reserve must have been remarkably ephemeral. A similar picture is gleaned from the diaries of those working inside Mkomazi and other fundraising literature (Box 4.2).

Ironically, these accounts are indicative of the resilient environment that non-equilibrial ecology envisages, rather than the fragility the writers

Box 4.2 The miraculous recovery of Mkomazi

'In the beginning of November [1992] the waterholes were all dried out and cracked and their surfaces a maze of cracked, hard impenetrable mud. The roads were washed with several inches of dust ... It was impossible to imagine there was anything nutritious left at all for the animals to eat or the vegetation to soak up in the Reserve. Any grass that had been left to dry out had by mid November burned due to natural fires or deliberately set ones. Then during the second week of November the clouds began to build and on the 11th, rain kissed the frog and the bush transformed.

The fairytale began. Magic permeated every drop of rain that sprinkled the Reserve. ... The animals weakened from the drought were now faced with not enough strength to stand up in the downpour nor ability to cope with the outrageous extravaganza. Many perished by the side of the road. ... Literally, within 2–3 days new grass shoots sprouted throughout the Reserve, and every bush and tree peeled back their surfaces to reveal their buds. Like Mardi Gras, the insects and birds took to the streets. I have never seen such wild ecstasy – the insects were multiplying on the wing and coming from EVERY-WHERE and birds all the way from Europe were enjoying the moveable feast. ... Not only are all the waterholes and korongos (riverbeds) full, but also standing water is prominent throughout the Reserve. And the bush – wow! – it is so green and thick with vegetation. The grass stands over 6 feet tall in places where you could never have thought a seed of grass could have lodged let alone grow.'

Kim Ellis, former partner of Tony Fitzjohn, Field Officer of the Trusts, newsletter, early 1993

'Mkomazi was gazetted in 1950 and maintained as a Game Reserve until around 1970 when extensive human encroachment was not combated. By 1988 Maasai *bomas* covered much of the Reserve. ... Mkomazi was verging on a wasteland ... by the beginning of last year [1993] we could honestly say that a spectacular environmental recovery had taken place, the elephant population had gone from 11 to 300 and even 900 at certain wet season times of the year, and everything else was on the increase.'

Tony Fitzjohn, Field Officer of the Trusts, speech to the Royal Geographical Society, 1994

'In all some 78 species of mammals have been recorded [in Mkomazi] ... That so much wildlife remains is a miracle. By the late 1980s Mkomazi was in steep decline. Heavy poaching had wiped out its black rhino and elephant popula-tions. Overgrazing, deliberate burning and illegal hunting had also taken their toll. ... in 1989 the Mkomazi Project was born ... The result has been a spec-tacular success. One of the most fragile, threatened and beautiful parts of Africa has been reborn. Already the years of hard work have had a profound effect on the animals living in the Reserve.'

GAWPT, fundraising literature, *circa* 1994

thought they had saved. This is an environment that can recover from grazing pressure because its vegetation dynamics are driven by rainfall, and only to a lesser extent by grazing pressure. The accounts are doubtless coloured by enthusiasts' eagerness to write positively about an environment that is now free of people. Nonetheless, they are possibly the strongest evidence of all these observers that the environment at Mkomazi is resilient, and that its dynamics may be best explained by non-equilibrial ecological theories. They suggest that the impact of grazing and livestock was short-lived and did not degrade the environment. However, they give little information about the vegetation dynamics involved. The transformation of Mkomazi into an environment that conservationists like does not refute the hypothesis that livestock changed vegetation dynamics, or that soil erosion rates have decreased since eviction.

Rainfall
Mean rainfall at Same town and Voi is less than 600 mm. Close to the eastern (windward) side of the Pare mountains more than 700 mm are recorded (Table 4.3), but rainfall further out on the plains is thought to be similar to Same and Voi.[21] This makes the Reserve, with the exception of its mountains, a semi-arid area. The coefficients of variability at all sites underline how unpredictable rainfall is here. These are above the 30 per cent level suggested by Caughley and colleagues to indicate ecosystems likely to be explained best by non-equilibrial dynamics.[22]

Figure 4.1 makes the same point. Rainfall totals are commonly far from the mean. These are data described better by their variability than their averages. The graph also shows that there have been no long-term trends in rainfall in and around the Reserve area between 1935 and 1990. Data are patchy, but no overall trends are evident.[23] If there has been environmental change, it is unlikely to have occurred because of climatic change.

Table 4.3 Rainfall at sites around Mkomazi.

Station	Mean / mm	Range	Coefficient of variability (%)	Years of data
Same	566	243–1057	32.9	60
Kisiwani	734	330–1605	49.4	18
Gonja	894	427–1443	31.0	44
Mnazi	782	470–1554	32.5	28
Voi	556	180–1203	36.4	87

Sources: East Anglia Climate Research Group; Dar es Salaam Meteorological Office; Same Town Meteorological Station; Harris, 1970.

Livestock numbers
What data exist to support the dominant view that cattle are deleterious to Mkomazi's environment? Is there evidence to suggest that herd condition has suffered as a result of the degradation cattle were causing? Presumably, if there were a deterioration in pasture quality, this would be

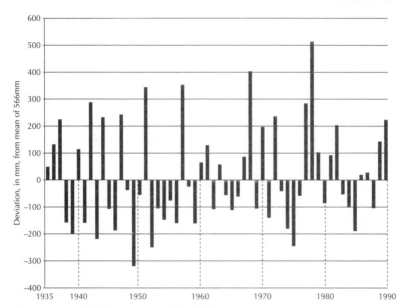

Figure 4.1 Rainfall at Same Town, 1935–1990.
Source: district records.

reflected in cattle numbers and fertility. The impact of cattle on the Reserve was examined in the 1960s. Unfortunately, a number of problems with the research make it hard to tell exactly what was happening.

In 1967 Dr G. Anderson, a government research officer, wrote a report evaluating the current use of the Reserve and discussing future plans.[24] Anderson referred to 3,000 to 5,000 cattle 'grazing within the Reserve' (which at the time meant only the eastern portion). He asserted that:

> Because of the restricted range and more selective grazing habits of cattle, they exert a very destructive force on the ecosystem. Neither the habitat nor the cattle will be able to withstand this grazing pressure for long. The habitat will continue to deteriorate until herders will be forced either to move into denuded areas or localities outside of the Reserve (Anderson, 1967: 15).

But by Anderson's own criteria the Reserve was understocked. He gave the Reserve's size as 600,000 acres. If the cattle were using one-quarter of the Reserve (none of the western part and only some of the east), 5,000 cattle would give a stocking rate of one animal per 29.8 acres. Anderson stated that suitable stocking rates varied from ½ acre per animal in a few choice areas to over 8 acres per animal over the majority of the Reserve. Where the grazing had been destroyed he said that a mature animal would require 20–25 acres' grazing. Anderson's claim that cattle were damaging the environment is not supported by the number of cattle he said were present, nor by his estimated ideal stocking rate. More puzzling still, Anderson underestimated the size of the Reserve by 200,000 acres. This means that the 5,000 cattle, had they been using a quarter of the Reserve, would have had 40 acres each.[25]

Why did he think that so few cattle were causing so much damage? The most obvious answer is that Anderson underestimated the number of cattle using the Reserve. Although he described overcrowding around the Reserve's boundaries, he appears not to have thought that these animals were also using the Reserve.[26] If cattle outside the Reserve are included, the stocking rate was much higher (Table 4.4).[27] It may be that the effects that alarmed Anderson were the consequence of much higher stocking rates than he realised.

But if stocking rates were higher than feared, what were their long-term consequences? How did they affect the long-term ability of the ecosystem to support livestock? We have seen that for 25 years before the evictions, cattle censuses show an increase in stock in and around the Reserve (Table 3.1). Smallstock populations remained relatively stable (Figure 4.2). Cattle censuses offer only a snapshot of a fluid situation, but with an increase of this magnitude the census data are likely to reflect a reality on the ground. The magnitude of this rise in the Reserve cattle population may be a little misleading. It is composed of a fluctuating population in Lushoto combined with 14 years of growth in Same District (1970–1984), which followed the opening of the western half of the Game Reserve. The increase is not the result of one area sustaining greater herds, but of more places supporting more cattle.

The implications for the environment of such a growth in cattle populations are equivocal. Such an increase must have affected the environment in some way. Yet it is hard to see how it could have been causing the damage Anderson feared. The eastern half of the Reserve sustained a population of 15,000 to 40,000 cattle, far higher than he thought possible, for over 30 years. Whatever changes were occurring were not damaging the ability of the ecosystem to support cattle.[28] The environment was able to sustain the growth.

The problem of interpreting the environmental impact of cattle is essentially one of scale. Figures for the whole of the Reserve and its environs tell us little about cattle–vegetation dynamics in particular places. It may well be that herds were overgrazing one pasture and moving on within the area censused, but the effects were sufficiently localised or temporary not to impede the growth of livestock populations. More detailed studies of how livestock affect vegetation in this environment are needed to refute the hypothesis that cattle graze, overgraze and move on.

Vegetation change
A central weakness of Anderson's report is that it offers no data that describe what cattle actually did to the vegetation. There were two

Table 4.4 Cattle resident in Umba Division, 1951–1968.

Year	Location	District records	Game Ranger reports
1951[a]	The Reserve and its environs	–	'A few thousand Wakwavi cattle and a small number of herdsmen lived in the Reserve and on the south bank of the Umba outside the Reserve near Mnazi and Lelwa. There were a small number of Sambaa and Kamba etc., cattle owners at Kivingo, Mnazi, Kamba and Lelwa.'
1952[b]	Parakuyo cattle estimated to go to cattle camps at the Katamboi water holes	5,000–6,000	–
1952[c]	Total Parakuyo cattle on the plains north of the mountains	8,000–19,000	–
1952[d]	Cattle population on the plains as a whole	15,000	–
1952[e]	Parakuyo, Kamba and Sambaa cattle at Mnazi and Kivingo	11,690	–
1952[f]	Estimated cattle population on the plains from census data	17, 829–30,564	–
1953[f]	Estimated cattle population on the plains from census data	16,503–28,291	–
1953[g]	Cattle population on the plains north of the mountains	10,000	–
1954[h]	Estimated cattle population on the plains from census data	19,746 33,850–	–
1960[i]	Umba Division plains	21,984	–
1960[j]	Mnazi, Kivingo and Lelwa	16,000	–
1963[k]	Around the Reserve	26,200	
1963[l]	In the Reserve	–	4,300
1964[m]	Aerial count of cattle in the Reserve	–	3,235
1964[n]	Plains north of Usambaras	14,000	–
1964[o]	Reserve-adjacent villages	32,721	–
1965[p]	Mnazi and Kivingo area	30,000	–
1965[q]	Outside the Reserve	38,561	–
1967[i]	Umba Division Plains	45,245	–
1966–7[r]	Aerial count of cattle in the Reserve	–	1,350–3,000
1968[l]	In the Reserve	–	21,080

[a] Reported by David Anstey to Director of Game, TNA, G1/7, 24/1/67.
[b] Reported by PC Tanga to PC Mombassa, TNA, 11/5, vol III, 19/5/52; DC Lushoto's request for grazing in Kenya, TNA, 723, vol III.
[c] DC Lushoto to PC Tanga, TNA, 723, vol III, 23/6/52; stated in a meeting of Tanganyikan and Kenyan officials to discuss the Katamboi affair, TNA, 11/5, vol III.
[d] DC Lushoto's request for grazing in Kenya, TNA, 723, vol III.
[e] Estimated from rinderpest vaccination data. Young calves were vaccinated and these commonly constituted 20 per cent of the herd. This figure has been obtained by multiplying the number of vaccinated calves by five. TNA, 962/15.

Table 4.4 Continued

ᶠ TNA, 6/1, Lushoto District Annual Report, 1953. Estimated from district census data. In Lushoto District, the plains north of the Usambara mountains lie entirely within Umba Division. The proportion of the cattle of Lushoto District found in Umba Division varies between 28 and 48 per cent between 1960 and 1984. These figures in this table represent just under 28 and 48 per cent of the Lushoto District cattle populations. They have been further modified to reflect the fact that, according to the 1984 census, 2 per cent of Umba Division's stock were not located on the plains, but on the hills on the northern slopes of the Usambara mountains.

ᵍ Reported by the PC Tanga to the Member for Agriculture and Natural Resources, TNA, G1/7, 17/10/53.

ʰ Tanga annual veterinary report. Census data modified according to note g above, TNA, 962/15.

ⁱ District Census, Lushoto District Livestock Office wall-chart, modified as note g above.

ʲ DC Lushoto to a lawyer hired by Pare and Sambaa herders, TNA, G1/7, 15/2/60.

ᵏ Note in TNA, G1/7, 6/6/63.

ˡ Reported by the Game Ranger, TNA, G1/7, 17/4/68.

ᵐ Counted by the Game Warden, TNA, G1/7, 17/1/64.

ⁿ Estimated by the Regional Veterinary Officer, TNA, G1/7, 11/5/64.

ᵒ A count reported by the Regional Agricultural Officer, TNA, G1/7, 11/7/64.

ᵖ Estimated by the Regional Veterinary Officer, TNA, G1/7, 9/9/65.

ᵠ Reported by the District Agricultural Officer, TNA, G1/7, 2/1/68.

ʳ Harris, 1970: 113.

studies that attempted a small-scale analysis of the impact of livestock on vegetation. They date from March 1966 and August 1967, and were made outside and along the borders of the Game Reserve, in the Kalimawe Game Controlled Area and around the Umba river, respectively. Five points were surveyed in Kalimawe on three different types of soil. Nine sites were sampled along the Umba river, with no indication of how the soil type varied between sites.[29]

The researchers recorded the vegetation cover of a 0.75 inch diameter wire loop (attached to the end of their shoe) at two-step intervals along a 200-step transect.[30] When a live plant fell within the base of the loop a

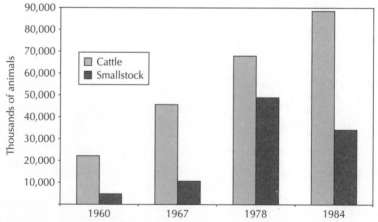

Figure 4.2 Livestock census results.

Source: district records.

Note: no data are available for Same District in 1960 or 1967. But numbers were low at this time and are unlikely to alter the trend.

'hit' was recorded. Vegetation was divided into forage (perennial grasses) and 'plants' (other live vegetation). Dead vegetation litter was recorded as 'ground cover' and soil termed 'bare ground'. The results of these two studies and four (undated) surveys in Tsavo are shown in Table 4.5.

The authors compared these records of vegetation cover with data from the Sandhill Prairie rangeland in the Western USA (Table 4.6). As most of the Mkomazi range examined by these researchers, according to these American criteria, was in poor or very poor condition they concluded that it was overgrazed. Appropriate stocking densities were also derived from the Sandhill Prairies. They suggested that one cow on Sandhill Prairie required 192 acres of grazing a year and that, on the basis of the 1965 census, the Umba river area was 14–19 times overstocked. Other stocking densities from Kenya were also cited, which

Table 4.5 Range condition for Acacia–Commiphora areas, sorted according to forage density.

Site	Number of transects	Forage density	Plant density	Ground cover (%)	Bare ground (%)
Umba river (6)	7	3	9	51	49
Umba river (5)	7	3	7	51	49
Umba river (7)	7	4	10	57	43
Tsavo – n. of Loosioto Hill	2	4	11	22	78
Kalimawe – red soil	8	5	7	23	77
Umba river (2)	11	5	16	58	42
Umba river (9)	7	6	19	77	23
Umba river (3)	6	6	18	54	46
Umba river (1)	9	7	20	67	33
Kalimawe – red soil	8	8	16	40	60
Kalimawe – *mbuga*	8	9	21	41	59
Umba river (4)	7	9	17	57	43
Umba river (8)	7	9	16	67	33
Lake Jipe – east side (Tsavo)	10	10	12	43	57
Kalimawe – *mbuga*	8	10	16	35	65
Kalimawe – grey clay	8	13	16	38	62
Tsavo – Murka	13	18	22	63	37
Tsavo – Pump Station	9	27	28	68	32

Source: Robinette and Gilbert, 1968.

Table 4.6 Evaluating range condition.

Range condition	Forage hits per 100
Excellent	25
Good	22–24
Fair	15–21
Poor	8–14
Very Poor	0–7

still left the area 10 times overstocked. They therefore suggested that the range be destocked.

But there are a number of problems with both methods and conclusions. First, only perennial grasses were counted as fodder, not annuals, although annuals can make a useful contribution to livestock's diet.[31] Second, browse was not included. Third, there was no indication of recent rainfall, nor discussion of the problems of comparing data collected in March with that of August, nor any information about the timing or previous rainfall of the Tsavo surveys. Fourth, these surveys were snapshots of a highly variable system, and there is no mention of how range cover varies through the year. Fifth, there were no data on the herding patterns followed by the livestock of the area; it is not certain how many animals were using the areas sampled, and how often. Sixth, there was no sense of what local herders make of the situation. Seventh, it was impossible to say how representative these data are as there is no indication of how the sites of the transects were selected.

The advised stocking rates are also questionable.[32] Stocking rates are intimately related to the goals of production. The rates cited were from the Western USA where stock farming was geared towards beef production. This maximises productivity per animal, minimises losses during droughts and attempts to produce a high-quality product.[33] Subsistence dairy herding is different. Productivity is maximised per hectare by keeping a higher stocking rate, which lowers productivity per cow but raises it per unit area. A high stocking rate also allows the herder to take advantage of a highly variable productivity. Low stocking rates fail to capture all the resources that can become available in the wet season. Moreover, a large number of animals minimises risk, as more are likely to survive a drought to provide for the families' needs and produce offspring in the following years. Subsistence dairy herders therefore operate stocking rates that are higher than beef ranching. The comparisons offered were not appropriate.[34]

More recent data on a larger scale are available in Cox's preliminary study of vegetation change in western Mkomazi between 1975 and 1988, using two Landsat images. The data cannot offer any explanations of vegetation change in the Reserve, but can be used to generate hypotheses.[35] These are that during 1975–1988 the extent of grassland remained unchanged, thinly wooded grassland (2–40 per cent canopy cover) decreased and woodland (>40 per cent canopy cover) increased (Figure 4.3). The thickening of bush to become woodland suggests that one of the driving forces behind vegetation change at Mkomazi could be the decline of the elephant populations of the Tsavo ecosystem. An increase in bushland would have been consistent with overgrazing since pressure on grass populations results in an increase in bushland. Herders recognise that cows could 'bring bush', and counteracted this by burning to improve pasture quality and reduce lion habitat.[36]

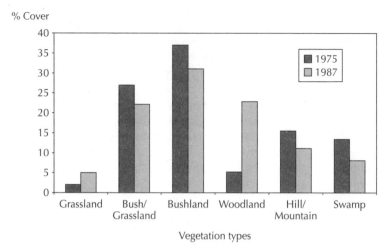

% Cover

Figure 4.3 Percentage changes in land cover in the western half of Mkomazi Game Reserve, 1975–1987.
Source: Brockington and Homewood, 1999.

No conclusions can be drawn from such data, which merely serve to generate ideas. It is important to emphasise the effect of the elephant decline, because this impact has not been mentioned in some of the literature on the Reserve. There has been a tendency to blame all changes on livestock.[37] A more authoritative study is in preparation that may make it possible to offer an account that takes the effect of both changes into account.[38]

Biodiversity

Mkomazi is celebrated for its biodiversity. It was anticipated by Dr Coe (the leader of the RGS research team) to be 'one of the richest savannas in Africa, and possibly the world' for plants, birds and insects.[39] This perception has taken root in the Department of Wildlife. In a draft management plan it describes the Reserve as:

> one of the richest savannas in Africa and possibly in the world in terms of rare and endemic fauna and flora (MNRT, 1997: 18).

These claims are used to bolster and justify current policies, but how was it affected by the presence of livestock? I argue here that there is no clear evidence about the effect of people and their stock on the biodiversity of the Reserve. It remains possible that they enhanced it.

Biodiversity is a widely used word with many meanings and no single precise definition.[40] Guyer and Richards describe it as a 'boundary object' in science, that is, a concept that:

... both inhabit[s] several intersecting worlds ... *and* satisf[ies] the informational requirements of each of them. Boundary objects are objects which are plastic enough to adapt to local needs and constraints of the several parties employing them, yet robust enough to maintain a common identity across sites (Star and Griesemer, 1989: 393, cited in Fujimura, 1992: 173).

The imprecision and ambiguity of 'boundary objects' makes them useful for all sorts of agendas; they serve to unite different groups of people behind a common purpose. Guyer and Richards attribute the term to the biologist E.O. Wilson, who used it as a way of protecting research into whole organisms.

Biodiversity comprises a number of key ideas.

1. Number of species. This can be either a simple count of species or a hierarchical measure of their distribution across higher order of taxa.[41]
2. Relative abundance. This is a measure of the number of rare species and of the domination by a few species.
3. Endemism. The degree to which species are unique to this location.

There are a number of problems with the concept of biodiversity that stem from its status as a boundary object.

First, it is quantitative, but unquantifiable.[42] Species diversity can be counted, but biodiversity figures are usually estimates of the number of species to be found. It is always an extrapolation. Second, it is imprecise. Diverse forms of life – birds, vegetation, animals and insects – are lumped together. Meanwhile other aspects of biodiversity such as agrodiversity, the variety of species found on farmers' land, enjoys less attention.[43] This points to a final difficulty. There is often conflict about which aspect of biodiversity, which type of habitat, what group of species is to be promoted. In savannas, grassland species may prosper at the expense of woodland, and agricultural species at the expense of both. It may not be possible to conserve all aspects of biodiversity.

Biodiversity and savanna woodlands

What produces biodiversity? In general, it is enhanced by environmental heterogeneity. Topographic diversity, variation in the substrate or water availability, and small-scale disturbances fostering a dynamic mosaic of vegetation all augment biodiversity. Over long time-scales persistence of environments may enhance speciation and thus diversity. For example, the high degree of endemism that characterises the Eastern Arc mountains of Tanzania is attributed to the age of their habitat.

The processes of vegetation change and response to disturbance in savanna woodlands, through which biodiversity is encouraged or diminished, are poorly understood.[44] However, long-term studies in other savanna ecosystems suggest that long-term fluctuations between relatively dense canopy and open grassland are common in East African savanna woodlands.[45] Savanna species are generally widely distributed in contrast to their forest counterparts, and are often well adapted to deal with fire and other perturbations.[46] Savanna plant biodiversity appears resilient, with individual plant species, communities and vegetation formations re-establishing themselves, despite major fluctuations.[47]

The impact of people on the vegetation and biodiversity of savanna woodlands is disputed. Local land-use has been thought deleterious to both, but its effects may in fact be negligible compared to 'natural' factors. Human use of savanna woodlands may be highly destructive in some cases. However, it may even underpin regeneration and the dynamic mosaics of vegetation that foster high biodiversity.[48] Change is characteristic of savanna ecosystems and not always symptomatic of degradation.[49] Strict protection may not be necessary to protect the biodiversity of savannas.

Biodiversity is driven by ecological processes that take place in an historical setting. The history of Mkomazi and the borderland plains over the last 200 years, the repeated presence of people and stock, and the great numbers in which they were present before eviction make it necessary to consider the role of people in maintaining or restricting the habitat and its diversity, and in creating disturbances that foster or limit biodiversity.

The biodiversity of Mkomazi
One would expect Mkomazi to be species-rich. African savannas tend to be.[50] Their plant diversity is thought to rival that of African forests. Their large mammal diversity is renowned.[51] Mkomazi is also topographically diverse, close to centres of endemism such as the Pare and Usambara mountains, and at the edge of the eastern Sahel, and thus likely to house species from neighbouring ecosystems. What is at stake is whether it is as uniquely rich as has been claimed, and the role of people in creating, maintaining or limiting that diversity.

Between 1994 and 1997 Mkomazi was subject to intensive surveys of its biodiversity.[52] The published results offer a list of the species present, which is the basis of the evaluation of its biodiversity status. No such surveys were done before the eviction of people. This work only gives us a snapshot of its present condition.

There are limitations on the comparisons that can be made. Comparisons require good species distribution and good sampling.[53] Here data are incomplete, and, for most taxa, are not available in a form that allows direct comparison of sampling with that of other savanna areas within Mkomazi's vegetation category.[54] It is not possible reliably to estimate species richness for the majority of taxa investigated. It is also difficult to derive species-area curves for animal species in savanna protected areas, because, unlike forests, protected savannas merge seamlessly with surrounding rangelands. Species-area curves reflect the area of the ecosystem available to a species, rather than the area demarcated by the administrative boundaries of a park or reserve.[55] This chapter therefore limits discussion to putting Mkomazi species richness in a biogeographic context.

Vegetation

On the basis of White's analysis of African phytochoria and regional centres of endemism, Mkomazi would be expected to have plant diversity consistent with the Somali–Maasai regional centre of endemism (RCE) of which it is part, moderated by species-area relations and topographic/habitat diversity.[56] On continental terms the Somali/Maasai RCE is of comparable diversity to the neighbouring Zambesian RCE, but not a 'hot spot' of African diversity like the Karoo–Namib or Afromontane forests (Table 4.7).

Although White lists the Serengeti as a detailed instance of the Somali–Maasai RCE, exemplifying its Acacia–Commiphora vegetation, Davis and colleagues list only Somali sites as special centres of plant diversity.[57] Centres of plant diversity are defined as sites of global importance, having in excess of 1,000 vascular plant species of which >10 per cent are endemic either to the site or to the phytogeographical region, with at least some being strict site endemics. Mkomazi has 1,307 vascular plant species. None have been identified as endemic, although 159 remain to be identified.

Current data suggest that Mkomazi, while species-rich, has no special plant diversity status within the Somali–Maasai RCE, nor the wider array of African savanna protected areas, whether in the Somali–Maasai phytogeographic region or in other RCEs.[58] There is certainly good reason to believe that the Mkomazi flora is more diverse than the much drier Tsavo East and the small but rich Kora and Meru areas (Table 4.8). But this comparison does not allow for differences in sampling intensity, methodology or completeness of coverage of different habitats in the different areas. It is not possible reliably to determine Mkomazi's

Table 4.7 Diversity in regional centres of endemism.

Name	Area (million km²)	Vascular plant species	Percentage of species endemic
Sudanian	3.7	2,750	35
Zambesian	3.7	8,500	54
Guineo–Congolian	2.8	12,000	80
Somali–Maasai	1.9	4,500	31
Afromontane	0.7	4,000	75
Karoo–Namib	0.66	>7,000	35–50
Mediterranean	0.33	4000	20
Maputaland–Pondoland	0.2	7,000	>20
Cape	0.09	8,600	68

Source: after Davis *et al.*, 1994: 106.

Table 4.8 Comparison of actual and predicted plant species numbers for Mkomazi with other dryland areas.

Site	Area (km²)	Numbers of species observed	Reference
Mkomazi	3,400	1,307	Coe, Vollesen *et al.*, 1999
Tsavo East	13,000	937	Greenway, 1969
Kora	1,788	717*	Kabuye *et al.*, 1986
Meru	870	605	Ament and Gillett, 1975; Gillett, 1983

*The main survey was carried out during two months July–September 1983, with further sporadic collections up to 1986 (Coe & Collins, 1986).

national or international importance using currently available data on species richness, endemism and sampling effort.

Birds
There has been a concerted effort to identify areas of outstanding bird species richness and endemism. Endemic bird areas (EBA) are defined as areas that encompass the overlapping breeding ranges of restricted-range bird species, such that the complete ranges of two or more restricted-range species are entirely included within the boundary of the EBA. Savannas are less likely to host site-endemic bird species than are forests. The Usambara mountain forests adjacent to Mkomazi are listed as an extremely important EBA, but Mkomazi itself has no site endemic bird species.[59] Mkomazi's 402 bird species are mostly widespread in East African savannas (75 per cent), and include many birds of passage.[60] Six species have been recorded here in Tanzania for the first time, but they are also present further north.

Mkomazi's birds are potentially of importance to Tanzania, but not of global importance. Other savanna protected areas are equally rich. The 428 km² of arid savanna Samburu-Buffalo Springs-Shaba Reserve complex in Kenya has 369 bird species. The 3,810 km² of Amboseli National Park and reserve has 459 bird species.[61] Lake Baringo in the Rift Valley is an inland drainage area with wetlands extending over a few score square kilometres, surrounded by arid rangeland: at least 458 bird species are known in this small area, which includes wetland, dry rangeland and Acacia woodland.[62] These bird-diverse East African savannas owe their richness in part, as does Mkomazi, to their position on ecotones, to the proximity of other centres of habitat diversity and endemism, and to their continuity with a much wider extent of savanna than is enclosed by their administrative boundaries.

Invertebrates
Problems of commensurability are perhaps best illustrated by the data collected on spiders and insects. The Reserve is thought to be home to up

to 90,000 species of insects and spiders.[63] Mkomazi is clearly species-rich, but given the lack of comparable sampling elsewhere, it is premature to infer that Mkomazi's arthropod biodiversity outranks that of other (little studied) sub-Saharan savannas. The study of savanna tree canopy arthropods in the Reserve 'represents the biggest single study of savanna tree canopies ever undertaken'.[64] This study collected an estimated 500,000 specimens from 266 trees, the runner-up being a 1980s study of Kora National Reserve, which collected 6,742 specimens from 49 tree canopies. The huge difference in the relative numbers of specimens collected is not thought to be an indication of Mkomazi's biodiversity, so much as the sampling effort.[65]

There are also problems in assessing the degree of endemism because of our ignorance of the distribution of species:

> Relatively few spider families in Africa are sufficiently well known that the distribution of their species can be mapped with any reliability … for two of the larger families from Mkomazi … a relatively high proportion (43–63%) of all species have a poorly known distribution as they have been either recorded only from the type locality or from very few sites (Russell-Smith *et al.*, 1997: 20).

All the diversity at Mkomazi tells us is how little we know about what else is out there.

Mammals

The impact of people on Mkomazi's large mammals may be more evident, although there are still few data to give an accurate idea of the trends involved. The best data are available for changes to the elephant populations (Table 4.9). Though elephant counts are not available frequently, they do indicate that elephant populations were higher when the Reserve was less occupied (before 1968), plummeted after 20 years of pastoral dominance, and recovered after the Reserve was cleared. This suggests that elephants declined because of pastoralism.[66]

But this is not the only possible inference. Elephant populations at Mkomazi owe much to events in the broader Tsavo ecosystem, which experienced a decline in elephant numbers following drought and extensive poaching.[67] Moreover, there were significant populations of

Table 4.9 Elephant populations in and around Mkomazi Game Reserve.

Year	Month	Season	Count	Std. error	Source
1968	June	End of long wet	2,760	Unknown	Watson *et al.*, 1969; Huish *et al.*, 1993
1988	February	Short dry	93	Unknown	WCMD, 1988
1991	June	Start of long dry	273	198	Huish *et al.*, 1993
1991	October	End of long dry	1,719	1,568	Huish *et al.*, 1993
1994	April	Long wet	477	304	Inamdar, 1995

elephants in the east of the Reserve in 1968 after many decades of pastoral occupation of that area.[68] There are also other disturbances to consider. In 1968 and 1969, 598 elephants were rounded up by helicopter and light aircraft and shot in the Reserve as part of research into the dynamics of herd growth and in a bid to control their numbers.[69] This may have had the effect of encouraging elephants to leave the Reserve, at least in the short term.

Data about changes to the other fauna are not available. There is no baseline to indicate how numbers have changed, except for rhinoceros, which went extinct during the poaching crisis of the 1970s and 1980s. There are two general impressions as to the effect of eviction on wildlife numbers. The first is that, in the absence of people and livestock, they have recovered. Elsewhere in East Africa, livestock are excluded from pasture by the presence of wildebeest whose calves carry malignant catarrhal fever that is fatal to cattle.[70] At Mkomazi there are no wildebeest, and interactions between livestock and wildlife may accordingly have favoured livestock.

A less popular view among wildlife conservationists, voiced by one researcher who has studied the general populations of the broader Tsavo ecosystem, is that wildlife densities in Tsavo are generally low compared with other protected areas like Maasai Mara, the Serengeti or Tarangire.[71] When Mkomazi was gazetted, it was mainly praised for its rhinoceros population. It is unlikely that there were large concentrations of wildlife present in the Reserve for the livestock to displace. The presence of people may still have served to reduce the low densities that were there.

Conclusion

Conservation policies at Mkomazi have assumed that people threaten the environment and biodiversity. This interpretation of the human impact has not been supported by the data analysed here. Problems with the precision and scale of the data make it difficult to say exactly what the environment was doing, but they do suffice to suggest an alternative explanation.

The rapidity of the Reserve's recovery, considered a triumph by conservationists, suggests that it may not have been badly damaged in the first place. But these are only hints, counter-interpretations that the imprecision of the data permits, but which, for that very reason, they cannot further clarify. We can be sure that cattle numbers increased throughout the period of anxiety over their impact. A deteriorating environment could not have supported such an increase. But it only tells us what was going on at the regional scale, over thousands of square kilometres. There are no good data on the detailed, small-scale impact of livestock on vegetation at Mkomazi. Herders may still have been grazing, overgrazing and moving on, but the impact on soil, vegetation and cattle numbers has not been visible at the current temporal and spatial scale of analysis. The large-scale health of the ecosystem may have entailed local and temporary degradation and recovery. We have no data to refute or support that hypothesis.

If that was the case, at what level would cattle populations become too dense to allow degraded patches to recover? We have argued that the 'limits' suggested for livestock were too low. But does that mean there are no limits? There must be some limits to resilience. The concept risks being used without sufficient definition, parameters or support; it risks being abused as 'degradation' has been. What limits to cattle populations should be set?

Long-term records of livestock populations in Baringo and Ngorongoro suggest that livestock populations do not continually increase but fluctuate up to a certain level.[72] They are repeatedly depressed by drought and disease, and frequently constrained by poor rainfall. Cattle populations only rarely and briefly attain levels where populations are sufficiently dense to have a sustained and widespread impact on soils and vegetation. Cattle populations in the east of Mkomazi between 1960 and 1984 also show fluctuations. Our hypothesis therefore is that no limits need be set because populations are already restrained by aridity. Before the cattle can damage the environment, the droughts kill the cattle.

As regards biodiversity, Mkomazi is species-rich for plants and birds, but not outstanding in global or regional terms. Invertebrates are numerous, but evaluation of its relative conservation value awaits better research in similar ecosystems.[73] The Reserve is species-rich, but it cannot be said to be 'one of the richest savannas in Africa and possibly the world'. Yet the Tanzanian Government has taken this conclusion to mean that Mkomazi is a centre of endemism, that it is the richest area in Tanzania in terms of rare and endemic fauna and flora, and migrant birds, although no species has so far been shown to be endemic.[74] Together with crisis talk about degradation resulting from human land-use, these statements encourage management based upon exclusion.

Yet we have seen that for the best part of 20 years there were large numbers of cattle in the western half of the Reserve before the eviction operation, and that livestock were present in the east for much longer. The documenting of high biodiversity values within a few years of alleged degradation raises questions about the real impact of people on biodiversity. We shall never know whether biodiversity has increased, decreased, was prevented from decreasing or remained the same because of the evictions. We do know that people have been present in the area for a long time. It is not reasonable to assume that they cause the loss of the plant, bird and insect species for which Mkomazi is currently celebrated.[75]

The role of anthropogenic impacts on savanna and other rangelands remains poorly understood, but is increasingly thought to be less deleterious than has been assumed.[76] Fairhead and Leach have suggested that forest patches in Guinean drylands are fostered by village land-use.[77] Coppicing potentially creates and maintains a patchy habitat without threatening tree survival.[78] Studies of savanna woodland/grassland dynamics, and of the factors underpinning biodiversity, do not suggest that local land-use threatens Mkomazi's biodiversity. Pasture management by grazing and burning, and moderate use of dry forest species for fuel and construction purposes, could arguably have a role in creating and maintaining biodiversity. Excluding grazing and controlled burning may allow accumulation of dry matter, triggering damaging, hot, late dry season fires.

The data I have considered are not sufficient to determine how these new theories apply at Mkomazi. Indeed, it may be impossible ever to understand the Reserve's environment. The disputes over Mkomazi are about more than the impact of cattle on the environment or how nature should be conceived; they also involve conflicting agendas for use of the Reserve's resources.[79] In one sense it is not possible to determine which of these viewpoints portrays 'the truth' about the environment of the Reserve. Different groups have constructed images of the environment and environmental change that work for them. The proposition that pastoralists degrade or do not degrade environments is an integral part of beliefs about what the environment should look like, or how it should be used to benefit people, the state or the world. Conservationists celebrate Mkomazi as a reclaimed wilderness, a landscape restored to what it should look like.[80] Former residents and their supporters claim it as their home. They say herds flourished within the Reserve, that the environment was not damaged and that pastoralists' presence deterred poachers.[81] These social constructions of 'nature' are not really within reach of Popperian refutation. They exist and persist for reasons in which 'hard evidence' or 'data' will not necessarily figure, or in which they will be treated in special ways.

But social constructions of nature make statements about the environment that can be tested. The view of the environment examined above is proclaimed to be true. And it is as a result of it being dangerously and urgently true that such levels of coercion were exerted by the state and so much money has been raised abroad. It is as saviours of the environment that the government and Trusts have cast themselves. If they are saviours, then my concerns about the social and economic consequences of eviction are trivial. Eviction would be regrettable but absolutely necessary if the ecosystem were to have a future. It has therefore been essential to consider the veracity of their claims.

The data considered here raise doubts about the severity of degradation at Mkomazi. These doubts have an important corollary. We have seen that previous considerations of people's needs were contingent upon their perceived impact on the environment. Where their resource use destroyed the environment, those practices could not be tolerated. Given that there is little evidence of damage it is important to look again at their needs, and the impact of conservation policies upon their livelihoods. To this we now turn.

Notes

1 Leach and Mearns, 1996.
2 Variation in livestock numbers on a given range would drive vegetation communities up or down known seres in predictable ways. A sere describes the development of vegetation communities towards a steady state. The concept comes from Clements' succession theory, which holds that in a given ecosystem bare ground will be colonised by successive assemblages of plants, each altering the environment in preparation for its successor until the most suitable vegetation for this climate, the climatic climax, is reached (Clements, 1916). The principal mechanisms at work are interactions between biotic elements of the ecosystem. See Illius and O'Connor (1999) for a recent review advocating this.
3 Sinclair and Fryxell, 1985; Coe, 1990; Prins, 1992; Hardin, 1968.
4 Scoones, 1995; Behnke, Scoones and Kerven, 1993.
5 Dyson-Hudson and Dyson-Hudson, 1969; Dyson-Hudson, 1980.
6 Homewood and Brockington, 1999.
7 Western, 1982; Homewood and Rodgers, 1991.
8 There are two principal differences between these ideas and succession theory. First, the long-term importance of changes to the environment wrought by fauna is doubted. Second, vegetation assemblages do not change in predictable ways as the sere concept suggests.
9 Ellis and Swift, 1988; Westoby *et al.*, 1989; Behnke and Scoones, 1993; Sullivan, 1996. The relative importance of infrequent and weak but nonetheless occasionally density-dependent interactions is the focus of ongoing debate (Illius and O'Connor, 1999; Sullivan and Rohde, forthcoming). Empirical evidence for the relatively minor role of grazing pressure on long-term environmental change in arid and semi arid areas is mounting (eg. Sahel: Turner, 1998a, 1998b, 1999; Namibia: Sullivan, 1999; 30-year analysis of Serengeti–Mara ecosystem: Homewood *et al.*, forthcoming).
10 Berkes, 1989; Bromley and Cernea, 1989; Ostrom, 1990, Ostrom *et al.*, 1999.
11 Ostrom *et al.*, 1999.
12 Mace and Houston, 1989; Sandford, 1983; Western and Finch, 1986.
13 Brockington and Homewood, 1996.
14 Anderson, 1984.
15 Tiffen *et al.*, 1994.
16 Homewood, 1994.
17 Potkanski, 1997; De Souza and De Leeuw, 1984; Peacock, 1987.
18 There were some indications that there were rival sources of authority operating that made control over pasture difficult. Herders within the Reserve

preferred to set aside pastures on the Reserve boundary (nearer water) for their calves. But these were precisely the areas that were more likely to be grazed by herders who did not have permission to enter the Reserve and who lived outside it, but could send their animals a short distance inside on a daily basis. Interview, MN, 1/4/96.

19 Some interviews also indicated that the reserved grazing area management could be weak: MM, 10/5/96.

20 Indeed, part of their power as emotive statements, as clarion calls for action and celebrations of success, stem from the fact that they are so fuzzy. Within some limits, readers can envisage what they want to imagine.

21 McWilliam and Packer, 1999: 17.

22 Ellis, Coughenour and Swift, 1993: 33.

23 McWilliam and Packer, 1999: 17.

24 Anderson, 1967.

25 Anstey (1958: 68) said that the Reserve was about 1,100 square miles (285,000 ha) in area. Anderson (1967: 18) gave a figure of 597,770 acres (241,918 ha). Harris (1970: 3) gave the size as 3,276 km² (327,600 ha, 809,488 acres), which Coe (1999: 7) reports is almost the same as the area calculated from current maps.

26 Anderson, 1967: 29–30.

27 Indeed, this table suggests that the Game Department continually underestimated the number of cattle using the Reserve. The number of stock Anstey recalls present in 1951 is much lower than all the other estimates for the 1950s.

28 cf. Bell, 1987.

29 Hemmingway *et al.*, 1966; Robinette and Gilbert, 1968.

30 Anderson, 1959; Parker, 1951.

31 Mace, 1991.

32 For a start they are quite diverse, cf. Anderson's rates above.

33 Behnke, 1985; Sandford, 1983.

34 In this regard it is instructive to note that the researchers suggested that the 'Tsavo pump station site' was a model of ideal range condition while at the same time noting that it has 'escaped livestock use during the past few years'. It was almost as though range at Mkomazi could only be 'good' if it was untouched.

35 Brockington and Homewood, 1999.

36 Interview, MK, 29/4/96. Bushy land would be set aside in a good rainfall year when grass was abundant. This would result in a hotter fire in the dry season to keep down the bush.

37 Brockington and Homewood, 1996; Coe and Ndolanga, 1994.

38 Canney, 2001.

39 Coe, 1995: 1.

40 Blaikie and Jeanrenaud, 1997: 67.

41 Pielou, 1975

42 Guyer and Richards, 1996: 1.

43 In some conservation circles, but see Altieri, 1993, 1999; Brookfield and Stocking, 1999; and Liang *et al.*, 2001 for discussions of agrodiversity.

44 Grainger, 1999.

45 Dublin, 1995; Pellew, 1983.

46 Davis *et al.*, 1994; Stattersfield *et al.*, 1998; Huston, 1994; Braithwaite, 1996.

47 Belsky, 1987; Dublin, 1995.

48 Western and van Praet, 1973; Wijngaarden, 1985; Dublin, 1995; Hoffman *et al.*, 1995; Leuthold, 1977, 1996; Ribot, 1998; Shepherd, 1992; Abbot and Homewood, 1999; Nyerges, 1996; Fairhead and Leach, 1996.

49 Kramer *et al.*, 1997; Hoffman *et al.*, 1997; Davis *et al.*, 1994.

50 Davis *et al.*, 1994.

51 Menaut, 1983.

52 Coe *et al.*, 1999.

53 cf. Prendergast *et al.*, 1993.

54 This, following White, 1983, is the Somali–Maasai phytochorion.

55 Western and Ssemakula, 1981.

56 White, 1983; Davis *et al.*, 1994.

57 (1994, *ibid*).

58 See species lists and analyses: Coe *et al.*, 1999.

59 Stattersfield *et al.*, 1998.

60 Lack, 1999.

61 Williams *et al.*, 1981.

62 Hartley, 1986; Little, 1996.

63 *Guardian*, 25 May 1998.

64 Russell-Smith *et al.*, 1997: 39; Kruger and McGavin, 1997.

65 Russell-Smith *et al.*, 1997: 39.

66 Coe and Ndolanga, 1994.

67 Inamdar, 1996.

68 Watson *et al.*, 1969: 14.

69 Parker and Archer, 1970.

70 Homewood and Rodgers, 1991: 183–4.

71 Inamdar, pers. comm.; Inamdar, 1996.

72 Homewood, 1994; Homewood and Rodgers, 1991.

73 cf. Howard *et al.*, 1998.

74 MNRT, 1997: 16–18.

75 cf. Brown, 1998.

76 McCann, 1999; Hoffman *et al.*, 1995; Sullivan, 1998, 1999; Turner, 1998a, 1998b, 1999; Little, 1996.

77 Fairhead and Leach, 1996.

78 Nyerges, 1996.

79 Sullivan, 2000.

80 Watson, 1991. The views of conservationists are divergent. By labelling this viewpoint 'the conservationist position' I do not wish to imply that all conservationists think like this.

81 Mustaffa, 1997.

5
People

The foresters clung still to the lowest rungs of a hierarchy of use-rights. While their own rights were inconsequential beside those of the great users, they were more numerous than the great; they knew every pathway and spinney in the forest, and they exploited each faggot, turf, and hare until these added up into a livelihood. With its tree-fellers and hewers, its sawyers and hurdlers, its spoke-choppers and faggoters, its lath-renders, rake-and-ladder makers, and what not, the forest found food for hundreds of families. ... Little money passed among foresters; they did not go to a butcher for their meat. It was because they pursued not a luxury but a livelihood that encounters between them and the keepers were so grim.

E.P. Thompson, *Whigs and Hunters*

On ordinary Nkwo days the voice of the market carried far in all directions like the approach of a great wind. Today it was as though all the bees in the world were passing overhead.

Chinua Achebe, *Arrow of God*

A comparison of livelihoods before and after eviction requires good baseline data against which to compare the current state of affairs. These are rare. At Mkomazi we have been fortunate to recover some data that make 'before and after' comparisons possible, and some that allow a historical reconstruction of changes since eviction. We can also compare indices of household and herd well-being against similar indices for other populations, based on a year-long repeat round survey of 52 households. We can document uses of the Reserve's resources whose prohibition law-abiding citizens would find obstructive, and which make it more costly, in terms of bribes, imprisonment and fines, for others. These reveal some changes brought by the details of the eviction of people and livestock from the Reserve. From these a picture of the cost of eviction begins to emerge.

This chapter falls into four parts. First, I consider the impact of exclusion on pastoral livelihoods. Second, I look at how the regional live-stock economy was affected. Third, I examine the benefits offered by tourist revenues and outreach programmes, and consider how far costs have been offset by the advantages of the Reserve. Fourth, I discuss the reactions to the benefits offered by the Mkomazi's authorities, and the resistance to them.

Livelihoods

Lack of data makes it difficult to evaluate livelihood change. The unreliability of some sources compounds the difficulty. Accounts of the immediate and subsequent impacts of eviction on livelihoods are contested by herders and the state. What people say has to be carefully evaluated.

The evictees allege that the operation to clear the Reserve was violently and rapidly executed, with no compensation and inadequate provision of alternative places to live:

> We did not want to move but they moved us by force and burned houses. They just left us there on the road. … We were just taken out. … No cattle were taken by the Government but a lot of cattle died and we got a loss. Some cattle were sold by the Government saying they were sold to pay for the expense of keeping the livestock. … There was a lot of cattle sold and a lot died (Juma and Mchome, 1994: Appendix One).

I heard many stories like that. The High Court accepted that the evictions had been improperly carried out, stating:

> game scouts and militiamen effecting the eviction assaulted pastoralists, harassed their families, mothers with newly born babies had to be dumped into the bush in the rush of the eviction, cattle, donkeys and calves strayed into the wilderness where they were lost or devoured by beasts; *bomas*, huts, kraals, cattle, domestic articles, food stuffs, veterinary medicines, cash and ornaments got lost or razed down by the fires the game scouts started. Families were dislocated and broken up. In short the plaintiffs were seriously inconvenienced, put to a great crisis and thrown out of the reserve without assistance for resettlement in terms of alternative land (Tenga, 1999: 61).

The court awarded compensation of 300,000 Tanzanian shillings (approximately US$ 400 at the time of the trial) to 27 evictees for damage they experienced during the removals.

The Reserve had probably been a good place to rear cattle. The immigration pressures into the east and west of the Reserve in the 1960s and 1970s indicate that pastoralists found it so. Oral histories proclaimed the Reserve to be excellent pasture, with a mixture of 'sweet' and 'salty' grasses that enhances livestock productivity. It was relatively free of trypanosomiasis and East Coast Fever.[1] Herders bought in stock from dry areas in central Tanzania, which are not known for their disease resistance but perform well in drier lands.[2] Herds benefited from transhumant grazing, which allowed the exploitation of wet season pastures

---

Box 5.1 Eviction experiences

Elena was a bright, educated woman from Monduli who moved to Mkomazi after her marriage in 1986. Initially, she went to live with her new husband at Kisiwani, where they practised transhumance using Kavateta dam and the Kisiwani river as their main sources of water. Her experience of the eviction was typically unpleasant. Her home was burnt along with others, some of them with smallstock and calves still inside. They were given no chance to prepare to leave the house. Numerous household goods were lost. There was no reception area for evicted people. Cattle were herded on ahead by men and game guards until they arrived south of the Pare mountains where they were abandoned. Elena and her family spent three days near Same Town with no proper accommodation. She said that in some cases children were separated from their parents in the confusion. She and her family moved to Ndea, where they are now living. In this they are luckier than most. Others went to the Ruvu valley first and lost many cattle to tick-borne diseases. Others tried to settle in Kenya and were evicted to Ndea.

Source: Igoe and Brockington, 1999.

---

in the plains and pastures near the mountains in the dry season. These may be rose-tinted views but probably reflect an underlying reality.

Since the operation, herds have been concentrated around the edge of the Reserve. Law-abiding herders could use only the thin strip of land between the Pare and Usambara mountains and the boundary. The Reserve is not fenced and many enter it illegally, but a well-enforced exclusion policy backed by heavy fines makes that a risky option. The herders no longer have access to the fertile wet season pastures so important for their herds' condition.

Herders claim that livestock died after the evictions for lack of grazing, and through exposure to disease.[3] In a letter of complaint to the government they said:

> ... we people, your citizens, are in great danger of losing our income and so likewise people's lives for the same reason. We ask that you investigate this issue, look carefully through it and inspect it in much more detail since we have been deprived of rights, we have not been treated as original citizens of this country. If it is possible let the Game Reserve be divided and areas be given to livestock, or herds can enter and leave in order to find grazing (Parakuyo pastoralists to the Prime Minister of Tanzania, 10 July 1988).

This is the complaint that we must examine most rigorously. To what extent was it accurate? Is it still true?

Damage to herds straight after the evictions (when the herders wrote to the Prime Minister) appears to have been accentuated by conditions immediately following the evictions. In the first few months, animals were crowded together with insufficient grazing. There is evidence of high herd mortality. In September 1989, 49 Maasai and Parakuyo pastoralists of Umba Division met to record the deaths of livestock since eviction; they noted the loss of a total of 7,700 cattle and 2,200 small-stock.[4] The numbers cannot be checked and are probably exaggerated, but the fact and record of the meeting indicates that something unusual had happened. Two relatively impartial accounts suggest that the immediate effects of the evictions were indeed deleterious to herds: two Lutheran missionaries in Kivingo in 1989 found that their Easter service was disrupted by the stench of dead cattle;[5] and the Divisional Livestock Officer of Umba noted that the high concentration of cattle outside the borders of the Reserve resulted in the rapid spread of disease.[6]

The immediate aftermath of eviction appears to have been sufficiently severe for many herders to move away.[7] Unfortunately, it appears that those who remain still face problems. Considerable data suggest that live-stock production has continued to be adversely affected, with a reduction in herd size and a decline in herd performance.

Livestock census data of 1984 can be compared with the stock counts made during my research.[8] This shows a sharp reduction (Table 5.1). It is clear that, before the evictions, the Reserve housed wealthy herders compared with similar communities elsewhere. Zaal and Dietz use White and Meadows' data to show that, in 1980–1 the average herd size on one (relatively prosperous) ranch in Kajiado District was 236 tropical livestock units (TLU) per household.[9] Some herders at Mkomazi were considerably richer. However, after the evictions there was a stark decrease in household herd size. In Same District, this is not surprising given the constraints on space at Kisiwani. It is impossible to tell how much of the decrease reflects the large number of absent animals. In Lushoto District fewer animals are sent away and trends are more reliable. Household herd sizes here have decreased to between 3 and 38 per cent of their former size, with an average of 75 TLU per household. In comparative terms, the wealthiest are still better off than other Maasai groups, but the poor are poorer. Zaal and Dietz report an average of 84 TLU per household in Kajiado in 1994–5, but state that the poorest household had 9 TLU.[10]

Averages conceal an uneven distribution of livestock wealth in the sample. It is highly skewed, and well over half do not have the lowest estimated minimum number of cattle per capita (four) needed for subsistence (Table 5.2).[11] While wealthier households at Mahambalawe are still almost as wealthy as those at Kisima (Same District) were before the evictions, those at Kisima (Lushoto District) are considerably poorer than their neighbours. In Lushoto only 5 per cent of the households qualify for the wealthiest bracket, and nearly 70 per cent belong to the poorest. Rutten found livestock holdings were evenly distributed across the three

Table 5.1 Household herd sizes in Same and Lushoto District before and after eviction.

Year	District	Village	Sub-village	Cattle keepers	TLU	TLU per household
1984	Same	Kisiwani	Kavateta	12	11,300	942
1984	Same	Kisiwani	Kisima	16	2,402	150
1984	Lushoto	Kivingo	–	92	32,761	356
1995–6	Same	Kisiwani	–	26	633	24
1995–6	Lushoto	Mng'aro	Mahambalawe	10	1,341	134
1995–6	Lushoto	Lunguza, Mng'aro	Kisima, Mazinde	10	101	10

Source: District Census data, 1984; Household survey data, 1995–6.
Calculation of TLU follows Buhl and Homewood (2000) who use Little's (1985) measure of 1 TLU = 1 bovine or 6 small ruminants. There are other measures. Fratkin and Roth (1990: 393, footnote 5) state that Dahl and Hjort follow the FAO production yearbook of 1 TLU = 1 camel, 0.8 cattle or 11 smallstock, but that the UNESCO Integrated Project in Arid Lands uses 1 TLU = 1 cattle, 0.8 camel or 10 smallstock. Homewood and Rodgers (1991: 212) cite formulae for standard stock units (SSU) of 1 mature bovine = 2/3 SSU; 1 immature bovine = 1/3 SSU; 1 small ruminant = 1/10 SSU and 1 donkey = 2/5 SSU. Grandin (1988: 4) also gives a formula for livestock units (LU), which are equivalent to one 250 kg animal; accordingly, one cattle = 0.71 LU and 1 sheep or goat = 0.17 LU. Potkanski (1997: 71) uses 1 LU = 1 cattle or 7 smallstock. Ensminger (1992: 82–3) takes 1 TLU to be equal to 1 cattle but converts either 5 or 6 smallstock to 1 TLU according to their value. Zaal and Dietz (1999), citing Peden (1984), Bekure et al. (1991) and Kilewe and Thomas (1992) report that the most commonly used measure in Kenya is 1 TLU = 1.42 cattle, 10 sheep or goats or 1 camel. I follow Buhl and Homewood as this measure is closest to those used in the 1950s at Mkomazi.

wealth classes in Kajiado District in 1990.[12] Zaal and Dietz do not give figures for the distribution of livestock per capita for Kajiado District in 1994–5 but state that 21 per cent of the households had less than 4 TLU per capita. At Mkomazi the inequalities are more marked than elsewhere.

The inequalities recall Fratkin and Roth's work on the impact of drought among the Ariaal in northern Kenya, and Roth's work amongst the Rendille. They note that richer families tend to lose more livestock, both absolutely and in terms of the proportions of their herds. However, they do not suffer the same consequences as the poor. The size of their pre-drought herds keeps them within minimum subsistence requirements even after a drought.[13] They are not reduced to the famine avoidance methods forced on poorer families. Families that start 'poor', or middle-income families that finish 'poor', are reduced to circumstances from which recovery is slow. Ensminger shows a similar pattern among the Galole Orma of Kenya. In the 1974–5 and 1983–5 droughts, the poor and middle-category families lost a greater proportion of their

Table 5.2 Household livestock ownership per capita around Mkomazi, 1995–1996.

Location	0–4.99 TLU/AAME	5–12.99 TLU/AAME	≥13 TLU/AAME
Lushoto	13	4	2
Same	25	3	1

Source: Household survey.
AAME: average adult male equivalent. Calculations follow Grandin, 1988; ILCA, 1981. Wealth categories follow Rutten, 1992: 335.

livestock than did rich families. Similarly, the recovery rate of herds after the drought was much higher for the rich families than for herds of their poorer neighbours.[14]

The same principles are applicable to Mkomazi. The consequences of impoverishment following eviction would have been most severely felt by poor and middle-income families. A number of households may have been able to remain rich following the evictions, as at Mahambalawe. Yet eviction has also resulted in concentrations of impoverished pastoralists, such as those found at Kisima and around Kisiwani, who cannot rely upon their herds. This is not to argue that wealth was equally distributed before eviction. The point is that eviction has accentuated the inequalities, by making poorer families even poorer.

The decline in livestock at Mkomazi is reflected in a fall in the bride price. Normally a high bride price is an indication of wealthy times.[15] In late 1990 a group of Maasai and Parakuyo elders from Kapimbi in Kisiwani met to agree a new bride price. They decided that because of the general impoverishment, the bride price should be reduced from 15 cattle to between 10 and 12. They communicated their decision, by letter, to the three leading Parakuyo elders in Lushoto District.[16]

Data on herd performance were collected by interviewing people about the lives of their cattle. Cattle are the subject of intense interest, and women in particular can remember the fate and history of each named animal in the herd allotted to them, for some time. This store of knowledge is a valuable source of information about the history of herds and the fertility and mortality of individual cows. Compiling these histories into a year-by-year record allows a chronology of herd performance to be constructed (Table 5.3 and Table 5.4).[17]

This method over-represents survivors, as we could only begin to ask about cattle that are still alive. It under-represents infertile animals, as we could only ask about named cattle, and cattle are only named when they give birth. The mortality rates are therefore minimum estimates, and fertility rates maximum estimates. In comparison with other areas, these errors tend to make these indices appear healthier than they really are for Mkomazi. Evidence of poor herd performance relative to other areas is likely to be robust and not an artefact.

Fertility and mortality data are compared with other cattle populations in Table 5.3. De Leeuw and Wilson have observed that Maasai calf mortality is low when compared with West African pastoralists. They suggest this is owing to better calf management and provision of reserved calf pastures.[18] To keep factors relatively constant, I have compared the data from Mkomazi with other Maa-speaking pastoralists. Table 5.3 shows that, while calving rates at Mkomazi can approach and even exceed levels elsewhere, in general they do not compare favourably with other populations. Calving rates were particularly low during a dry spell of 1991, and

Table 5.3 Cattle fertility at Mkomazi and elsewhere.

Year	Place	Fertility	n	Place	Fertility	n
1981–3	Kajiado[a]	0.6	120	NCA[c]	0.61	153
1982–3	Baringo pre-drought[b]	0.83	68	–	–	–
1983–4	Baringo drought[b]	0.69	76	–	–	–
1988	Same[d]	0.47	8.5	Lushoto[d]	0.52	34.5
1989	Same	0.7	11.5	Lushoto	0.46	44
1990	Same	0.33	15	Lushoto	0.52	51.5
1991	Same	0.29	25	Lushoto	0.31	61
1992	Same	0.46	35	Lushoto	0.4	80.5
1993	Same	0.59	44	Lushoto	0.47	105
1994	Same	0.67	58	Lushoto	0.51	125
1995	Same	0.7	68	Lushoto	0.57	135
1996	Same	0.71	35	Lushoto	0.37	65.5

Note: n = number of cattle monitored for Kajiado, NCA and Baringo (1982–3) and number of 'cow years at risk of giving birth' for the data of Same and Lushoto (see Appendix 2).
Source: [a] Bekure *et al.*, 1991; Homewood, 1992; [b] Homewood and Lewis, 1987; [c] Homewood *et al.*, 1987; [d] this survey.

considerably lower than the rates recorded at Baringo during the first year of a drought.[19] Calf mortality figures in Table 5.4 show that rates in Lushoto District are on a par with those elsewhere; in Same District, however, they are similar to those of the Ngorongoro Conservation Area, where high levels of tick-borne disease were recorded. The dry year of 1991 appears to have had relatively little impact compared with that recorded in Baringo.

These data concur with statements made by residents and veterinary officials. Before evictions, herds had access to fertile, relatively disease-free pastures on the plains. After eviction, grazing was less accessible.

Table 5.4 Calf mortality at Mkomazi and elsewhere.

Year	Place	n	Mortality within 2 years	Place	n	Mortality within 2 years
1981–3	Kajiado	678	0.09*	NCA	no data	0.26
1983–4	Baringo drought	no data	0.89	–	–	–
1988	Same	6	0.17	Lushoto	29	0.17
1989	Same	13	0.15	Lushoto	32	0.06
1990	Same	12	–	Lushoto	34	0.12
1991	Same	12	0.25	Lushoto	27	0.04
1992	Same	20	0.20	Lushoto	33	0.09
1993	Same	28	0.36	Lushoto	50	0.18
1994	Same	39	0.28	Lushoto	65	0.06
1995	Same	47	0.19*	Lushoto	77	0.18*

*within 18 months only.
n for Same and Lushoto data is the number of calf-years-at-risk of dying.
Source: as for Table 5.3.

Herds spend more time on less nutritious pastures and are exposed to more disease. Household heads without the experience, health, connections or plain nous to change their herding patterns are at greater risk of losing animals. We observed the herd of one ill pastoralist at Kisiwani decline from 20 cows to zero during the course of this study. Elsewhere around the Reserve, herds declined owing to wasteful selling by drunkards or profligate youths.[20] Evictions have reduced the margin of error available to herders and their dependants.

A key indication of the importance of livestock to families' needs is the amount of milk used. This is less open to manipulation than cash sales of animals, because it does not involve sensitive questions about income and is measured at source. Average milk yields in Mkomazi are low compared with other locations. Milk availability averages 0.42 and 0.16 kg/reference adult/day in the wet and dry seasons in Lushoto District, and 0.41 and 0.26 kg/reference adult/day in Same. At Mkomazi, milk makes a low contribution to calorie intake levels compared with other pastoral populations. If the recommended calorie intake is 2,530 k/cal/day, these figures translate to 4.7–12.4 per cent of recommended intake in Lushoto and 7.7–12 per cent in Same. This can be compared with Ngorongoro, where dry season milk intake averages 34 per cent, and with Kajiado, where annual averages were 48 per cent of the recommended calorie intake.[21]

There are noticeable differences within the study sites. Some households had little, if any, milk for daily use. Others had considerable quantities. In Same District some men had many animals, but did not keep them near their homes because there was insufficient grazing and the disease risks were high. Women in these households would complain that they were unable to milk animals kept so far from home.

Stock kept far from home have more milk for their young. In Kenya, Grandin has shown that rich and poor households tend to take similar amounts of milk from the herds, even though the rich have many more animals.[22] She concludes that the richer households are investing in the herd by leaving extra milk for their calves. Sikana and colleagues report other examples, and note that when wealthy households reside in towns, they leave their herds in more distant camps, so that the dairy economy declines in importance.[23] The resulting shortfalls in food supply are made good by sale of stock and purchase of grain. This strategy entails splitting herds: some animals are retained to provide milk, the rest are sent away. It allows pastoralists to take advantage of the greater productivity that mobile herds can enjoy, but depends on having much labour power and many animals. The strategy reflects the fact that men and women control different spheres of economic activity.[24] Men have the final decision over the disposal of livestock and control the proceeds of their sale. Women are responsible for milking the beasts and control its allocation to their children, guests and husband.[25] By sending animals to distant camps men are denying women access to milk. This can have knock-on effects on women's earnings and expenditure.

As Kiwasila has shown, exclusion from the Reserve affects a large number of other resource users in different ways.[26] She found that agropastoralists used over a hundred species of wild plants for food or fuel, which could be gathered inside the Reserve. The latter were particularly important for poorer families who also sold wood. Wildfoods were eaten on 20 per cent of 373 meal-days. Some wildfoods were also sold. *Msele* (*Fagara holtziana*), a local tree leaf, often gathered in Vumari in the west of the Reserve, was most popular. It was principally sold by women and schoolgirls, the latter using it as a source of income for exercise books and pens. Village government levies on the sales were over Tzsh 100,000/= during the year of the study period. A lucrative form of income was honey gathering. A litre of honey could sell for as much as Tzsh 1,200/= (then US$ 2). The Reserve was valued as a relatively safe place to hang hives. Many resent the restrictions the Reserve places on these activities. Farmers also perceive it to be a safe haven for crop raiders. Many wish to see the boundaries moved further north, away from the mountains.

These data all suggest that livelihoods have suffered as a result of the evictions. The problem with the data is that they are based on a relatively small sample. How can we tell that the problems found are typical of livestock keepers more generally? For indications of broader changes to the livestock economy it is necessary to look at livestock markets.

Regional consequences

We have seen that the influx of livestock into the western half of the Reserve in the 1970s resulted in the establishment of a cattle market at Kisiwani. This rapidly gained business to become the most prominent in the district. Local entrepreneurs and traders at Kisiwani remember the days of the cattle market as a boom time. What happened to this market and its neighbours after the evictions?

Livestock markets occur every fortnight or month, with records kept of each month's performance. The records used here extend back to the early 1970s. These data are therefore useful as an indication of long-term changes in the livestock economy before and after eviction. They are an unusual, if not unique, source of information. The older records in particular were a serendipitous find by district staff amid a jumble of files in district and regional headquarters. Although sales at official markets represent only a small proportion of the actual trade going on, they can be used as an indication of events in the wider economy. The type of animals that herders are prepared to sell, and the prices they are prepared to accept, will be reflected in the official markets. The records provide quite detailed information about the condition of the livestock economy.

There are several problems to consider with these data. First, the prices reported may be underestimates of the money actually exchanged. Sale is not by auction but by mutual agreement between buyer and seller, who then report the taxable price to the government officer present. Second, there are inconsistencies, which suggest that the amount of money collected from markets was sometimes underreported by district officials. Third, the records are not continuous. Sometimes this is because data are missing, making interpretation of long-term trends difficult; sometimes it is because the market was temporarily in abeyance. They are also geographically patchy, with the best data coming from Same District. Records from Lushoto District are more sparse and sporadic. The northern plains of Lushoto District are not well served by formal livestock markets. Records from Mwanga District are largely incomplete. Fourth, the spatial aggregation of the records also varies. Most of the time data are available for individual markets, although sometimes only district-level data are available. Finally, the type of data available is not uniform. Sometimes records provide highly specific data on the type of animals sold and the average, highest and lowest prices recorded. On other occasions only the number of animals sold and the average price are given.

These problems, however, neither prevent the detection of patterns nor create spurious trends. Overall, both prices and volume of sales can be taken as minimum estimates, as there is a consistent incentive to underreport both. Here I will explore what trends in livestock sales are visible in Same District, where the best data are available, and which explanations can most usefully account for them.

There are four livestock markets in Same District – Same Town, Makanya, Hedaru and Kisiwani. Since pastoralists were evicted from the Reserve there has been a decline in the number of cattle sold in the four markets as a whole. Figure 5.1 shows the number of animals sold between 1974 and 1996. Mean monthly sales before 1986 (when moves to evict herders began) were over 261 animals. After 1986 the average fell to 146 animals. The differences are statistically significant (see Table 5.5).

Although it appears that cattle sales are generally much lower after eviction, the value of cattle varies and it is necessary to control for changes in the relative worth of stock. Here I will measure cattle value in terms of maize.[27] The buying power of cattle with respect to maize has fluctuated, with no overall trend visible (Figure 5.2). Comparing the number of cattle sold and their value in terms of maize produces the relationship shown in Figure 5.3. This shows the classic reverse response to demand of pastoralists who sell cattle to meet short-term needs and accordingly sell fewer stock when their value is higher and more when they are worth little.[28]

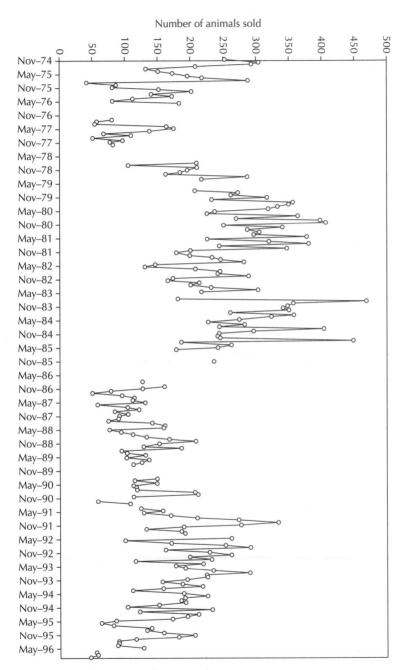

Figure 5.1 Cattle sales in Same District markets, 1974–1996.

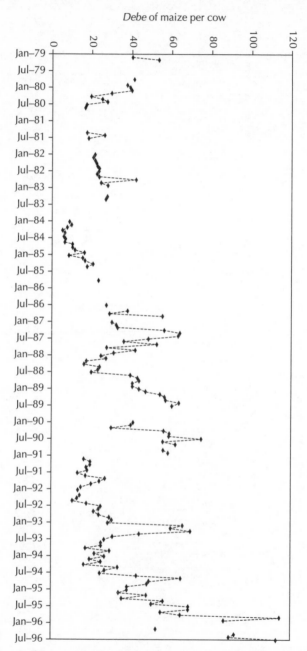

Figure 5.2 The value of cattle in terms of maize.
Note: A *debe* is a measure of grain used in markets. It weighs approximately 20 kg.

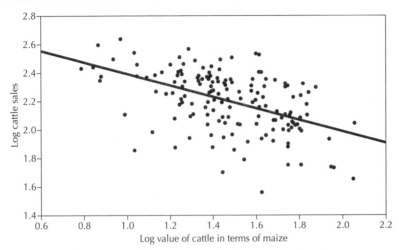

Figure 5.3 Log cattle sales and log average cattle value in terms of maize.
The variables have been logged to show a linear relationship.

Examining changes in the relationship shown above takes account of the variation in sales due to the changing worth of cattle. Figure 5.4 shows that, when controlling for value in terms of maize, cattle sales were greater before 1986. Modelling the difference using multiple regression shows that the decline in sales remains strongly significant even accounting for the changing value of the cattle (F-statistic 45.95, P<0.0001). Although cattle are worth more, and so fewer sales are expected, this change cannot account for the decline in sales. For a given value of cattle, more animals were sold before evictions than after. Another factor must be sought to explain the decline.

Cross-border sales may rob Tanzanian markets of their business, and produce a decline in sales, but trends elsewhere suggest this is unlikely for this period. Potkanski noted that a fall in the value of the Kenyan shilling in late 1992 boosted Tanzanian sales in and around Ngorongoro;

Table 5.5 Sales of cattle in Same District.

Period	Months of data	Mean	Std Dev
All period	192	194.85	89.22
11/74–10/85	81	261.72	78.94
7/86–7/96	111	146.06	59.95

Periods compared	't' test for separate variance	Degrees of freedom	P
11/74–10/85: 7/86–7/96	11.06	143.07	<0.001

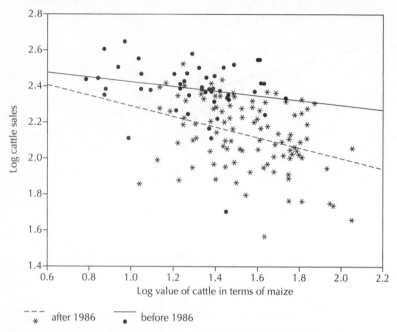

Figure 5.4 Log cattle sales and log average cattle value before and after 1986.

at Mkomazi they were lower than before.[29] The most likely explanation for the change is simply that there were fewer cattle in Same District available to sell. The stock have moved to other pastures.

The strength of the 'absence of cattle' hypothesis is apparent if we disaggregate the data slightly. In three markets located west of the mountains – Same Town, Makanya and Hedaru – there is no real change in the number of animals sold. Indeed, there even appears to be an increase in sales after 1986 (Figure 5.5; Figure 5.6). This increase is overshadowed, however, by the collapse of sales at Kisiwani, which declined to zero in 1995 (Figure 5.7). At the time of my research this market was no longer viable. Thus the decline in the sales of stock in Same District is explained by the collapse of the Kisiwani market, which had flourished during a brief period when the west of the Reserve was opened to cattle.

There are other factors involved. As well as the supply of cattle drying up, Kisiwani became relatively inaccessible, compared to the other markets, after the road west of the mountains was tarred. The market had begun to weaken before the evictions took place; indeed, Pare people appealed to local Maasai leaders to bring more cattle to their market in 1985.[30] The death of the market was inevitable, however, after the loss of the cattle that had caused its creation.

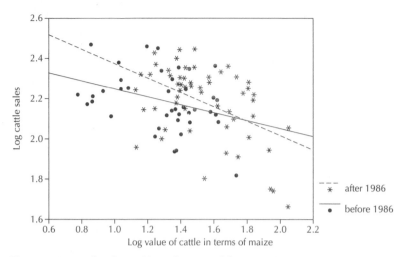

Figure 5.5 Log cattle sales and log value west of the mountains.

The decline in sales has damaged the local economy of Kisiwani. Less money is earned in the village and less spent than before. Shopkeepers and bar owners bitterly resent the lack of custom, which they saw as directly related to the closure of the market.[31] Some businessmen at Kisiwani blame the market's decline for causing local economic depression.

The changes at Kisiwani were local. But there are also indications in the market data of more widespread changes to the livestock economy following the evictions. These are found in the ratio of male to female animals sold. Pastoralists normally sell more male than female cattle. This is expected for a subsistence pastoral population, where males are sold to raise cash. Cows, the source of milk and calves, are rarely sold or slaughtered.[32] The corollary is that high sales of females are indicative of stress in the pastoralist economy. It indicates that pastoralists are selling off the productive nucleus of the herd. It suggests a loss of flexibility and lack of choice of which animals to sell, and when to sell them. It shows that pastoralists have no surplus animals to sell, and need to dispose of their basic means of production to supply their household needs.[33] It may result from poor herd performance, with lower fertility rates and higher mortality rates reducing their options. This can happen during droughts, or when good-quality pasture is unavailable, as after the evictions.

Figure 5.8 shows that the proportion of female cattle sold increased considerably after 1986. Before eviction 2.57 males were sold for each female. After it, 1.76 males were sold. The difference in the ratio of male: female animals is statistically significant (Table 5.6). It is more remarkable

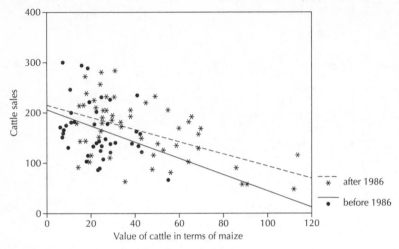

Figure 5.6 Cattle sales and cattle value west of the mountains.

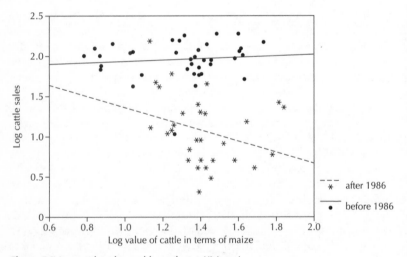

Figure 5.7 Log cattle sales and log value at Kisiwani.

given that the terms of trade for cattle (their buying power in terms of grain) were improving at that time (Figure 5.9). Even though pastoralists found that their cattle were worth more in terms of maize, they sold more female animals.

There were also changes in smallstock sales, but these are harder to interpret. Smallstock ownership is more extensive than cattle ownership,

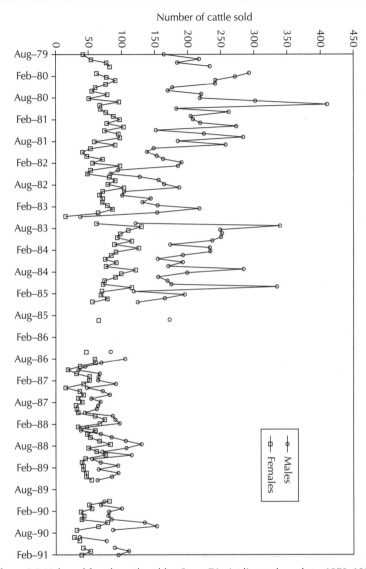

Figure 5.8 Male and female cattle sold at Same District livestock markets, 1979–1991.

and informal sales are considerable. The formal sales, recorded at livestock markets, represent a much smaller proportion of the total business, and caution is needed when interpreting these data. Sheep sales are not well recorded and only sales of goats are represented. There is a clear pattern of goat sales increasing considerably in 1986 (Figure 5.10). This occurred at

Table 5.6 Comparing the male: female ratio of cattle sold before October 1985 and after July 1986.

Period examined	Months of data	Mean ratio	Mean % females	Mean rank	U	P
All data	119	2.23	31%			
11/74–10/85	69	2.57	28%	76.32	599	<0.0001
7/86–3/91	50	1.76	36%	37.48		

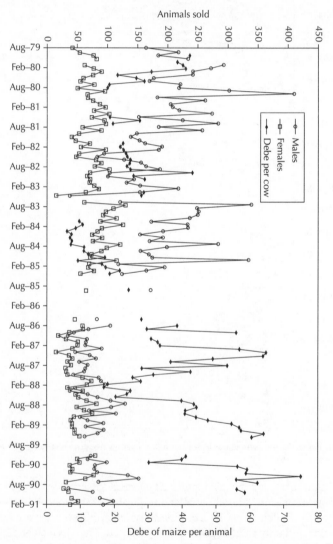

Figure 5.9 Value of cattle and the number of male and female animals sold.

the same time as cattle sales decreased. The difference between sales before and after 1986 is again statistically significant (Table 5.7).

Several authors, for both empirical and theoretical reasons, have suggested that reliance upon, and investment in, smallstock are both indicators of stress in pastoral economies, an indication of poverty and a useful strategy for those who are trying to rebuild their herds.[34] Increased sales could be a consequence of pastoralists selling more smallstock in order to avoid selling their cattle. It would be difficult, however, to draw that conclusion from these data without corroborative evidence. The livestock markets serve a large number of agropastoralists who own smallstock and are heavily reliant upon agriculture as well. Their sales of smallstock may reflect decision-making linked to agricultural liveli-hoods, not herd management. So many sales take place informally that it would be hard to interpret trends in the wider economy on the basis of these data alone.[35]

However, when changes in the sale of smallstock are considered along with changes in the male: female ratio of cattle sales, the two indi-cators suggest there has been a decline in the viability of pastoralists' economies. These changes and indications of stress coincide with the eviction from the Reserve. Given the indicators of impoverishment recorded elsewhere and the simple logistical problems that herders faced when excluded from such an extensive area, this would be the simplest explanation.

It is misleading to attribute too much change to one cause. The patterns described here began when there were still some pastoralists inside the Reserve. They also coincide with national economic changes and struc-tural adjustment programmes that were widely criticised for the burdens they imposed on rural dwellers. Education costs, for example, rose as government expenditure on services was reduced.[36] Perlov notes that education expenses accounted for 30 per cent of stock sales among Samburu herders in Kenya.[37] Food needs accounted for only 18 per cent of sales. The changes recorded here also reflect these forces. Nevertheless it is hard to avoid the conclusion that eviction from Mkomazi has had considerable costs for local herders.

There are, therefore, indications of considerable problems afflicting herders at a household and regional level as a result of the evictions. But what of the financial benefits that the Reserve brings to the nation and to locals? Are local costs offset by national gain? What about the services offered by extension activities? Any evaluation of the costs and benefits of the Reserve must consider these goods, and it is to these that we now turn.

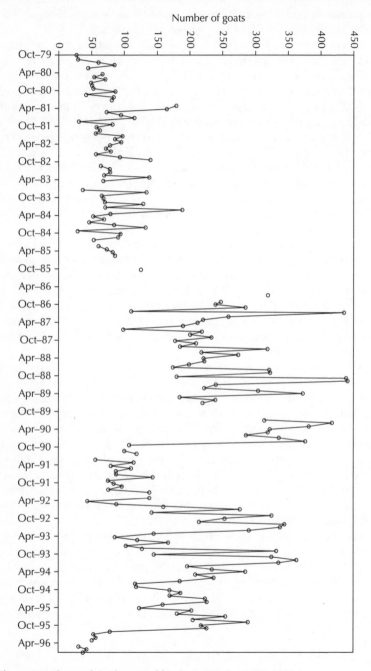

Figure 5.10 The number of goats sold in Same District, 1979–1996.

Table 5.7 Comparing sales of goats in Same District, October 1979–October 1985 and July 1986–July 1996.

Period	Months of data	Mean	Std Dev
All period	174	157.89	99.61
10/79–10/85	63	81.44	33.62
7/86–7/96	111	201.28	98.59

Periods compared	't' test for separate variance	Degrees of freedom	P
10/79–10/85: 7/86–7/96	−11.67	148.63	<0.001

Benefits

We have seen that if goods or services are to promote good relations between protected areas and their neighbours, the benefits offered should at least match, if not exceed, the costs incurred by the protected area. If that is not the case, it is difficult to envisage on what economic basis good relations could be built.[38] But even if revenues from conservation are not well distributed, they may indirectly benefit many citizens of a cash-starved state. Mkomazi Game Reserve's revenues are part of a broader plan for national development, and must be considered in the national context. Here we will examine the Reserve's contribution to the national economy first and local needs second.

Tanzania is promoting its tourism industry. Tourism brought in $332 million in 1996, equivalent to 30 per cent of export earnings and 10 per cent of GDP.[39] The government hopes that the number of visitors will continue to rise, and it is keen to promote 'high-class' tourism that generates much income per visitor, while minimising local impact. Mkomazi is seen as an ideal site to further that goal.

Unfortunately, Mkomazi has only attracted a few tourists (Table 5.8). Gate receipts between 1991 and 1994 were low, and did not meet the Reserve's operating costs (Table 5.9). Mkomazi currently has camping facilities only, no hotel and none of the services expected by the high paying tourists Tanzania seeks to attract.[40] It is not generating any revenue.[41]

Tourist facilities are set to improve, but numbers are unlikely to be significant.[42] The estimated bed size of an initial venture at Mkomazi is small (Table 5.10), and the Reserve is unlikely ever to become a major attraction. Its concentration of wildlife is low. Mkomazi is a wet season dispersal area for mammalian wildlife, unlike currently popular dry season concentration areas like Manyara, Ruaha and Tarangire.

Table 5.8 Tourism figures at Mkomazi Game Reserve, 1966–1980.

Year	Number of visitors
1966	< 200[1]
1969	554[1]
1970	740[2]
1971	776[2]
1972	870[2]
1973	1,018[2]
1975	1,773[2]; 417[3]
1974	1,266[2]
1976	1,059[3]
1977	934[3]
1978	981[3]
1979	1,045[3]
1980	662[3]

Source: [1] J. Barry Turner, 1967. 1966 figure is exclusive of school parties. The size and number of these parties is not given. [2] Ibeun, 1976: 49. [3] Abu-zeid, 1981: 19.

Table 5.9 Gate receipts in Mkomazi Game Reserve, 1990–1994.

Year	Fees from tourist viewing (Tzsh)	Equivalent in £ sterling and US$
1991	1,390,450	£3,600; $5,400
1992	1,558,150	£2,980; $4,500
1993	1,188,900	£1,950; $3,000
1994	928,900	£1,250; $2,000

Source: Game Reserve files.

Table 5.10 An assessment of Mkomazi's potential.

Facility size	Obvious attractions	Linked to	Linking problems	Success potential	Appeal rating
20 beds	Vehicle game viewing	Kilimanjaro (120 km)	None	A+	All visitors
	Walking safaris			(80–100%)	
	Plant life	Usambara Mts (100 km)	None		
	Bird life				
	Large mammals	Lossongoi Plateau (80 km)	River crossing		
	Geology				
	Scenic wilderness				

Source: Oliver, 1994.

Another means of generating revenue from African wildlife is hunting. This was attempted at Mkomazi for six months in 1994, and brought in over Tzsh 16,600,000/–(then worth $41,500).[43] Some of this revenue – Tzsh 1,313,650/–(then worth $2,400) – was later returned to villages in

Same District in 1996 as part of the government policy of redistributing wildlife revenue to districts. The bulk of the money was allotted to water projects and primary school development projects at sites around the edge of the Reserve.[44]

Hunting aroused considerable controversy, however. Many felt that the Reserve had only recently been saved and restored, and that hunting was inappropriate. With such low wildlife populations it is difficult to set a sustainable and profitable offtake rate. Moreover, the hunting companies were alleged to be unscrupulous, and to owe their tenure at Mkomazi to their relations with the Minister of Natural Resources, Tourism and the Environment. The affair aroused the attention of the press.[45] Eventually Parliament banned hunting.

What of local benefits? Clearly, no significant income can be derived from tourism. Currently the main sources of outreach funds for local people come not from Reserve revenues but government funds and donor support. The Reserve management has undertaken extension activities in the form of high-profile projects aimed at meeting local needs. These are funded by the Tanzanian Wildlife Protection Fund, a central fund of the Department of Wildlife, and separate applications are required for each project. They include Tzsh 4,000,000/– ($6,700) for the construction of a new laboratory at Same secondary school and Tzsh 2,800,000 ($4,700) for the construction of a dam on the west side of the Pare mountains to provide an alternative watering point for pastoralists in the Ruvu valley. In addition, the World Wide Fund for Nature (WWF) was committed in 1996 to spending nearly $95,000 on extension activities on the Reserve.[46] While each of these is an important contribution, it is difficult to maintain that these benefits compensate for the losses suffered by some sections of the Reserve-adjacent population. Too many people and too many costs are involved.

Outreach was also initiated with the help of the Trusts' Field Officer and implemented by two Dutch expatriates and since taken over by the Department of Wildlife. It has primarily been active in Kisiwani, Mkonga Iginyu and Pangaro, providing goods and services to those near the Reserve. It has offered help to schools, clinics and women's groups, and recently assisted the completion of the Kisiwani secondary school.

The work done is valuable and necessary, but it has to replace benefits lost from the Reserve if it is to form the material basis of an alliance. At Mkomazi the benefits offered are not great when compared to schemes elsewhere, and the people more numerous. There are several examples of private tourist companies that offer more substantial benefits to local communities in return for their setting land aside for conservation purposes. For example, Oliver's Camp gave $14,076 to one village between October 1992 and April 1995, and $4,809 to another between September 1993 and April 1995.[47] The inhabitants of the two villages leasing land to Oliver's Camp number 3,000 and 2,500[48] (Table 5.11). There is greater potential here for dealing adequately with the costs of giving up the land. The CAMPFIRE scheme in Zimbabwe distributes valuable returns from tourist hunting revenue to relatively few people. The high value of the resource means that it is relatively easy to make it worthwhile for local residents to conserve.[49]

Table 5.11 Private community conservation schemes currently in operation in Tanzania.

Name	Nature of the scheme	Source of revenue	Beneficiaries	Source
Oliver's Camp	8,000 acres of land is leased from two villages by a private tour operator for an initial 15-year period.	Tourists coming to the camp pay an extra fee a night, which is split between the two villages.	The money is paid into a bank account to which several elected village officials are signatories.	Dorobo Tours *et al.*, 1994; interviews with Paul Oliver and business partner Jim Howitt.
Dorobo Tours	Several schemes are operated. One village receives a set sum when the company comes into the area as well as bed night fees.	Bed night fees and the set sum come from tourist revenues.	The money is paid into a bank account to which several elected village officials are signatories.	Interviews with J. Peterson, in charge of Dorobo tours; Larma, pers. comm.
Cullman Wildlife Project	Rewards are paid for the destruction of snares and for information leading to the arrest of poachers or destruction of poachers' camps by village-based anti-poaching schemes. Village development projects are funded.	Fees paid by tourist hunters fund the rewards and development projects.	Rewards are paid to individuals. Development schemes are planned at village level with a Cullman scheme employee and then funded.	Interviews with Cullman Wildlife Scheme employees.

Even if hunting were possible, if wealthy tourists flocked in numbers to Mkomazi, if revenues soared, it would not be possible adequately to compensate for the needs denied by the Reserve. One of the starkest problems about Mkomazi is its geography. There are over 50,000 people living around its borders.[50] The mountains south and west of the Reserve concentrate these people into a narrow strip of land. There is no buffer zone. The needs without the Reserve for the resources within are great. Eviction and exclusion were expensive. Significant sections of the community feel they have lost a great deal. Tourism cannot realistically be expected to meet these costs.

Resistance and protest

It is against a background of economic decline and inadequate compensation that resistance to the Reserve becomes intelligible. It is best understood as peasant resistance and opposition to policies inimical to their survival and prosperity. Here I follow Neumann's application of Scott's arguments (in *Weapons of the Weak*) to resistance of Meru villagers to the Arusha National Park.[51] He observed that rural groups resort to 'everyday forms of resistance' that effectively nullify the regulations.[52] These were viewed in the context of a moral economy that views threats to livelihoods, posed by exclusion or raiding by wildlife, to be a greater wrong than poaching or illegal grazing. Peasants do not encroach on parks; rather, 'the park is seen to be encroaching on the Meru villages'.[53]

> The 'crime' of poaching is not a crime at all, but a defense of subsistence, and the 'real crime' is that park animals are allowed to raid crops with impunity (Neumann, 1998: 187).

Resentment at the restrictions imposed by the Reserve was continually evident. There was frustration that people had been treated unreasonably and had suffered deprivation at the hands of the government as a consequence of eviction:

> In 1990 many cows died because they were grazing in diseased pastures. The cows finished until now, 1996, you can stay here and maybe come across 3 or 5 cows. Right now there are 6 cows in the entire village. Now because of the Reserve we herded on diseased land and the cows are finished (ASM 20/5/96[54]).

For pastoralists the constant refrain is '*Tumebanwa na hifadhi*', 'we have been squeezed by the Reserve', or '*Tunaonewa*', 'we are being oppressed', or, as one put it, 'we are left living like people waiting to die':

> ... sometimes the cattle go astray and enter into the reserve. What the Game reserve does is to capture them and put them in a *boma* (compound). This has brought hardship not only for the cows but also to people. Children do not get

milk because the milking cows have been captured and retained until you pay 100,000 shillings. Cattle have also been dying because they are not let out to feed and are put in the sun without water or care. We are left living like people waiting to die. It is very difficult to control the cows from rushing into the Reserve to graze. Especially during the dry season. It has reached the stage where livestock lack food to the extent of eating clay. To say the truth, we are very uncomfortable ... This whole problem has been the result of Mkomazi Game Reserve (Juma and Mchome, 1994: Appendix One).

The resentment is manifest in several levels of conflict around the Reserve. The most frequent is low-level contravention of Reserve regulations, particularly extraction of firewood, hunting and grazing. Sporadic entries in Game Reserve files record offences committed (Table 5.12). Not all those who act illegally are caught. Not all those caught are recorded. Nevertheless it provides an indication of the pressure on the Reserve. It also shows what risks people are prepared to take to use its resources.

One of the most frequent transgressions is grazing inside the Reserve, either as daily incursions by Reserve-adjacent herders or as longer-term invasion by large herds, housed in illegal compounds inside the Reserve, often from villages many miles away. The main pressure is felt between October and March, during the short and long rains, when herders from the south and west move north of the Pare and Usambara mountains for wet season grazing. The fines for illegal grazing are considerable and frequently equivalent to one or two cows. These severe fines cause intense resentment among the pastoral community. Illegal grazing is countered by rangers operating alone or in conjunction with the Trusts' Field Officer. The accounts of anti-grazing operations are less violent than clashes that occur in other protected areas.[55] But they nonetheless provide colourful reading and offer some impression of the interactions with local people that can occur (Box 5.2).

Opposition to the Reserve's rules is also expressed in protests to the Reserve's authorities and other local government officers. This has been the case throughout the Reserve's history by all ethnic groups, and before its existence, when other forms of state intervention restricted livelihoods. We have seen that for Maa-speaking pastoralists, evasion and resistance of state regulations on cattle movements long pre-date the Reserve. Some of the older pastoralists at Mkomazi have spent their entire lives avoiding regulations designed to control their residence and movements. They have variously circumvented the Kenyan boundary and national park regulations, Tanganyikan and Tanzanian game laws, veterinary regulations concerning the movement of stock, colonial rules dictating which tribes live in which areas, and local regulations governing the use of dry season pastures. Some have been imprisoned or fined many times.[56]

Table 5.12 Contravention of Reserve regulations.

July 1991	Two herders fined Tzsh 121,000 and 21,000, respectively (equivalent to US$ 470 and US$ 77)
September 1992	Fines recorded for illegal grazing (from Fosbrooke, 1992): Tzsh 26,600; Tzsh 27,200; Tzsh 42,200; Tzsh 40,000; Tzsh 65,500; Tzsh 91,500; Tzsh 91,500; Tzsh 40,000 (US$ 75 – US$ 250)
November 1993	Lorries smuggling beer are caught in the Reserve (they pass through it to avoid paying tax at village customs duty posts). The value of the beer transported was Tzsh 36,000,000 (US$ 90,000). The smugglers were fined 10 per cent of the value
April 1994	A shotgun was confiscated after it was used for poaching
July 1994	9 elephant tusks weighing 48 kg and worth Tzsh 960,000 (US$ 4,800)
November 1994	Two herders caught and fined Tzsh 65,000 and Tzsh 70,000 (US$ 105 and US$ 126)
July 1995	1 herder arrested and fined Tzsh 40,000 (US$ 75)
August 1995	1 herder arrested and fined Tzsh 50,000 (US$ 91)
September 1995	2 herders arrested and fined Tzsh 10,000 and Tzsh 20,000 (US$ 18 and US$ 30)
October 1995	2 herders caught and fined Tzsh 40,000 each (US$ 75)
November 1995	2 herders caught and fined Tzsh 60,000 and Tzsh 47,000 each (US$ 110 and US$ 90)
December 1995	3 herders caught and fined Tzsh 50,000 (twice) and Tzsh 3,000 (US$ 95 and US$ 6).
January 1996	4 herders caught and paid fines of Tzsh 50,000–70,000 each (US$ 95 – US$ 130)
	2 herders caught and paid fines of Tzsh 85,000 each (US$ 160)
February 1996	2 herders paid fines of Tzsh 60,000–70,000 each (US$ 110–US$ 130)
March 1996	2 herders paid fines of Tzsh 60,000 and Tzsh 100,000 each (US$ 110 and US$ 230)
April 1996	1 culprit paid Tzsh 100,000 (US$ 230) for an unspecified offence
May 1996	1 poacher caught with 33.5 kg ivory

Source: Homewood *et al.*, 1997.
Systematic records of Reserve-related offences are confidential and documented in patrol reports and Reserve receipt books. The list is not complete and is no measure of the extent of contravention of Reserve rules. It does give an idea of the type of opposition the Reserve faces and the type of punishment exacted. These records are extracted from Reserve files.

Pare, Sambaa and Kamba herders were excluded from use of Mkomazi's resources when the Reserve was established. Boundaries were redrawn to ensure that no huts were found inside the Reserve and people would have no right to live there. They responded with vigorous opposition. Herders at Gonja successfully lobbied to have land excised from the Reserve (see Box 3.1). Others hired lawyers to plead on their behalf. Pare pastoralists were also successful in gaining more access in the late 1960s and early 1970s, when a series of dry years made its resources all the more important.

Box 5.2 Coping with illegal grazing: Reserve policing after the evictions

Extracts from *Newsletter 5*: Kim Ellis, former partner of Tony Fitzjohn,
Field Officer of the Trusts,
September 1992

24–25 January 1992

'6am. Talk with Mungure (Game Warden). Rangers had confiscated wire snares and encroaching livestock near Ngurunga and herded it to Kampi ya Chauka. The camp was attacked in the night by intruders. Kisinza (officer in charge) was beaten unconscious and several others injured. All taken to hospital in Same. Caught two prisoners.

'Seems herdsmen came to break into the livestock compound. The rangers refused them entry. They offered them a bribe. An argument ensued and the herdsmen pulled out clubs, *rungas* (wood clubs) and *pangas* (machetes). Thankfully, there were no guns.'

15 February 1992

'3:30 pm about to sit down for lunch when Mungure calls them to say he and Mr Tarimo ran into over 3,000 head of livestock at Kavateta Dam on their recce and they are trying to contain them, seven guys ran off but they got 3. Needs help from some of our guys till the rangers can get them.

'Head off with Semu, Efatha and Zakaria and we are about 7 miles out when Mungure calls again and Fitz [Tony Fitzjohn] too – who's at Kisiwani on his way in. Mungure decides there is far too much stock and it's getting too late as the sun is going to set soon, he must give up. I head back to camp. Tony offers to find the rangers in Kisiwani and chase up the game lorry to go and relieve Mungure. Fitz finds Hassan and they round up the guys and lorry. Then he and Hassan drive in to meet Mungure … Fitz gets a half-hour flight in before dark to check Kavateta situation. Gives livestock a warning buzz and home by dark.'

Since the clearance of the Reserve, protests have become more urgent. The people of Vumari have challenged the recently cleared Reserve boundaries, disputing the identification of the local mountain peaks used as markers. The dispute warranted a visit from the Presidential Commission of Inquiry into Land Matters, but no clear recommendation was offered.[57] There is also a well-documented sequence of Maasai and Parakuyo protests recorded in material collected by the late Henry Fosbrooke. The documents testify to a sustained campaign against the evictions between 1988 and 1992 in which evictees appealed to numerous leading members of Government, including the Prime Minister, the Minister of Home Affairs, the Regional Commissioner and the Government Party headquarters.[58] Delivering the letters involved delegates travelling hundreds of miles to seek help.[59] Nothing aroused an effective response.

In 1993 Tanzanian and international NGOs supporting Maasai pastoralists elsewhere began to offer help to the evictees at Mkomazi. The presence and guidance of the NGOs, and their international

Highlights

'In the early morning of the 30th I dropped the Kisima workers off in Kisiwani for the day so they could go to church, and Tony went flying with Nick. They spotted hundreds of head of encroaching livestock heading towards Kaveteta dam and several herdsmen with spears ... The ranger force was spread thin and none were in the vicinity of the livestock. If the herds had a chance at the water they'd finish it and there'd be nothing left for the wild animals, who would then wander outside the Reserve and face the consequences. Tony radioed headquarters straight away, but everyone was busy trying to fend off the fire, which had already burned part of the new office. So he arranged to move a handful of rangers who were stationed at Kifukua, 25 km from us, to Kaveteta dam.

'They were set up at Kaveteta by 2.30 pm. The handful of rangers at Ndea – which is on the northern border towards Lake Jipe – were alerted and they agreed to move in by foot and patrol their surrounding areas. We were satisfied at a good job done. At 5.30 we flew to see how the rangers were and where the encroachers were. We spotted a lovely herd of 30-plus elephant heading to the dam for a drink. A couple of kilometres away the herdsmen were settling in for the night. We descended to take a better look and the herdsmen began throwing spears and rocks at the plane. We feared the elephant might not be able to approach the dam due to the proximity of the herdsmen for they are right in their path.

'As we circled a last time to pull up and inform the rangers a blast came hurtling through the aircraft's windscreen and shattered it. The break occurred on my side and I automatically ducked, and thank goodness Tony kept flying. He cut the power a bit and flew straight and level before pulling up for more altitude. Everyone was okay but the compass was lost and the windscreen had a huge hole (in) it, half the normal size. It looked like and sounded like a bullet hit us, but we found pieces of rock inside – a lucky shot?'

Source: Homewood *et al.*, 1997.

sponsors, altered the nature of resistance to the Reserve.[60] The principal NGO active at Mkomazi is called *Ilaramatak Lolkonerei*. It was established in 1991 in Simanjiro District on the Maasai Steppe, west of the Pangani river, in order to counter land losses to commercial agriculture.[61] Together with a number of other Maasai NGOs, it attracted support from foreign donors such as the International Institute for Environment and Development (IIED), Survival International, Pilotlight and DANIDA, the aid agency of the Danish Government. It was part of a huge expansion in NGO activity in Tanzania, whose numbers leapt from 17 registered in 1978 to 813 in 1994 as donors and aid organisations sought to invest in Tanzania's civil society.[62]

The leader of *Ilaramatak*, Martin Saningo, visited Mkomazi with Henry Fosbrooke in 1993. Fosbrooke had advocated that both Maasai and Parakuyo be allowed to stay at Mkomazi (and Toloha) in the 1950s. He was concerned by the results of the eviction and the failure to provide for the evictees. He alerted the Legal Aid Committee of Dar es Salaam

University. This resulted in cases taken out in the High Court at Moshi in 1994 and 1995 against the Ministry of Tourism, Natural Resources and the Environment.[63] *Ilaramatak* assisted with collecting evidence and communicating the results and progress of the trial to the evictees.

Fifty-three evicted herders put their names to the cases. They demanded compensation for the losses caused by the evictions and alleged that their constitutional right to live on their customary lands was denied them. The second claim was the most important. The herders had been evicted from the Reserve according to the provisions of the 1974 Wildlife Conservation Act. The claimants argued that this general act, which covered protected areas throughout the country, was not sufficient to extinguish their right to live on their customary lands.

As we have seen, the cases won slight compensation but no right to use of the Reserve. They were unsuccessful for surprising reasons. The claimants, who were both Parakuyo and Maasai, made their claim under the collective name 'Maasai'. The High Court treated their claims according to its interpretation of Maasai history. It denied 'the Maasai' any ancestral claim to any part of the Reserve on the grounds that:

> ... the Maasai ... began to reach the area in the second half of the 1940s and their presence was still scanty at the time the Mkomazi Game Reserve was established in 1951 ... the Maasai community in question did not have ancestral customary land title over the whole of the Mkomazi Game Reserve (Judgment on Civil Appeal no. 53 of 1998).

This history does not describe the lives of the older residents of the Reserve or their forebears.

The legal cases marked a qualitative break in forms of resistance to conservation at Mkomazi. We have seen that local groups had previously hired lawyers to represent their needs to the government. But these protests contained an implicit idea that the state was powerful and could not be stopped, only persuaded.[64] The Moshi cases profoundly challenged the legitimacy of state actions. If they had won the case the implications for the rest of the country's protected areas would have been momentous. The existence of many protected areas is dependent upon the eviction of people who might also be in a position to claim ancestral rights. A great deal had hinged upon whether or not the Reserve had been the herders' customary home. It is perhaps not surprising that they failed.

In part, the judgment reflects the character of Tanzanian courts.[65] Shivji and Kapinga have argued that such cases, pursuing precedents on behalf of a group of people, are ill-advised and unlikely to achieve the gains sought. Courts do not readily support the claims of peasants who allege they have been wronged by government actions. They tend to pursue narrow technical lines of argument, which defeats the claims.

There are a number of other cases like that pursued at Mkomazi that have also been lost on a technicality.[66]

It would be wrong, however, to suggest that all of Mkomazi's neighbours lost when the court case was defeated. As we have seen, only Maasai and Parakuyo herders were represented in the legal action. *Ilaramatak* does not work with evicted Pare, Sambaa or Kamba pastoralists, some of whom are less keen to confront the government in this manner. Others are wary of the consequences of an influx of powerful herders, fearing an increase in stock theft.

As we saw at the beginning of the book, these divisions are central to Mkomazi's dilemma. Community conservation here has to work with divided peoples. But this is precisely the detail that is lost on an international stage. Human rights attention to land loss at Mkomazi now focuses on Maasai pastoralists to the exclusion of other groups. This is typified by an article in the London *Observer* newspaper, which discussed only the plight of Maasai pastoralists. Other groups, far more numerous, were not mentioned. Kiwasila offered a strong rebuttal (Box 5.3). Neumann notes that contesting the evictions means promoting a history of the Reserve that endorses and celebrates pastoral use of it, rather than, as conservationist history does, its transformation following exclusion of people.[67] Pastoralists are indeed offering such an alternative history of the Reserve, but theirs is not a multi-ethnic account. Igoe has found that, in Simanjiro, attention to the plight of 'marginalised Maasai' acts to the detriment of the poor within multi-ethnic communities, with Maasai elites using donor support to expropriate resources from more marginal, non-Maasai villagers.[68]

International attention changes not only the representation of Mkomazi's contests but also the workings of the NGOs themselves. It creates a new constituency – international donors – to which the NGO leaderships are now answerable. Since the international NGOs provide the Maasai NGOs with most of their funds, the latter can become more orientated towards their donors than to those whom they represent. Igoe has suggested that test cases in court can have more value as sources of prestige and donor funds than as means of establishing legal precedent. He argues that the NGO leaders' actions are best seen as 'strategies of extraversion' where alliances are sought with outsiders to enhance local authority. The groups become little more than vehicles for the ambitions of their leaders and are rarely united. Much of their activity dissolves into 'an ongoing saga of ascendancy and intrigue'.[69]

It also makes compromise harder as there is a danger that NGOs have a vested interest in lobbying and protest. Compromise, and solutions, mean less funding and less business. The needs of the mouthpiece supplant those of the body. The failures, or as Foucault would put it, dysfunction, of the NGO work is useful to the NGOs' interests. As Chabal and Daloz

---

Box 5.3 Representations of people at Mkomazi

The soil is parched, the acacia bushes and trees are dying and the Masai of northern Tanzania are suffering severe malnutrition on the perimeter of a rhino park run by a British charity. In a land littered with fly-infested, stinking animal carcasses, children with distended bellies stand in glum groups near a huge white stone pillar marking the boundary of the 1,400 square mile Mkomazi Game Reserve. Beyond the boundary are the grazing lands where the Masai have roamed for centuries. The tribes have been banned from entry since 1988 when the Tanzanian government evicted some 8,000 Masai and 75,000 head of cattle to make way for the "sanctuary". Now the Masai are fined if they "trespass" in the game park. Aid workers say malnutrition, TB, malaria, pneumonia and dysentery are rampant.'

Lucy Johnston, 'Barred from animals' kingdom', *The Observer*, UK, 6/4/97: 12

'Hasty research leads to shallow conclusions. "Barred from animals kingdom" ... demonstrates both. I am a Tanzanian with 23 years' experience of community development in my country. For two years my colleagues and I have visited villages, consulted villagers and local leaders and reviewed archives and monitored resources use around Mkomazi Game Reserve (MGR). From this research I realised that the area is not just a Garden of Eden for the Masai. Other ethnic groups such as the Pare and Sambaa have longer historical roots there. These groups are forgotten whenever MGR is discussed. ... Tanzania has 120 ethnic groups. We have always had a peaceful country. Groups in the Mkomazi area have co-existed, managed resources and solved conflicts for many years. Our disputes can be resolved by Tanzanians using broad research. Focusing on one ethnic group is not the Tanzanian way; it impedes conflict resolution.'

Hilda Kiwasila, 'Not just a Masai Garden of Eden', *The Observer*, UK, 13/4/97: 2

---

have found in other contexts, the rise of NGOs does not indicate a flourishing of civil society, but rather the ready availability of money and resources to support NGOs. They state that:

> it would thus be naïve to think that the advent of NGOs necessarily reflects a transition from the more ponderous world of state bureaucracy to that of more flexible 'civic' associations operating beyond the clutch of the state ... it is rather the reflection of a successful adaptation to the conditions laid down by foreign donors on the part of local political actors who seek in this way to gain access to the new resources (Chabal and Daloz, 1999).

Crucially, Igoe argues, the situation is not just useful to local NGO interests.[70] The existence of 'indigenous peoples' organisations provides a suitable target of intervention for western donors. They are therefore fundamental to the international donors, who have to be seen to be spending money suitably and efficiently. Local NGOs, born out of local reaction to adverse circumstances, fit the bill exactly. But the results may serve the donors and the NGOs more than the original protesters.

Pastoralists protesting their eviction from Mkomazi are caught in a bitter irony. Their opposition to evictions was rooted in the impoverishment it caused. They expressed their discontent to numerous government officials though various channels, before any outside organisations became involved. They turned to NGOs and international support as a means of representing their problems to the government. Yet international support made their situation more intractable. The NGO leaders become caught up in factional disputes and political infighting. Compromise becomes harder and the evictees have gained nothing materially.

Conclusion

The preservation of Mkomazi has hurt its neighbours. Until the evictions the Reserve's resources had been used by a large number of people for a long time. They derived benefits from that use and built their livelihoods upon it. Exclusion has impeded their use of gathered wild resources, reduced household herd size and performance, damaged the local livestock economy, and caused serious hardship to thousands of people. These grievances are strongly felt. Communities around the Reserve are preoccupied with obtaining use of land inside the Reserve for grazing, cultivation or gathered resources. Villages are negotiating directly with Reserve authorities, pursuing legal cases and in many places using Reserve resources illegally. International assistance to indigenous peoples' NGOs has failed to make substantial gains.

The Reserve does not earn the tourist revenue to pay for its own conservation. It is highly unlikely that it will earn revenues sufficient to win the support of its neighbours by paying for goods and services. The revenues will be too few and the people too many. This suggests that the only possible material basis for an alliance between the Reserve and its neighbours would be to permit some use of the Reserve's resources.

The human costs of saving this wilderness have not been carefully considered yet at the same time Mkomazi's preservation after the evictions has been hailed as a success. The omission and oversight has come at a time when conservation rhetoric in Africa is dominated by concern for 'community conservation'; for setting up partnerships between people and protected areas; for providing benefits to the rural poor from wildlife. The story of conservation at Mkomazi challenges the ideals of community conservation. The exclusion policy pursued by the government and endorsed by international organisations flies in the face of proclaimed trends. It is necessary now to examine more carefully the implications of Mkomazi's 'success' for current trends in African conservation.

Notes

1 Interviews: KM, 18/2/96; LK, 20/2/96; Lky, 9/5/96; MM, 10/5/96; ML, 5/9/96; group discussion, Antakaye, 10/5/96.

2 Field notes, 15/5/96; Giblin, 1990b: 414–15. Cows bought in from Dodoma and Singida, and named after places there, were reasonably common in the herds of the families I worked with.

3 The higher incidence of disease was reported by a number of sources, notably by the Divisional Livestock Officer, 1/3/96. Also interviews: KM, 18/2/96; PP,AO,KP,LN,KL, 18/7/96.

4 Fosbrooke's papers, 20/9/89.

5 Interview: CK, December 1995.

6 Interview: MK, July 1994.

7 Group discussion, Antakaye, 10/5/96.

8 Figures may seem high but they are supported by oral history accounts and archival data. My own research continually brought up the wealth of herders before the eviction. Onesmo-Zacharia (1990: 61) suggests that herders owned at least 2,000 cattle each. The data are suspect because they were subject to a compensation claim at the time of evictions and herders were wont to use the research as a vehicle for lobbying. However, high herd sizes are supported by data collected in 1983 in preparation for a visit by the District Commissioner of Same.

Stock ownership of pastoralists at Kisiwani.

	Cattle	Goats	Sheep	H'holds	Mean TLU per h'hold	Range	Mean h'hold size	Range per capita
Pare	3,400	445	200	6	585	106–1,548	8.33	5–20
Maasai/P'kuyo	14,149	6,380	2,790	35	448	28–1,217	11.43	3–21

Source: KWLF, 11/10/1983.

9 Zaal and Dietz, 1999: 186; White and Meadows, 1981. Zaal and Dietz state the figure is 166 TLU per household, but use a formula where 1 TLU = 1.42 cattle. This would be equivalent to 235.7 cattle.

10 Zaal and Dietz, 1999: 186. They report 59 TLU per household. The same adjustments have been made.

11 Dahl and Hjort (1976: 175–6) suggest that the minimum herd for self-sufficient subsistence is 12.8 animals. Kjaerby (1979: 58–60) suggests that a family of 7.1 adults may be able to get by with a herd of 43 cattle. McCabe *et al.* (1992: 357) cite Harris's (1980) calculations that each member of a pastoral family needs 5.5 cattle, 9.5 goats, 10 sheep and 0.7 donkeys; not counting the donkeys, this is

equivalent to 8.7 LU per reference adult (calculations of reference adults and LU both follow Grandin, 1988). Pratt and Gwynne (1977: 34–43), cited in Fratkin and Roth (1990: 394), estimate 4.5 TLU per capita in arid lands; for a brief comment on these estimates, see Fratkin and Roth (1990, footnotes 6 and 7). Zaal and Dietz (1999: 167) suggest four head of cattle could suffice for each person but note that this is based on average yields in environments where the variability of productivity is the main constraint. It also does not take into account problems of social obligations or disease.

12 Rutten, 1992: 337.

13 Fratkin and Roth, 1990: 397–8; Roth, 1996: 221–2.

14 Ensminger, 1992; 82–3.

15 Fleisher, 1997: 121–2; Potkanski, 1997; 73; Maddox, 1991: 40.

16 Letter from EF to MM, 3/11/90.

17 See Appendix 2 for details of their calculation.

18 De Leeuw and Wilson, 1987: 380.

19 Homewood and Lewis, 1987: 628; note that the 1982–3 figure in Baringo is unusually high owing to a delayed recovery to a previous drought.

20 Interview: LM, 15/5/96. cf. Potkanski, 1997: 102–3; Talle, 1988: 265; Spencer, 1988: 10–11, 237–8.

21 Homewood, 1992: 71.

22 Grandin, 1988: 11–16.

23 Sikana *et al.*, 1993: 10–12.

24 Guyer, 1986: 83; Hay, 1976: 90; Maddox, 1991: 40.

25 Rigby, 1985: 148; Talle, 1988: 205, 211.

26 Kiwasila and Homewood, 1999.

27 The details of maize price data are given in Appendix 3.

28 Baker, 1967,

29 Potkanski, 1997: 85.

30 KWLF: meeting between villagers of Kisiwani and Kavateta pastoralists, 26/2/85.

31 Homewood *et al.*, 1997.

32 Dahl and Hjort, 1976: 161

33 cf. McCabe *et al.*, 1992: 359.

34 Spencer, 1988: 9; Mace and Houston, 1989; Hogg, 1980: 304–5; Dahl and Hjort, 1976: 230–7.

35 This was Anderson's error in 1967 when he evaluated alternative uses of Mkomazi. He took sales reported at livestock markets to represent total commercial sales. Given that 216 sheep and goats were sold in Pare District in 1965 and there were 72,930 shoats in the district, he concluded that offtake was only 0.3% and could be improved 100 times! Informal sales and slaughter need to be included better to appreciate the importance of small-stock for livelihoods.

36 Havenik, 1993: 299.

37 Perlov, 1987: 256

38 Where that basis is lacking, Marks observes wildlife officers should not be blamed. The failure of wildlife to generate revenue locally is not the fault of the wildlife staff, but of broader state decision-making, which treats wildlife as an exploitable resource to generate revenues for state coffers (Marks, 1984: 132).

There are many other reasons, however, which may impede acceptance of benefits from conservation. People may not be prepared to tolerate the environments conservationists wish to see because wilderness or wildlife can be associated with poverty, or lack of 'civilisation' (Alexander and McGregor, 2000).

39 *The Times*, UK, Spotlight on Africa, 25/4/97, page 14.

40 CHL, 1996: 11.

41 Mbano, 1999.

42 *Harpers Bazaar*, April 1993.

43 Homewood *et al.*, 1997: 59.

44 Meeting of the Ward Councillors of Same District, 26 June 1996.

45 Godwin 1995.

46 Stephenson, pers. comm.

47 Wøien and Lama, 1999: 22.

48 Howitt, pers. comm., 24/4/96; Wallace, pers. comm., 1996.

49 Duffy, 2000: 80, 100, 103–4.

50 48,000, according to the 1988 census.

51 Neumann, 1998; Scott, 1985.

52 Neumann, 1995a: 365.

53 Neumann, 1998: 203.

54 '*Tukakaa mpaka mwaka tisini, ng'ombe nyingi zilimalizika. ... kwa kula yale majani ya ndorobo ... ng'ombe zilimalizika tumeendelea mpaka sasa hivi tisini na sita unaweza kukaa hapa utakuta ng'ombe tatu au tano. Kwa sasa hivi kuna ng'ombe sita tu kijiji chote ... sasa hivi kwa sababu ya Risavu lakini tumechunga kule kwenye mandorobo, zimekwisha*' (ASM 20/5/96).

55 Peluso, 1993.

56 Interview: KK, 18/9/96.

57 URT, 1991: 86.

58 See also Juma and Mchome, 1994, and Mustaffa, 1997, where these papers are written up in detail.

59 Interview: MYK, 18/9/96.

60 Neumann notes that with the rise of indigenous NGOs '...pastoralists are moving away from "everyday forms of resistance" and protest toward more organised and formalized forms of political action' (Neumann, 1995a: 378).

61 See Igoe and Brockington, 1999 for more details.

62 Igoe, 2000, forthcoming a; Kelsall, 1998. In other situations the NGOs are perceived to be useful vehicles for applying community conservation goals built upon democratic principles of ground-up participation. For example, around the Tarangire National Park the AWF linked up with a Maasai NGO named *Inyuat-e-Maa* to try to promote community conservation goals in the Maasai steppe. See Igoe, 2000; Igoe, forthcoming b and Igoe and Brockington, 1999 for a critique.

63 *Lekengere Faru Parutu Kamunyu and 16 others* v. *The Minister for Tourism and Natural Resources and Environment and three others*, case no. 33 of 1994; *Kopera Keiya Kamunyu and 44 others* v. *The Ministry for Tourism, Natural Resources and Environment and three others*, case no. 33 of 1995.

64 Neumann, 1998: 179.

65 cf. Lobulu, 1999.

66 Shivji and Kapinga, 1998: 63.

67 Neumann, 1995b: 375; cf. Mduma, 1988a and b.
68 Igoe, forthcoming c.
69 Igoe, forthcoming a, b, c. 'Strategies of extraversion' is from Bayart, 1993: 22.
70 Igoe, 2000 and forthcoming b.

6

A Desert Strange

Conservation is about handling change, and about the transition from past to future. Here I have suggested that our understanding of nature ... is 'made', by science and by society. That creative process is of central importance to conservation. Conservation is about nature, but it is also inextricably about culture. Conservation is not about trying to stop the 'human impact on nature', but about negotiating that impact.

W.M. Adams, *Future Nature*

We have seen something of the flaws in the internátional image of Mkomazi. We have not yet seen quite how successful it has been. The extent to which it is both wrong and successful poses taxing questions about the aspirations of the community conservation movement. Let us briefly consider the Trusts' activities at Mkomazi and the image of the Reserve they project internationally.

The Trusts' work has paid for the construction of roads and airstrips and equipped Reserve rangers with radios and uniforms. The main focus of their activities is the reintroduction of endangered species. A compound has been constructed to contain African Wild Dogs (*Lycaon pictus*) brought in from the Maasai steppe west of the Pangani river, and a sanctuary has been built to care for Black Rhinoceros (*Diceros bicornis michaeli*) brought in from South Africa. These activities are under the direction of the Trusts' Field Officer, Tony Fitzjohn.

We have seen that the Trusts raise money partly by appealing to wealthy Europeans' and Americans' desires for preservation of the African landscape. Mkomazi is proclaimed in fund-raising literature to be a 'restored wilderness', a 'recovered pearl', a corner of Africa brought back from the brink of destruction and given a new lease of life. The excerpt from a newspaper article written by a Trustee is typical:

For years its remoteness and inaccessibility consigned it to the sidelines, but Mkomazi was always worth saving. Its northern boundaries lie up against Kenya's vast Tsavo national park and together the two reserves cover more than 8,000 square miles, forming one of the largest ecosystems on earth. ... The sense of space is overwhelming. To the south, the Usumbura (*sic*) mountains form a dramatic backdrop. To the north lie the rust-red game trails and blue faraway hills of Tsavo; and to the north-west looms the snowcapped Kilimanjaro. Its tourism potential, as yet untapped, is enormous. At present there is nowhere for visitors to stay; but there are plans for an eco-friendly safari lodge or tented camp. When it is built Mkomazi will be well on the way to becoming a Tanzanian Tsavo. Yet until the late Eighties Mkomazi remained forgotten. By then it had become badly degraded. Poaching, overgrazing, deliberate burning and unregulated trophy-hunting had taken their toll. Its black rhinos had been wiped out. Fewer than a dozen elephants survived and the future of the reserve itself hung in the balance. Only since 1988, when the Tanzanian government reassessed its value, has Mkomazi's true importance been recognised. A decision was taken to restore the reserve and save its remaining wildlife (Jackman, 1999[1]).

It is also worth repeating the excerpt reproduced at the beginning of the book:

> Mkomazi is potentially one of the most beautiful and important game reserves on the continent. ... Until 1988, it represented a classic example of ecological decline and degradation, over grazed, persistently eroded and the subject of indiscriminate and widespread poaching. ... Since 1988 the entire resources of the Trust have been devoted to the project. ... One of the most fragile, threatened and beautiful parts of Africa has been reborn ... The Mkomazi Project has a unique aspect. The rebuilding of Mkomazi Game Reserve, the rehabilitation of its wildlife, the endangered species programmes and the outreach programmes do not simply attempt to 'hold the line' on conservation. They are an endeavor to re-establish a complete ecosystem and thus positively reverse the damage that has been done (GAWPT (UK) fundraising document, *circa* 1994).

We have seen that this is not the only interpretation of Mkomazi's history and environment.[2] It is by no means certain that the environment was 'degraded' as a result of human occupation. The notion of wilderness is itself problematic.[3] Portraying Mkomazi as a wilderness unspoilt by people denies its history and the many ways it was used by a variety of people long-resident in or near it. 'Wilderness' is much more a western notion of what Africa should be like than of what the plains have been to its residents. Through the claims made in fundraising documents, the Trusts are recasting Mkomazi in the minds of their funders in the mould of a world view formed in Europe and America.

The Trusts are creating a myth about Mkomazi. By that I do not mean a set of ideas that are false – there are true myths. Rather myths are charismatic ideas that motivate people to action and direct their activity.[4] It is true that some elements of the Mkomazi myth are flawed, misleading or wrong. But no deception is involved. The Trustees and their supporters passionately believe their literature. They are people of integrity, with a strong and active concern for important causes. It is because they see their interpretation of Mkomazi to be cogent and urgent that they have taken on the costs and responsibility of saving the Reserve. It is because this is such a powerfully convincing and persuasive myth that the Reserve's conservation has been so successful. It is because such a flawed image can persist so success-fully that we must consider its implications.

The myth's power is evident in the stories circulated during the prepa-ration of the rhinoceros sanctuary, which was built in 1996 and stocked with Black Rhinoceros in 1997. The sanctuary is part of a broader strategy to set up well-guarded breeding populations throughout East and Southern Africa. Rhinoceros from the Addo Elephant National Park in South Africa, which has held the East African sub-species (*Diceros bicornis michaeli*), go to Mkomazi and other sites leaving valuable rhino habitat available for the Southern African sub-species (*D.b. bicornis*).[5] The Addo authorities plan to buy the Southern African sub-species from Namibia so that Namibian farmers can be financially rewarded for conserving Black Rhino on their land.

The plan is straightforward, but at Mkomazi it involved the sanctuary's advocates taking a peculiar stance in the contests surrounding the Reserve. The conflicting claims made on the Reserve were not adequately represented in the early stages of the project. A report on the sanctuary for the International Union for the Conservation of Nature (IUCN) African Rhino Specialist Group stated:

> There appears to be limited resentment towards the Mkomazi Game Reserve by the Msaai [sic], as they were well aware that their permission to graze within the reserve was only a temporary one (Harrie Simons and Truus Nicolson, pers. comm.) ... The more numerous Wapare and Wasambar [sic] tribe members within the Kisiwane [sic] and Uzambaras [sic] areas were never historically associated with the reserve and thus have no negative feelings towards it ... it would appear that the introduction of black rhino into the MGR would be: ... little affected by the limited to dwindling negative feelings towards the surrounding communities (Knight and Morkel, 1994: 6–7[6]).

This is wrong. But what is more extraordinary, given the proposed origin of the rhino, is that, at the end of 1996, South African members of the African Rhino Specialist Group appeared to be unaware of the report's inaccuracies two years after evicted herders had brought their first court case.[7] When the South African authorities made further enquiries about the problems in 1997 they were told by Tanzanian government officials that the court cases of evicted pastoralists were being brought by Maasai 'originating from Kenya'.[8] Recent drafts of a management plan for Mkomazi also invents history:

> When the Mkomazi/Umba Game Reserves were established, six pastoral families were living inside and they were compensated in order to move to areas outside the reserve (MNRT, 1997: ii).

Meanwhile international representations of the Reserve continue to combine a concern to provide for its neighbours with literature down-playing the evictions and their costs, both social and economic. Some fundraising documents fail to mention the legal conflicts surrounding the Reserve; others did not say that people were evicted, and just stated that the Reserve was 'rehabilitated'. The Chairman of the British Trust has questioned the severity of the consequences of eviction, saying that:

> The lot of the local villagers is no better and no worse than that of most of the rural population in Tanzania (Eltringham, 1997: 30[9]).

The international representation of Mkomazi ends up being an almost Orwellian rewriting of the Reserve's, and its people's, histories.

It is frequently said that conservation uses 'depoliticising scientific rhetoric' to 'escape the complex ethical and political considerations that lie at the heart of policies that ultimately result in land and other resources being targeted for wildlife conservation'.[10] Depoliticised debates make it difficult to discern whether or not harm is being done and to whom. Depoliticised goals and organisations are idealised. They have more space, freedom and power to act. But Mkomazi's case endorses Friedman's warning that 'the power to do good is also the power to do harm ... what one man (*sic*) regards as good another may regard as harm'.[11] At Mkomazi, scientific opinions on the degradation of the Reserve and expert ecologists' endorsement of the sanctuary have been used to further the conservation cause, evading politically sensitive issues.[12] But depoliticising rhetoric is not the only means of evading political sensitivities. Freedom and idealism have been enhanced by stories about the Reserve's history and current circumstances that were not accurate. Political neutrality has been promoted by fictions.

The case of Mkomazi suggests two reasons for the strength of fortress conservation. The first is that myths work. The Mkomazi myths can bring in much revenue. They result in the enforcement of exclusion and the creation of wilderness in the image desired by its creators. Myths may be wrong, but that is not the point. Myths are powerful. They motivate people; they help them to organise and understand their worlds; they provide structure and meaning; they are the source of beliefs, hopes and plans.[13]

Myths are not overturned by facts. Facts are judged by their accordance with myths.[14] Groups subscribing to myths often have criteria as to what constitutes good knowledge. In a sense the conservationists at Mkomazi and their allies can be seen as a 'folk' with their own culture, history, lore, standards, values and definitions of who arbitrates truth. Cohen, writing on the nature of knowledge among Shetlanders of Whalsay who are continually dealing with, and denying, outside 'experts' advice about how to fish and manage their fishing industry, observes that:

> For the Expert Outsider, salient knowledge is substantive: problems may be resolved by having 'knowledge' applied to them. For locals, the disputation

with experts may not call into question the *substance* of their knowledge, but its appropriateness. The sense of a discrete local knowledge does not deny that outsiders could know '*what* we know' but, rather, that they could know '*as* we know'. In viewing the world across their conceptual boundaries, Whalsay people argue for a kind of relativity of knowledge, insisting that while facts may well be facts, their interpretations and implications are culture bound (Cohen, 1993: 33, emphasis in the original).

Compare that description of local knowledge and expert opinion with this statement about the value of 'local conservationist' observations and the problems of expert wildlife knowledge:

> Wildlife statistics are always difficult and flawed. In Africa they are highly suspect. ... Real evidence comes from the field from those who are able to observe clearly on a daily basis patterns in populations and movement and the effect of natural and human influences and from those who are neither reluctant nor afraid to both record and share this information (Tony Fitzjohn, 20 June 1996, to the Sub Committee on Fisheries, Wildlife and Oceans, Committee of Resources, House of Representatives, Capitol Hill).

If Fitzjohn's views are representative of a wider body of conservation society then there are similarities between the Whalsay and conservation communities over what constitutes 'real' data. Depoliticising expertise may be promoted, but expertise that is perceived to threaten the authority of raw experience is not. History gleaned from local accounts or records, or concerns for the statistical representativeness of the field observations, are sidelined. Instead there is an intense, visceral knowledge of what the environments are like and should look like.

If facts are grounded and created in myth, then I cannot agree with Adams and McShane when they state that 'conservation based on myth is bound to fail'.[15] The power of the fortress conservation narrative, its emotive appeal and the hard certainties it offers may well ensure it persists long into the future. Conservative conservation policies preserve not just a dream of Africa, but also reproduce and sustain its supporters. Protected areas and their supporters live in symbiosis, each sustains the other.

Adams and McShane's judgement is too sweeping. There will probably be more diversity in practices and outcome. Even if 'normal' practices change and become more inclusive of local needs, the old views will still exist. Conservation practices will be a patchwork of reactionary and tolerant regimes. Indeed, old practices, even if replaced, may resurface. Suppose some conservative regimes do fail, and their protected areas are overrun by people, as happened at Mkomazi in the 1970s and 1980s. Yet repressive policies could still arise, fed by a groundswell of western dreams and the alliance between international conservation organisations and the state. It would be an ironic resurrection. If 'dying' protected areas can be resuscitated, it is because they are resilient and not threatened with imminent destruction. They are continually vulnerable to being saved, recreated and restored to the pantheon of 'last wildernesses' upon which fortress conservation thrives.

The second reason for the success of fortress conservation is that the necessity for participation is limited. Communities are heterogeneous and divided. The numerous peoples who live around Mkomazi have divergent interests. Few may profit from the Reserve, but the pastoral groups, who have lost considerably, are relatively weak locally. It is possible to ignore those who do not benefit.

The practice of rule, and the operation of power, revolves very much around such divisions. Conservation is about controlling people and their environments. It is about exercising power over how people use land, and how they change their land-use and how they lobby their government to allow them to change their practices. There may be powerful ethical reasons to try to make this process as inexpensive as possible, but it may also be a project for which there are unavoidable expenses to be paid. Those paying the costs may resist, but such opposition is likely to come from rural groups who are unorganised and poorly equipped. Unwelcome policies can be imposed.[16]

Marks declared that:

> The romantic vision of keeping Africa as an unchanged paradise teeming with wildlife is a foreign nonsense, for to ask East Africa to perpetuate such an image is to ask it to stay poor and undeveloped (Marks, 1984: 130).

But surely he errs if he expects the poverty to cause the vision to fail. If the poverty is only experienced by the rural poor, and if the benefits are experienced by elites at home and abroad, then the vision has a good chance of success. Foreign it may be, but it remains much at home in the protected areas of East Africa.

In Zimbabwe, Duffy has suggested that when conservation NGOs try to operate in a social, economic or political vacuum their projects may fail as the local politics of conservation activities begin to take effect.[17] In Tanzania, however, local factors have only a weak influence compared to the power of the state and the resources of internationally funded conservation. The continual local attempts to use resources or secure use rights are rebuffed with little consequence to conservation objectives.

A resilient environment would again, ironically, help maintain such a state of affairs. Exclusion usually has to deal with mass civil disobedience, when neighbours will flout its laws as often as necessary. The deterrent of rangers' presence and fines will curtail this activity to some extent. But a resilient environment is well able to absorb the impacts of the low-level and intermittent use resulting. Because the environment is not as fragile as exclusion policies assume, the situation works.

The problems of community conservation

But how typical are the problems of Mkomazi? Is it a good representation of conservation in Africa, or elsewhere? There are two reasons to suggest that it is atypical.

First, I have referred in this book to a generic group of 'conservationists'. I have painted a monochromatic picture of their views that ignores the diversity of interests, theory, thinking and experience found in conservation. Moreover, it is a dynamic diversity. The values, and their relative strengths, change. The attitudes I have encountered at Mkomazi represent but one strand of that changing thinking. But it is a separate task, for which I am not qualified, to portray the full make-up and variety of conservationist thought.

Second, the case of Mkomazi is stark. The geography of the Reserve, the uncertainty of its environment, the proximity of the mountains, the numbers of people around it, Tanzania's weak economic position that makes opportunities of other employment so slender, and the shrillness of the debate, suggest it may be an unusual test case. There may be more physical and political room for compromise elsewhere.

But it is probably true that all protected areas are contested. Their use is disputed by groups who see different purposes for them. The ideals championed by conservation may overlook the people who live near, and often once inside, the protected areas. These people question the worth and legitimacy of such values, and the rights of others to appropriate aesthetic and financial benefits. The disputes are concerned with ideals of beauty, sustainability or 'good use' and who should benefit materially from the uses chosen. Here the very starkness and extremism of Mkomazi serve to clarify some of the problems inherent in constructing the alternative offered by community conservation policies to fortress conservation. The case of Mkomazi suggests responses to the three doubts raised in the introduction about community conservation (p.8).

First, Mkomazi shows that it can be well-nigh impossible for benefits from protected areas to match the costs incurred from lost resources. Mkomazi underlines an essential inequality in African conservation. The opportunity costs of protecting areas are borne by the rural poor, while the benefits accrue to national elites and wealthy foreign tourists.[18] Many rural groups know conservation policy as something that brings little good they can enjoy, and causes much hardship and suffering.[19]

Community conservation will become possible where it recognises that conservation can be valued by the rural poor only insofar as it improves their standard of living.[20] Attempts to 'educate' the rural poor about conservation are likely to fail unless their livelihoods are clearly and directly enhanced.[21] Livelihood enhancement needs to be central to the enterprise for community conservation to succeed.[22] Community conservation, therefore, is a development issue.[23] It involves conflict mediation, equitable distribution of benefits, accountability of leaders, subsidiarity, representation and tenure over, and access to, land and resources. The latter are particularly important. The case of Mkomazi shows that economic justice will not be possible unless the rural poor have direct access to the resources of protected areas.

But it must be recognised that economic benefits alone are not the end of the matter. Gibson and Marks have shown that rural hunters gain much more than simply economic benefit from hunting.[24] Hunting is part of their identity, through which they gain respect and power. Economic benefits encouraging them to cease hunting may miss the mark. Alexander and McGregor argue that the economic benefits of CAMPFIRE were rejected by communities whose vision of their own development did not entail living off wildlife. Economic benefits from wildlife were vigorously resisted by people who saw their history as progressing away from the disease and problems that wildlife could bring and who wanted to choose other ways of managing their lands.[25]

Second, it may not matter that costs exceed benefits if those who lose are politically weak. The heterogeneity and divisions of communities may make the politics of forging alliances easier. The international conservation agenda is rarely just imposed by powerful outsiders on weak and helpless villagers. Although rural groups are often weak, they are not powerless but have bargaining power.[26] Local groups have long histories of negotiating with 'outsiders' and ensuring that they do not lose as heavily as they might have done.[27] We have seen that not all protected areas' neighbours resent their presence. A problem with human rights lobbying at Mkomazi is that it is ill-equipped to deal with the diversity of needs in 'local communities'.

The third problem facing community conservation that Mkomazi illustrates is that it is an unnecessary and potentially dangerous option. Exclusion has been successful at Mkomazi. Opposition is weak and ineffectual. The new measures may not offer the security fortress conservation offers for the valued species and landscapes.[28] Fortress conservation depends on an international community of wealthy preservationists for its finance, ideas and motivation. The power and wealth of this community make fortress conservation sustainable. Devolving power over these havens to locals threatens their future and may not have the conservation community's support.

Some of the support offered to community conservation is marked by continuity with old agendas. For example, Adams and McShane take as their imperative for reform the threat to wildlife, not the needs of people.[29] For others it offers hope to conservationists who fear for the fate of species beyond the borders of protected areas.[30] Westerners and others take the protected areas as given and look beyond their borders for future reforms. They call for action from 'society as a whole' to cope with the current extinction crisis.[31] But who does 'society' include, and whose values will set society's agenda? What are the political processes by which rival views are resolved? At Mkomazi, social action has been encouraged to further a fixed, predetermined, conservation goal. Local people are invited to support that project and offered some incentives to do so by means of outreach activities. Much energy has been spent cultivating the support of international elites with the money and time to support the Reserve's rehabilitation and enjoy its wildernesses.

Mackenzie found in colonial Kenya that a 'discriminatory environmentalism' became crucial in the construction of power relations built on race.[32] Similarly, Beinart has observed that the measures to preserve wildlife, soil and vegetation become closely bound to prevailing segregation policies.[33] It could be argued that similar forces are at work in present-day African conservation. The division now is not race but that conjunction of wealth, class and international influence that determines which groups win or lose from conservation agendas. Currently, wealthy westerners are most able to consume the benefits of conservation and national elites benefit most from the tourism industry, but both are subsidised by rural groups who bear the costs of giving up land and resources.[34] The poor are discriminated against because their livelihoods are changed; the affluent remain untouched.

Fortresses do not just enclose wildernesses, they defend western lifestyles. They draw attention and activism to protected areas abroad and away from issues of energy consumption at home. They are therefore a powerful and far-reaching 'anti-politics machine' that 'whisks political realities out of sight', both with respect to the application of projects in Africa and the international setting of conservation.[35] Alternative models of conservation do not adequately deal with these international aspects. They can be grounded more in wealthy westerners' conservation ideals than rural Africans' needs. Adams and McShane, for example, advocate material self-denial that is inappropriate for the poorest countries of the world:

> The challenge for Africa, indeed for all regions of the world, is to reconfigure economic structures and community values so that people can improve the quality of their lives without the constant accumulation of material wealth (Adams and McShane, 1992: 250).

Secular western societies are not espousing this philosophy, despite environmentalists' exhortations; a western politician could not advocate it in his constituency and hope for re-election. Given current global patterns of resource and energy consumption, it is more appropriate to pioneer such principles in the USA, Europe, Japan or the wealthy Middle Eastern states than Africa.

An alternative?

There is a danger that talk about the changes community conservation can bring will remain just talk. It is in the face of this Machiavellian scenario that the basic challenge to fortress conservation becomes clear. The essential objection is ethical: it is not fair. The enforcement of exclusion entails injustice. It leaves many rural people, and observers, with a powerful sense of a wrong being done. It leaves increasing numbers of conservationists with the same impression.[36]

Exclusion entails more than just displacement and loss of livelihoods, but also the loss of homes and places of spiritual, emotional and cultural importance.[37] The takeover of territory, and the usurpation of power and authority to manage and inhabit the landscape, renders once-familiar places 'a desert strange and chill'.[38] These words, written in protest at the enclosure movement in England two hundred years ago, were part of a poem filled with the indignation and anger evictees know. They are apposite to Mkomazi, where people have been evicted and impoverished in order to cleanse a land reinvented as wilderness. The image of Mkomazi created for funders and tourists is 'a desert strange' to those whose home it was.

It is in such injustice that the power of the challenge to the myths of fortress conservation lies. If its images depend on comfortable myths, the ethical problems of its reality are too uncomfortable to be tolerated. But it is precisely here that community conservation needs to be evaluated carefully. If it only appears to address material needs and gives only the semblance of power-sharing then community conservation will just perpetuate the same injustices under new guises.

The case of Mkomazi shows that people have long been a part of the landscape and environment of the Reserve. It challenges the determinism that holds that people will necessarily degrade the environment. The uncertainty means it is less imperative to move people. If we do not know what the environment is doing then it is hard to cite environmental reasons to justify causing the impoverishment eviction brings. I have argued elsewhere that this uncertainty is likely to persist.[39] It is only with careful long-term research that we will know how Mkomazi's environment responds to people's use of it. It is also dangerous to deny that degradation could occur; it is necessary to respect the precautionary principles that guard against degradation.[40]

Mkomazi's situation also makes it clear that a just solution to people's needs must allow some form of use of the Reserve's resources. Any buffer zones outside the Reserve would just be an expansion of the Reserve's influence. The compromise has to take place within the borders of the Reserve. This would not require new legislation. Use of reserve resources is permitted at the discretion of the Director of Wildlife.

There are three caveats. First, rectifying injustice at Mkomazi would not mean allowing use to all people. Some locals may not want all the former residents back. I cannot say what complexion of rights and permits would be considered most just to most people, only that some use must be allowed. It may be easier in the east of the Reserve, where opposition to pastoralists is slighter, and 'biodiversity', tourism, and wildlife interests fewer. Second, how could people manage that use? One of the central concerns of those who fear degradation is that rural people do not know how to manage their resources. At Mkomazi there are institutions governing the communal use of water and pasture. However, we have also seen that such institutions are dynamic; they may be weak and can fail. They may not provide the security conservation and local users require. It may be useful to explore ways of supporting these institutions. Third, local use would occur in the absence of any clear understanding of how such use affects the environment. Some form of monitoring and observation would be required.

Sen argues that no matter what the intrinsic moral value of a particular 'good', empirical analysis of causes, effects and consequences of pursuing that good is essential.[41] Whether this good be the conservation of disappearing landscapes, or addressing the social injustices resulting from conservation policy, the same challenge applies. Just compromises will depend upon detailed analysis of histories, ecologies, social outcomes and politics. It is for this end that these pages have been written.

Notes

1 The article also gives strong support to the Trusts' Field Officer, which suggests that this portrayal of the African environment works not just by creating images of the environment, but also by celebrating larger-than-life personae through which exclusion's supporters can vicariously live their ambitions, and apply their dreams (I am grateful to Peter Rogers for this point). The article continues thus:

> But who could take on such a challenge? The job required someone who was comfortable at the cutting edge of conservation. It needed a man who could handle animals, who was fluent in Swahili, a skilled mechanic who could build roads, fly a plane, strip down a Land Rover, organise anti-poaching patrols, run a remote bush camp and deal with the endless bureaucracy. All this it demanded – plus the ability to establish breeding programmes for highly endangered species and beat the drum on fundraising trips to Europe and the US. In Africa today such people are even rarer than the black rhino; but eventually a choice was made. Tony Fitzjohn is one of those restless, swash-buckling Englishmen that only the wildness of Africa can satisfy ... 'there's a job to be done in Mkomazi and I intend to see it through. I meet people in Tanzania, from top officials to ordinary kids in the street, who say to me, Tony, we can't do anything about the way things are: but you can. I say to them, but look, I'm just a bloody *Muzungu* (*sic*), a white man. And they say, but you know how to play the game and we want you to do it for us.'

2 cf. Turton, 1996: 107.

3 Western, 1994: 18; Turton, 1987: 180; Anderson and Grove, 1987: 4–6; Adams and McShane, 1992; Brockington and Homewood, 1996: 93.

4 Roe, 1991: 288.

5 In addition, the transport plane that brought the animals to East Africa took others back to South Africa, increasing the gene pool there too.

6 The report authors stated that the information came from the then Mkomazi Outreach Programme staff.

7 Knight, pers. comm., 3/12/1996.

8 Koch, 1997. In fact, in their written statement to the court, the Tanzanian government explicitly accept that the plaintiffs are Tanzanian citizens.

9 Letter to the editor, *Tanzanian Affairs: Journal of the Britain–Tanzania Society*, no. 58, Sept–Dec. The problem with this claim is that it was based on regional health statistics dated from 1982 and 1972 (Eltringham to Lane, 4/11/97). These are not good data to use. The impact of eviction cannot be assessed from data gathered prior to its occurrence, and regional statistics are not appropriate to monitor effects at the local level. The remark is also discordant with other ideas that the Chairman has published, which stress the importance of wildlife paying for itself, and the unreasonableness of expecting people near protected areas to pay the expenses wildlife can bring (Eltringham, 1994: 168).

10 Duffy, 2000: 2, 173.

11 Friedman, 1962, cited in Fisher, 1997.

12 For example, it is quite clear too that the rhino sanctuary's purpose was not just to conserve the Black rhinoceros but also to enhance the Reserve's future. As the Field Officer put it: 'I do feel that a project as prestigious as the rhino sanctuary, plus some form of revenue from a small but exclusive tourist venture in the reserve, must be forthcoming within the next year for Mkomazi to survive as a game reserve' (Fitzjohn, 1993: 9).

13 Roe, 1991; Adams and Hulme, 2001a.

14 cf. Marks, 1984: 4.

15 Adams and McShane, 1992: 245.

16 cf. Peluso, 1993.

17 Duffy, 2000: 114.

18 Bell, 1987; Marks, 1984: 130.

19 cf. Mishra, 1982.

20 WCED, 1997; Blaikie and Jeanrenaud, 1997: 64. This is not to say that people are only motivated by economic gain. A complex web of beliefs, values and desires, explicit and hidden, drives our actions. But pursuit of survival and prosperity are strong driving forces of human behaviour. People will only abide poverty, or threats to their survival, in unusual circumstances.

21 Blaikie and Jeanrenaud, 1997: 64, 67.

22 Murphree, 1996: 162; Ghimire and Pimbert, 1997: 35.

23 Murphree, 1996.

24 Gibson and Marks, 1995: 950.

25 Alexander and McGregor, 2000: 624–5.

26 Neumann, 1991.

27 Illiffe, 1979; Waller, 1976; Mosse, 1997.

28 Kangwana (2001) notes that the ability of community conservation to achieve conservation goals is not clear.
29 'Conservation will either contribute to solving the problems of the rural poor who live day to day with wild animals, or those animals will disappear' (Adams and McShane, 1992: xix).
30 Adams and Hulme, 2001: 18.
31 Western *et al.*, 1989: 317.
32 Mackenzie 1998: 97, cf. Lal, 1995.
33 Beinart, 1989.
34 Norton-Griffiths, 1996.
35 The phrase is Ferguson's, 1990 (from 1994 edition, p. xv); cf. Brockington, 2001a.
36 Hulme and Murphree, 1999: 279.
37 Oliver-Smith, 1996: 78; Gray, 1996: 101.
38 Thornton, 1997: 68. The extract is from Clare's poem, 'Remembrances', of the mid-1840s.
39 Brockington and Homewood, 2001.
40 O'Riordan, 2000.
41 Sen, 1988.

7

The Livelihoods
of Evicted Pastoralists

What of the second story in this book? How have herders coped with the circumstances dealt to them by the evictions? In this chapter I examine previous research on the consequences of land loss to pastoral societies and set the changes that have occurred at Mkomazi in the context of these and other trends for change.

Existing studies

Despite the importance of land loss to the daily lives of many people in Tanzania and elsewhere, there are remarkably few enquiries into its consequences for livelihoods, particularly of pastoralists. Most of the attention in East Africa has focused on injustice or illegality of the dispossession, and the politics of disputes involved. Studies that detail the anatomy of the effects of sudden land alienation on the people evicted are rare.

Fortunately, there is work detailing the consequences of loss of access to land and herds through changes to land tenure or warfare. The most authoritative is Rutten's account of changing land tenure and access to resources in Kajiado District, in southern Kenya, which details the long build-up of pressure on resources during the twentieth century.[1] Livelihoods here now include greater reliance on cultivation, wage labour, intensification of husbandry – investing in improved breeds – and commercialisation of offtake. Many wage-earners take jobs as watchmen. This is mainly a temporary strategy used to earn money, and there has not been a flood of young men to towns. Cultivation is more widespread and more important; it is both the cause and consequence of loss of pasture. It became more important especially for the poorer herders, but Rutten does not detail differences in the type of farming practised by rich and poor herders.[2] Bekure and colleagues suggest that in the mid-1980s much cultivation was an expedient to allow herds to recover, and much agricultural labour was hired by pastoral families.[3]

Southgate and Hulme report that, since then, agricultural land and output have increased enormously in Kajiado District. More of the cultivation is now being done by pastoralists themselves.[4]

Zaal and Dietz suggest that the diversification of livelihoods, and particularly the commercial development of the livestock industry, is working to the advantage of the wealthier herders in Kajiado.[5] They contrast this with the practices of the Pokot of north-east Kenya, whose livestock sales are more a means of avoiding poverty and diversifying livelihoods than a pursuit of wealth. The Pokot have seen human populations rise *pari passu* with the fall in livestock populations through drought and raiding. Families are unable to live off their herds and are farming more, getting food aid, selling *miraa* (or khat, a local narcotic) and mining. Dietz argues that the primary goal is to defend livestock capital, but that this has proven impossible recently – here, pastoralism has been defeated.[6]

Dahl and Hogg have described the consequences of severe stock loss by the Waso Borana of Kenya following the *shifta* wars of the 1960s and subsequent droughts in the 1970s.[7] The impact of war and drought has been felt unequally. Wealthy families have been able to build up their herds again. They can profit from better access to markets, cutting out the middlemen and making trading more profitable.[8] Poorer families are unable to exploit market opportunities so strategically. Many have been pushed out of pastoralism. The poorer Borana are dependent on the sale of pastoral products – animals, milk and butter – and waged labour. Favourite jobs are with the army or police, otherwise they seek work as herdsmen, agricultural workers or night watchmen. Stockless families are likely to drift off permanently to the urban areas, where they burn charcoal, sell *miraa*, brew beer, beg or work as carpenters and ironmongers. Others seek work on larger farms and plantations. Cultivation has also become more important for the Borana. Dahl records that stockless and poor families began farming on irrigation schemes. Hogg states that the trend is more general and argues that all but the very rich families valued the opportunity to cultivate maize to bolster food supplies and insure against possible misfortune. He also observed wealthy Borana investing in agriculture as a means of diversifying their livelihoods.

Dahl provides much detail on the strategies followed by women unable to depend on pastoralism. In rural areas, single women maintain themselves through prostitution or selling *miraa*. In urban areas they have more options: formal or informal prostitution; gathering forest products or animal fodder; looking after school children whose families live far away; trade; charcoal burning; and making mats and baskets.

There have been fewer pressures on rangelands in Tanzania than Kenya, but they have accelerated since the late 1980s. The most detailed account of recent changes has been provided by Igoe, who has examined alienation of rangeland for private farmers in Simanjiro District.[9] He showed how piecemeal land alienation for large-scale farms combined with altered land-use for farming or mining, and loss of land to tsetse infestation, to force a change in the grazing patterns practised by pastoralists resident there. Many families are turning to agriculture and mining.

More attention in Tanzania has been directed at the impact of land alienation on conservation. The impact of conservation policy on rural people has caused considerable concern in some circles.[10] In particular, the impact of protected areas on pastoralists, especially Maasai pastoralists, is a *cause célèbre* among anthropologists and conservationists.[11] The most detailed data come from the Ngorongoro Conservation Area, which was established in conjunction with the Serengeti National Park.[12] At least 1,000 Maasai pastoralists, 25,000 cattle and 23,000 smallstock and donkeys were excluded from the park and moved to the conservation area in 1959.[13] Here they have been allowed to continue residence, but have subsequently lost access to areas around Olduvai Gorge, and important dry season pasture within the Ngorongoro, Olmoti and Empakaai craters, and the forest reserve. They also face restrictions on rangeland burning and, until recently, were forbidden to cultivate fields.[14]

Stock populations at Ngorongoro have not risen since the 1960s, while human populations have more than doubled in the same period. The restrictions on agriculture required pastoralists at Ngorongoro to depend entirely upon livestock. Yet the productivity of their animals has suffered for several reasons. Livestock must avoid wildebeest calves as these carry malignant catarrhal fever, which is fatal to cattle. Since the park was gazetted, wildebeest populations have increased more than fivefold. Since 1976 they have prevented cattle from using nutritious wet season grazing on the plains.[15] This has combined with a decline in the quality of the highland pastures.[16] In addition, problems with tick-borne fever have increased following the cessation of burning and through the lack of, and possibly rising resistance to, acaricides.[17] The result of the cultivation restrictions and poor herd performance was an unsustainably high rate of offtake, with high sales (49 per cent in 1989) of valuable reproductive animals.[18] Pastoralists became increasingly reliant on smallstock, which breed more rapidly than cattle and provided a surer source of income.[19] The relaxation of cultivation restrictions in 1992 saw many turn to agriculture. At least half of energy needs are now supplied by home-grown crops, and sales of reproductive stock have declined dramatically.[20]

One of the more detailed political accounts of eviction and conservation in this region concerns the Maasai at Amboseli National Park in

Kenya. This small (488 km²) national park was gazetted in 1974 and vacated in 1977.²¹ Its size belies its importance, for it contains valuable water, dry season grazing and salt deposits. The history of Amboseli National Park is a fiery one, with many conflicts between pastoralists, wildlife and park officials.²² Attention has concentrated on the fact of the loss of grazing and water, the nature of pastoral land needs, the disputes and negotiations that have attended the park's development, and the potential for compromise between conservation and local needs. However, the strategies that people adopted to cope with exclusion from the park have not been described in as much detail.

Other work gives general insights into impoverishment, and the way in which it impinges on people's lives and yet is also a normal part of their experience. Turton has written a series of papers on the changes to the Mursi of Ethiopia following long-term climatic change, drought, war and the establishment of national parks on Mursi territory.²³ Migration and displacement are integral to the history of this people – they are both the dilemma and the norm for groups in this area:

> They [the Mursi] see themselves as having made a journey, but the historical truth of the matter may be more accurately summed up by saying that a journey 'made' them (Turton, 1979). By this we mean that Mursi society is the temporary outcome of a movement of cattle herding people, going far beyond the present day Mursi in both space and time and in the general direction of the Ethiopian highlands. Generated by ecological factors and, in particular, by the need to reduce the uncertainties of pastoral and agricultural production in an environment in which there is a wide range of fluctuations around mean conditions, this movement of herders into higher, better watered land, unsuitable for cattle because of tsetse, gives rise, in the end, to new political and ethnic identities (Turton and Turton, 1984: 187²⁴).

However, it is hard to provide statistical data that bear out the impact of these adversities on Mursi livelihoods. In particular, the statistics on changing cattle numbers are anomalous to the general pattern of marginalisation and impoverishment. The data Turton cites suggest that cattle populations have quadrupled between 1970 and 1994 while human populations have increased from between four and five thousand to between five and six thousand people.²⁵ Turton himself suggests that these data are suspect, particularly his own cattle population estimate of 1970. It is difficult to interpret these data without more detailed information.

All these studies provide insights into the nature of impoverishment and livelihood diversification. None is concerned with the impact of large-scale, sudden loss of land. The most spectacular case of land loss involving pastoralists was that of the Maasai moves of 1904 and 1911. These reduced the Maasai lands from 55,000 km² before colonisation to 39,000 km². The second move entailed the displacement of 10,000

Maasai, 200,000 cattle and 550,000 smallstock. But there are no details of the impact on livelihoods. We only know that in the early 1930s livestock to human ratios would theoretically have allowed a purely pastoral existence for all residents.[26]

Studies of more recent cases of land loss are also relatively silent about their impact on livelihoods. In the 1970s the Barabaig lost large areas of valuable pasture to wheat and bean farmers, and more than 100,000 acres of their productive wet season pastures to a Canadian-sponsored wheat-growing scheme run by the National Food Corporation of Tanzania.[27] Kjaerby has documented how the gradual build-up of pressure on Barabaig lands progressively constrained their land-use prior to the wheat scheme. He noted that many Barabaig cultivated in order to reduce the sale of their cattle, or in order to ensure they had sufficient food. This caused problems for the household division of labour and restricted the mobility of herds and hence their productivity.[28] Lane has described the importance of the lost pastures for Barabaig herding and land management. The alienated lands were highly nutritious, wet season pastures, which enabled stock to recover their health after the rigours of the dry season.[29] Without these pastures livestock productivity declines.[30] Lane's informants estimated that one-third of the Barabaig cattle died between 1981 and 1987 as a result of land loss to the wheat schemes. Cattle productivity is reported to have declined, but no details are given. Anomalously, Lane records that the average herd size of the Barabaig has increased in the long run.[31] As with Turton's data, it is hard to interpret them without knowing more about trends in differentiation of livestock holdings or human migration from the area.

The Meru land case, which occurred just after the Second World War, is perhaps the most famous instance of land alienation in Tanzania. It involved the alienation of two farms from the Meru people for settlers in the heavily contested lands surrounding Mt Meru, taking out several thousand hectares of fertile land, and requiring the eviction of approximately 3,000 people, 7,700 cattle and 5,500 smallstock.[32] The effects were undoubtedly severe, but attention has focused on the political implications of the action, and of resistance to it.[33] More is known about the agricultural adaptations of the Arusha and Meru living on Mt Meru in response to land shortage than their response to the loss of these particular lands.[34] Neumann's work on the Arusha National Park, again at Mt Meru, looks primarily at resistance and opposition rather than transformations of livelihoods.[35]

In summary, the general forces of impoverishment, livelihood change, marginalisation and commoditisation within pastoral society are well recognised. The problems caused by appropriation of pasture by governments, conservation, 'outsiders' and other pastoralists are well-known.

But the detailed anatomy of livelihood change following large-scale land loss has not been studied. We should expect that it will follow the patterns of impoverishment described elsewhere, but we shall have to look at the processes of immiseration and proletarianisation it causes in the context of other structural changes.

Changes at Mkomazi

Long-term livestock population data in East Africa rarely show a steady increase. Human populations, in contrast, are steadily increasing. The consequence of this is a declining ratio of livestock to people.[36] Specialised pastoralism, which entails a minimum number of stock per person, is therefore on the wane. Unless pastoralists can 'slough off' surplus people, as they have done in the past, their livelihoods must change. Specialised pastoralism will prove to be a temporary blip in the long-term scheme of African pastoral history.

The demographic pressures form the background to a series of disasters and conflicts that have afflicted pastoral societies in East Africa since the 1960s. Wars, droughts, intensification of raiding and land loss to conservation and farming have forced many herders out of pastoralism and into other livelihoods. Observers have noted decreasing social mobility, as the poorer groups find it increasingly difficult to join the increasingly small proportion of families who herd for a living. Wealthier families are able to use their resources to invest in farms and businesses that buttress, and occasionally transform, their herding.[37]

Two problematic responses to this situation can be found in the literature. The first tries to call a halt to the change, to turn back the inevitable. For example, Rutten calls for a moratorium on Maasai land sales to outsiders in Kenya.[38] There is much abuse and corruption in the sale of land here; the cessation of sales to wealthy politicians would be a good thing.[39] Rutten's call, aimed at the corrupt, is framed in simple ethnographic terms – Maasai and outsiders. Ethnicity and its history are more complex than that. Outsiders include the farmers who have long cultivated on Maasai rangelands, often in cooperation with Maasai hosts.[40] The definition of an outsider is open to continual negotiation, and violent conflict.[41] There is a sense of trying to attempt the impossible here. Pastoral populations have often shed people they could not support. The same is happening now. The poorer and marginal groups, the politically expendable, are being forced off the land. Moratoriums on land sales will not change that.

My advocacy of letting local people use Mkomazi's resources is not a call to preserve a livelihood, but rather to retain options. Herds provide wealth and security. Nor is it a call for Maasai/Parakuyo-centred, ethnically reified division of resources. All groups need to use them. My suggestion is that conservation objectives be modified, that boundaries retreat and management seek compromises in order that the resources of the Umba plain serve more people.

The second response is to suggest that pastoral societies are experiencing a crisis. Watts's account of the deepening problems of West African herders paints a bleak picture for all but wealthy absentee owners. The poor lose through a combination of drought, declining terms of trade and sale of reproductive stock. He does not state if there is any way out of the difficulties. Herd reconstitution after disaster is 'problematic if not altogether impossible'.[42] Bonfiglioli has written of a crisis facing pastoral societies.[43] He is specifically pessimistic about the Maasai of Tanzania:

> The Maasai pastoralists in Tanzania, incorporated into national economic structures, have grown more and more vulnerable to forces beyond their control; their capacity to manage their own lives is decreasing and their very survival as an ethnic group is threatened (Bonfiglioli, 1992: 47–8).

Péron adopts a similar tone when writing about the Kenyan Maasai. He concludes his account of the impacts of recent political changes and group ranches on Kenyan Maasai with these words:

> It is ... likely that they will become landless and end up (if they are lucky) in low paid manual jobs, caught in a poverty trap. A sad prospect for a proud people (Péron, 1995, vol II: 231[44]).

I suggest these remarks err in two ways. First, they make broad generalisations where fortunes and responses are diverse; second, they are too negative and underestimate the resilience that can accompany people's responses to land loss.

Other authors writing about change in pastoral society have emphasised the resilience and endurance of people's coping strategies. Waller criticises ideas about marginalisation of pastoralists under capitalism, because they subsume pastoralism within a broader subset of rural societies, without considering its peculiarities or the thoughts or agency of the pastoralists themselves. He argues that this leads to a one-dimensional view of pastoralists as 'victims'. Instead, the pastoral viewpoint should be foremost in mind. Turton has shown that the Mursi experienced devastating losses in the droughts of the early 1970s, but argues that the Mursis' response to drought and impoverishment then and now shows 'resilience, technical sophistication, inventiveness and sheer human determination to survive'.[45] Notions of 'rehabilitating' refugees such as the Mursi risk overlooking these qualities. Fratkin argued that 'things do not necessarily fall apart' for the Ariaal, despite drought and development programmes.[46] Dietz showed that calorific terms of trade have not declined for Pokot herders in decades.[47] Ensminger found loss of stock and increasing inequality among the Galole Orma, but yet signs of economic well-being among the poorer families.[48] Hogg wrote about a 'crisis in pastoralism' resulting from the changes to the world around them and loss of land, but sets that in the context of pastoral resilience, and a great variety of responses by different pastoral groups.[49]

At Mkomazi, I was working with a great variety of families pursuing varied livelihoods with different strategies to enhance prosperity while minimising the risk of loss. There were Maasai and Parakuyo herders splitting their herds between several different locations in Kenya and Tanzania, and there were Pare herders sending animals down towards the coast. Women were selling firewood daily in Kisiwani, or travelling far to sell medicine, or selling milk from animals that they had lobbied to have brought back to the compound. There were old men dependent on stock loans from relatives after profligate sons had wasted their inheritance; there were young wives reliant on selling milk from borrowed goats; widows who sold medicine and beadwork on the one hand and managed their herds on the other. Pare farmers bought weak animals from Maasai herders during the dry season, and toiled continuously to weed their rain-fed farms. Alcoholics sold animals recklessly and their children ran away from home. There were vulnerable individuals with few relatives to rely on; stock-poor families who depended on wage labour; aging families who had to pay the cattle bridewealth of their sons' marriages, and others who experienced new-found prosperity when their daughters were married. There were stockless dependants living in other people's compounds, rich women whose adult sons controlled many cows and poorer co-wives who only had smallstock. There were wealthy elders renting irrigated rice fields, and poorer youths jointly investing in, or gleaning from, neighbour's lands. There were men engaged in stock trading, or buying improved stall-fed cattle, while others invested wages in goats, or sought careers with Maasai NGOs.

From this diversity there are three strategies that I would like to emphasise. The main change is an increase in agriculture.[50] People claimed that no pastoralists cultivated before the eviction.[51] The claim is hard to refute or confirm for lack of descriptions of previous livelihoods. However, it is likely that herds were large enough to forgo farming. Now, almost all families cultivate. The wealthier herders practise capital-intensive farming, paying labourers and investing in pumps for irrigation. Poorer farmers work the land themselves and rarely use paid labour. This accords with Little's account of farming in Baringo, Kenya, and Dahl and Hogg's work on agriculture among the Borana, where the wealthy invest in farming for their prosperity, the poor in their struggle to survive.[52]

McCabe likewise found agriculture had dramatically increased among herders in Ngorongoro. Cultivated grains contributed 50 per cent of calorific needs.[53]

Changes are also apparent in women's earnings. Women have long traded independently in these societies, and sales are valued because they provide women with their own income that they control.[54] In Lushoto District we found a two-fold division in income-earning patterns in the households surveyed. Women from wealthy households sell milk or chickens but only irregularly. Women from poor households sell firewood, cow's and goat's milk and traditional medicine more often. The poorest do so every day in neighbouring villages. In Same District the pattern was more complicated. In addition to the two categories of Lushoto District, there were some women who went on long journeys selling medicine in distant towns (Box 7.1). Some women needed to sell firewood or medicine because their stock were kept far away, and Pare

---

Box 7.1 Risks of new livelihoods.

Moses is an influential elder claiming direct descent from Kamunyu, the patriach of the Lushoto Parakuyo. When he was evicted from the Reserve he settled at Kapimbi, in Same District, a village particularly close to the Reserve. Here the boundary coincides with the road to the village. Moses's compound is about 100 m from the border. Moses has five wives and numerous children. His first children are now all men of marriageable age. In setting up marriages for six sons at once Moses was faced with numerous expenses, combined with stock losses after eviction.

Moses's family does not have access to irrigated fields nor the expertise to farm. The family depends on the women of the compound travelling to sell medicines. The women travel enormous distances, from Chalinze to Moshi, Dodoma and into Kenya down to Mombassa. They tend to travel on circuits, sending money home whenever possible. They told me that when they first started they had no experience of selling medicine. They had no place to stay in the towns when they arrived, and would rely on churches or helpful customers or seek help from Maasai and Parakuyo people working in the towns (often warriors employed as watchmen).

The women are often away for long periods; it was typical to find half of them absent when I visited the compound. However, they had to travel if their families are to have food and their children are to be educated. All travel is dangerous in Tanzania. On 10 September 1996 three women, Ruth, Yehobet and Elizabeth, were travelling to Marangu, on Kilimanjaro mountain, in a pick-up that veered off the road. Elizabeth died at the scene, and Ruth was seriously injured, but recovered and was able to return home. However, it is still not certain whether or when she will be able to support herself and her family by selling medicine again.

Source: Igoe and Brockington, 1999.

women are part of a localised dairy network that contributes considerable income to the home.

These different livelihoods resulted in differences in diet.[55] The families that depended on milk for sale consumed less milk themselves and ate produce bought daily from the proceeds of milk sales. This echoes Fratkin and Smith, and Fratkin, Nathan and Roth, who found that different levels of involvement in sales by women were manifest in people's diet.[56] Those who sold more milk consumed less at home and ate more grains and vegetables.

It is wrong to interpret women's sales as necessarily indicative of impoverishment.[57] But the frequent grievance voiced by the women was that income they had once used for their own purposes was now expected to support the whole family. These changes need to be seen in the context of household dynamics. It is common for men to seek to transfer some household expenses, otherwise met by selling animals, on to women, who have to meet them by selling goods. There were families like this in Same District. Men kept the herd away from the compound to reduce milk offtake. As a result the availability of milk and money from selling animals, and the respective responsibilities of men and women to provide for household needs, are hotly contested. Where there is no herd, or it is greatly reduced, there is less room to manoeuvre. At Mkomazi, the responsibility for buying food falls on women more than it used to.

One change is significant in its absence. Very few evictees have sought urban livelihoods.[58] Women do go to towns to sell medicine, but do not stay long. Only one young man was reported to have sought urban work as a watchman, despite a growing number of Maasai and Parakuyo guards in urban areas. A survey of 1,032 siblings revealed only two in non-rural occupations.[59] This is markedly different from Rutten's findings in Kajiado District.[60] Instead, as Bryceson has found elsewhere in Tanzania, people sought work servicing the rural economy, selling clothes, veterinary medicine or livestock, or employment in NGOs or building new NGO headquarters.[61] Livelihoods at Mkomazi manifest the same structural trends found elsewhere in the country, with farming and herding becoming relatively less important and the rural informal sector growing. These, however, are just early days. There is a growing trend for young Maasai and Parakuyo men to work in towns as guards. The numbers of people working in towns from Mkomazi will probably increase.

The picture that emerges at Mkomazi is not of terminal crisis, but of a people facing rapid change that leaves some members in hardship. It does not follow, however, that their new livelihoods are more secure. Diversification is a way of reducing risk, but it is also a manifestation of poverty, an indication that previous coping strategies have failed.[62] In the

context of variable environments and increasing pressure on rural livelihoods and resources, the new occupations of Mkomazi's neighbours will
not necessarily lighten their predicament. Here, people are poorer, the
livelihoods they follow are more precarious and they are more vulnerable
to misfortune.

Notes

1 Rutten, 1992.
2 *ibid*: 434.
3 Bekure *et al.*, 1991: 36.
4 Southgate and Hulme, 1996: 16–18.
5 Zaal and Dietz, 1999.
6 Dietz, 1987: 290.
7 Dahl, 1979; Hogg, 1980, 1986.
8 Dahl, 1979: 205.
9 Igoe and Brockington, 1999; Igoe, 2000.
10 Turton, 1996, 109; 1985: 344; McCabe *et al.*, 1992: 354; Anderson and Grove, 1987: 3.
11 Collett, 1987; Brockington and Homewood, 1996; Enghoff, 1990; Deihl, 1985; Homewood, 1995: 335–6.
12 Arhem, 1986; Homewood, Rodgers and Arhem, 1987; Homewood and Rodgers, 1991; McCabe *et al.*, 1992; McCabe, 1997; Potkanski, 1997.
13 Homewood and Rodgers, 1991: 71.
14 Arhem, 1986: 246–7; Homewood and Rodgers, 1991: 73; McCabe, 1997.
15 Potkanski, 1997: 48. The Maasai refer to this year as *Alari loo engati*: 'the Year of the Wildebeest'.
16 Homewood and Rodgers, 1991: 108–10, 253–4. The decline is probably the consequence of restrictions on burning.
17 Homewood and Rodgers, 1991: 134–5, 170–2; Waller and Homewood, 1997: 74.
18 Homewood and Rodgers, 1991: 167; McCabe *et al.*, 1992: 358–9; McCabe, 1997: 61.
19 Arhem, 1986: 247–8; Dahl and Hjort, 1976: 230–4.
20 Potkanski, 1997: 79.
21 Lindsay 1987: 156–8.
22 Western, 1994; Lindsay 1987.
23 Turton, 1977, 1985, 1987, 1988, 1995, 1996; Turton and Turton, 1984.
24 See also Turton, 1988; 1996: 105–6.
25 Turton, 1995: 8, 30.
26 Rutten, 1992: 177–82, 468.
27 Kjaerby, 1979: 31–4; Lane, 1996; Lane and Moorehead, 1995: 124. The Land Commission reports that in 1991 Lane estimated the acreage involved to be 70,000 acres (URT, 1993: 16). The difference is in part made up by the farms of individuals which have grown up in the area around the wheat scheme.
28 Kjaerby, 1979: 42–5, 47–8.
29 Lane, 1996: 109, 114.

30 Homewood and Rodgers, 1991: 182–3.

31 Lane, 1996: 47, 161.

32 Official and local estimates vary. Spear (1997: 222) reports that the British authorities stated that 1,000 people, 440 cattle and 1,200 smallstock were moved. He also notes that local estimates were considerably higher. They claimed that 2,993 people were evicted (*ibid*: 225). Luanda (1986: 305, footnote 3) cites evidence in favour of the latter. He reports that the Northern Province Settlement Committee recorded the figures cited above. A similar number of people were reported there by the Sub-Committee of the Land Settlement Board (*ibid*: 268, footnote 5).

33 The Meru brought the case before the United Nations with momentous implications for opposition to colonial rule in Tanganyika.

34 Luanda, 1986; Gulliver, 1961 and Spear, 1997 among others. Some interesting details are recorded by Meru leaders in a report to the East Africa Royal Commission, PRO, CO 892/10/2.

35 Neumann, 1991, 1998.

36 Western, 1994; Rutten, 1992; Homewood and Rodgers, 1991.

37 Hogg, 1986; Galaty *et al.*, 1994; Zaal and Dietz, 1999; Waller, 1999; Brockington, 1999.

38 Rutten, 1992: 460.

39 Rutten, 1992; Galaty, 1994; Galaty and Munei, 1999.

40 Knowles and Collett, 1989; Waller, 1993.

41 Dietz, 1997.

42 Watts, 1991: 23.

43 Bonfiglioli, 1992: 3.

44 *Il est plus vraisemblable que ceux-ci vont un jour ou l'autre être destitués du peu de terre qui leur reste, et finir (s'ils ont de la chance) par entreprendre un travail manuel sous-payé, pris au piège de la pauvreté. Une bien triste perspective pour un peuple si fier* (cited by Graham, 1989: 185).

45 Turton and Turton, 1984: 178.

46 Fratkin, 1991: 125.

47 Dietz, 1993.

48 Ensminger, 1992: 88–101.

49 Hogg, 1992: 133, 135.

50 Brockington, 1998, 1999.

51 Two people mentioned that there had been some cultivation by herders living in the Reserve, but there is no indication that it was significant for livelihoods (interviews: AA, 30/5/96; MK, 29/4/96). The main centre for pastoral farming in the east of the Reserve was well-known as a previous drought refuge for calves and only recently taken to agriculture (interviews: KL, 26/2/96; KK, 3/3/96).

52 Little, 1985; Hogg, 1980, 1986; Dahl, 1979.

53 McCabe, 1997.

54 Talle, 1988: 65; House-Midamba, 1995: 86.

55 For a complete discussion of the data and their implications, see Brockington, 2001 b.

56 Fratkin and Smith, 1995; Fratkin *et al.*, 1999.

57 Buhl and Homewood, 2000.

58 Dahl, 1979: 212–13; Hogg, 1980: 307–8.
59 Brockington, 1998.
60 Rutten, 1992: 431.
61 Bryceson, 1999; interviews: LK, YK, MK 5/3/96; P, S 11/5/96.
62 Bryceson, 1999; Bollig and Göbel, 1997; Davies, 1996.

Methods & Sources

Historical sources

In the nineteenth century the Umba Nyika was frequented by several explorers and missionaries. Their descriptions, and the broader history of the plains constructed by Waller and Berntsen, provide an account of the movement of people and livestock in the area up until the early 1890s.

For the twentieth century there are the letters, notes, diaries and reports kept in the Tanzanian National Archives (TNA), the Kenya National Archives (KNA), the Tanga Regional Archives (TRA), the Public Records Office at Kew (PRO), the Royal Geographical Society (RGS), the Cambridge University Seeley History Library (SHL) and the Colonial Records Project at Rhodes House of Oxford University (RH). These begin in the early years of the twentieth century. I have not looked at German records but have instead relied on Ekemode's dissertation, which discusses them extensively. I have also used papers and letters collected by Henry Fosbrooke when he visited the Mkomazi Game Reserve in 1991.

In addition, I conducted taped interviews with people now living around the Reserve, from Mahambalawe to Toloha and also in the Ruvu valley, and who used to work there. These provide many personal insights into the processes and events recorded in the archives. Most of these were with one or two people, but some were conducted in groups. Initial meetings in each village included representatives of the village or sub-village government who were in the discussions.

There are two problems with these sources, one pertaining to the records and the other to my use of them. First, certain groups are more visible in the records than others. Much of the attention of the archives and the more recent records has focused on pastoralists, and especially the Maasai and Kwavi people. They attracted attention largely because they controlled much of the cattle on the plains and because their movements proved so hard to govern. Although they probably dominated the use of the plains, herders from these groups were (and are) a minority in the area. Mention of Pare, Kamba and Sambaa stock owners is slight and probably not proportional to their numbers. In no sense therefore is this account a general history of the area and its peoples. It is about a dry country that was extensively, but not intensively, used by a small number of people who happened to generate much excitement in government circles.

Second, my involvement at Mkomazi was part of a research project into household economies. The focus of my work was current pastoral livelihoods. It mainly involved measuring diet, milk yields and herd use. The historical work I discuss here was incidental to that research project. Many of the records only came to light serendipitously, and then after the field research was complete. The findings I present are not 'proper' historical research. I have not been able to interrogate the records sufficiently, to go back and interview people who had been at meetings, to ask their opinions of minutes that had been taken, or devote sufficient time to collecting oral histories with the rigour I retrospectively desire. The importance of local people's actions is pre-eminent in the records, but their own views and versions of these events are not sufficiently represented.

Despite these problems, there is much to write. The archival data are particularly rich about a rather obscure tract of bush and a population whose presence and movements are normally rarely plotted in any detail. If the problem of the records is their excessive attention to Maa-speaking pastoralists, that is the weakness of their strength, for there is a wealth of material available.

The volumes of files arise because this part of East Africa is full of boundaries – tribal reserve boundaries, crown and settler land, international borders, game reserve and national park edges. These were either unrecognised, or seen as eminently crossable, by people living around them. They were, however, indelibly marked on the official mind and they created administrative hard edges that people were continually violating, generating all sorts of interesting reactions and reams of records.

Livelihoods and economic data

Livestock market records, cattle census data and other indicators of past conditions at Mkomazi are available, sporadically, in local government offices. Data on current livelihoods were gathered in two surveys. One, on agriculturalists and agropastoralists, was conducted by my colleague Hilda Kiwasila between January 1995 and February 1997; the other was conducted by myself among pastoralists and agropastoralists between April 1995 and June 1996.

To select the households for the pastoralist survey I first identified places where pastoralists were concentrated in a pilot study in 1994. In Tanzania, villages are divided into sub-villages (Swahili: *kitongoji* singular, *vitongoji* plural). Pastoralists tended to live separately from the rest of the village in their own *vitongoji*, often some distance from the main concentration of settlement.

Pastoral *vitongoji* tended not to be ethnically diverse. Different ethnic groups tend to live in different *vitongoji*. In Lushoto District I worked in three *vitongoji* closest to Mng'aro: Mazinde, Mahambalawe (both *vitongoji* of Mng'aro) and Kisima, a *kitongoji* of Lunguza. These were not Pare or Sambaa pastoral *vitongoji*, which were further west near Mnazi, their residents being only Maasai and Parakuyo. At Kisiwani I worked in five *vitongoji*: Kamadufa, Kamorei Chini, Kamorei Juu, Rambangondo and Kapimbi. Kamorei Juu was exclusively home to Pare pastoralists, the rest were Parakuyo and Maasai.

In both study sites I also administered the survey with Sambaa and Pare agropastoralists who lived in the main villages. These data have generally not been presented here as these pastoralists were not, nor had been, users of the Reserve. However, the survey work with them, and subsequent discussions, have informed my understanding of pastoralism and relations between pastoral groups in the area.

I met with leaders of the pastoral *vitongoji* to introduce the work and to identify suitable households for the survey. Through these leaders I was introduced to the people living in the pastoral sub-villages either in group meetings or individually. Households were selected on a stratified-random basis within each *kitongoji* thus: the leaders listed the households of their survey and grouped them into different wealth categories according to divisions that they felt appropriate. We then selected families within those categories randomly. The number of families selected in each category was proportional to the size of that category within each *kitongoji*.

Maa-speaking and Pare Muslim families usually consist of a man, his wives and other dependants. Each woman runs her own home. Sometimes families are grouped in compounds (Swahili: *boma*), which consist of several households sharing a common livestock enclosure, to which each family has a separate entrance.[1]

The economies of sub-households within a *boma* and within one family can be quite separate.[2] Indeed, for a large number of rural African societies, the concepts of 'family' and 'household' are problematic when researching resource use and economies. The physical space of settlements, compounds and houses can conceal a web of overlapping, but distinct, consumption and production units. Those who cooperate to produce food or earn income may not unite to share it or have equal power over proceeds.[3] Although 'households' structure data collection they may have analytical limitations.

In all, the main body of data presented here is derived from 20 households in Lushoto District and 32 in Same District (Table A.1). These were grouped into 38 *bomas* and contained 148 sub-households. Of the sample, the five households in Kamorei Juu were Pare pastoralists, the rest were Parakuyo and Maasai. All households had been present at Mkomazi at the time of eviction. They have not been grouped into wealth categories as analyses were based on ranking, not categorisation.

Families were visited five times in the course of the survey: in May, September and November of 1995 and February and May of 1996 in Lushoto, and in June, October and December 1995 and March and June 1996 in Same. Repeated surveys allowed me to see seasonal variations in livelihoods and household dynamics, build up a large number of observations and check impressions and ideas formed during the course of the research. The survey also helped me to get to know a number of families in different areas, and with different economic status. Through the relationships I established I came to understand more about the history and nature of pastoral resource use and economy in the area.

Data were collected on milk yields; 24-hour food recall; expenditure and selling at market; expenditure on veterinary medicine; offtake from the herd; agricultural yields; farm size and herd size. A register of cattle was established and their progress monitored during the course of the research.

Table A1 Outline of data collection: location and sample size.

District	Village	*Kitongoji*	Number of *bomas*	Number of households	Number of sub-households
Lushoto	Mng'aro	Mahambalawe	8	10	42
		Mazinde	3	3	4
	Lunguza	Kisima	7	7	13
Same	Kisiwani	Kamadufa	5	6	11
		Kamorei Chini	2	2	19
		Kamorei Juu	4	4	5
		Rambangondo	6	16	22
		Kapimbi	3	4	32
Lushoto total			18	20	59
Same total			20	32	89
Overall total			38	52	148

Notes

1 Spencer, 1988: 12–13; Homewood and Rodgers, 1991: 35–8.
2 Fosbrooke, 1948: 43–8.
3 Guyer, 1986: 93–5.

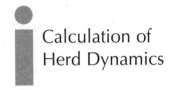

Calculation of Herd Dynamics

Fertility and mortality rates were calculated from these data in terms of the amount of time in which a cow is at risk of dying or giving birth. The unit of time is a 'cow year at risk'. The purpose of this is easiest to understand when considering fertility. For example, a herd of 20 cows may include 10 animals that are too young to give birth. Relevant fertility rates must only include the mature animals. Furthermore, it is important to know for how long each of these 10 mature cows is at risk during the year. Two cows may be sold in June and thus will only have been at risk of giving birth for six months, another may only have matured in May and so will only be at risk of giving birth for seven months.

These data recorded the timing of events by calendar year. It was not possible to determine when in the year an animal died. Assumptions had to be made when calculating cow years at risk.

If a fertile animal is present at the beginning and end of the year, there are 12 months at which it is at risk of giving birth or dying. If it dies, it is assumed to die in the middle of the year; it is present for six months, and at risk of giving birth for six months.

When an animal is born, it is assumed to be born in the middle of the year and so present for just six months. In the first year of its birth it is only at risk of dying for six months. An animal is considered to be fertile four years after it is born. In the first year when it becomes fertile it will only be at risk of giving birth for six months as it was born halfway through the year.

For most animals, I know when they were born, when they started giving birth and when they left the herd through death, slaughter, sale or as a gift. However, for some animals information is less complete. First, I do not know when some animals were born. For all of these, however, I know when they first gave birth. I assume that they were fertile, and at risk of giving birth, one year before they are recorded doing so. If these animals were reported to give birth before the year of the eviction operation, I assume that they remain fertile for half the average fertile life of an East African Zebu cow. I estimate that an East African Zebu could expect to live to be giving birth for about eight years, and that therefore cows of unknown age who first gave birth before eviction remained fertile for four years.

For the purposes of this analysis an animal that left the herd through any means is not included in the calculations of cow months at risk of giving birth. These results, then, are a record of the fertility of the managed herd, not of a cattle population.

Mortality rates are similarly calculated on the basis of cow years at risk of dying. Animals present throughout a year are at risk of dying for 12 months. Those that leave the herd or die were at risk of dying for six months, as are those that were born or entered the herd that year. Indices of mortality per cow year were calculated by dividing the number of deaths in a calendar year by the number of cow years at risk lived that calendar year. Additional rates of sale, livestock gift giving, slaughter and general offtake can also be worked out with similar calculations.

Maize Price Data

Maize price data were collected from Same and Moshi District records. Records were not complete, and some estimates have had to be made. The relationship between maize prices close to the Reserve and those far away from it were established empirically and then prices close to the Reserve predicted. Figure A3.1 shows the actual and predicted results; Figure A3.2 shows the data used in the analysis. The price of maize climbs in three jumps, with a rise at the beginning of 1980 followed by a plateau, the same at the beginning of 1984 and a further jump in 1990.

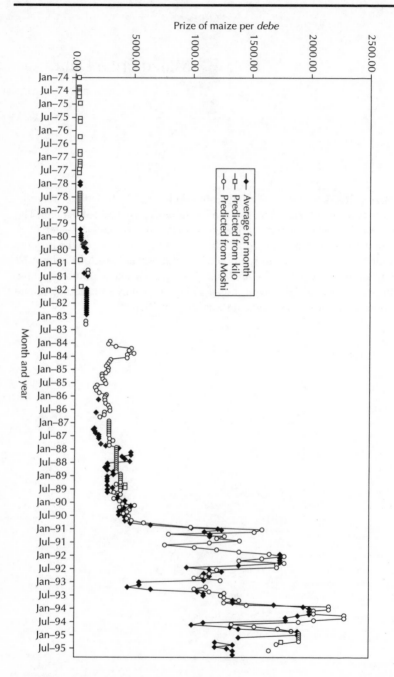

Figure A3.1 Actual and predicted maize prices, 1974–1995.

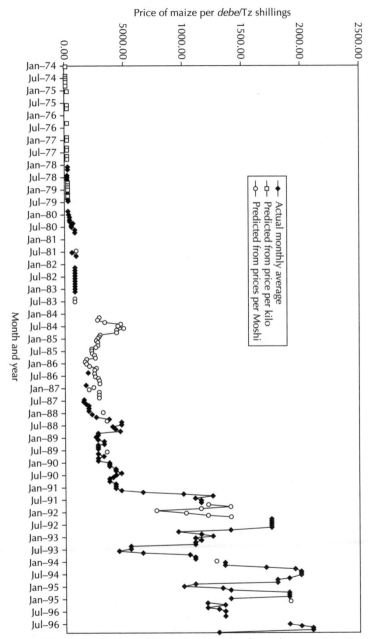

Figure A3.2 Actual and estimated maize prices used in the analysis, 1974–1996.

These data are mainly derived from the price of maize per *debe* (18 kg tin). Where this was unavailable, it is predicted from the price per kilo in Same District or the price per *debe* in nearby Rural Moshi District.

Primary Sources

Files consulted at the Tanzania National Archives
10273/II. Cattle raids. Secretariat File.
11/5, vol II. Movements of Masai and Kwavi. Accession number 19.
11/5, vol III. Movements of Masai and Kwavi. Accession number 19.
1733 (28). Annual report Lushoto District, 1928. Secretariat File.
35/3 1920. Tribes Maasai, 1920. Secretariat File.
35/3 1921. Tribes Maasai, 1921. Secretariat File.
35/3 1922. Tribes Maasai, 1922. Secretariat File.
35/3 1923. Tribes Maasai, 1923. Secretariat File.
451/I. Game. Accession number 4.
451/II. Game. Accession number 4.
451/III. Game. Accession number 4.
451/IV. Game. Accession number 4.
G1/7. Mkomazi Game Reserve. Accession number 481.
6/1. Pare District annual reports. Requisition number 19/6/1.
69/1, vol II. Livestock permits.
723, vol I. Movements of the Maasai and Kwavi. Accession number 4.
723, vol II. Movements of the Maasai and Kwavi. Accession number 4.
723, vol III. Movements of the Maasai and Kwavi. Accession number 4.
962/15. District and Provincial annual reports.
962/1953. Lushoto District Annual Report 1953. Requisition number 304/962/1953.
962/1954. Lushoto District Annual Report 1954. Requisition number 304/962/1954.

Files consulted at the Tanga Regional Archives
TA4 Box 12 G1. Untitled.
V.10/22. Lushoto District Veterinary Movements.
V.10/10. Lushoto District Veterinary Conditions.

The Kisiwani Ward Livestock File
This is held at Kisiwani village, Same District at the village office. The author has copies of relevant papers.

Files consulted at the Kenya National Archives
DC/TTA/1/1/3. Annual reports 1949–1958.
DC/TTA/3/8/37. Maasai grazing concessions.
DO/Tav/1/1/22. Maasai repatriation.
DO/Tav/1/26/13. Maasai cattle trespass.
DO/Tav/1/26/8. Movement of stock.
KW/23/30. Tsavo West 1949–56.
PC/Coast/1/1/112. Administration Maasai.
PC/Coast/2/11/64. Extra grazing for the Taveta.

Files consulted at the Public Records Office
CO/533/484/11. Kenya. Kilindi Harbour Wharfs and Estate Company Land Grant.
CO/533/551/2. Somalis in Nairobi National Park.
CO/691/27. Von Lettow-Vorbeck's private diary.
CO/892/12/3. East African Royal Commission. Notes prepared for the Royal Commissioners by the Provincial Commissioners.
FO 925/228/A. Anglo-German boundary in East Equatorial Africa, 1892.
WO/32/5819. Report on operations in East Africa during 1915.
WO/32/5820. General Smuts's report on his campaign.
WO/32/5822. Dispatches from General Tighe, 1915.

Papers consulted at Rhodes House
Mss.Afr.s. 1980. Popplewell's diary and notes.
Mss.Afr.s. 2156. Popplewell's recollections.
Micr. Afr. 472. Same District books.

Papers consulted at the Royal Geographical Society
Manuscript copy of Richard Thornton's diary. Journey to Kilimanjaro, 28 June 1861 to 10 October 1861. 300 pages of foolscap and illustrations.

Papers consulted at the Seeley History Library
Kenya microfilm reel 55. Taita District annual reports.

Fosbrooke Papers
Letters and testimonies collected by Henry Fosbrooke while he was working on the Mkomazi evictions in the 1990s (a copy of which is in the author's possession).

Secondary Sources

Abbot, J. & Homewood, K. 1999. 'A history of change: Causes of miombo woodland decline in a protected area in Malawi.' *Journal of Applied Ecology* **36**: 422–33.

Abu-zeid, M.N. 1981. 'Management programmes for the proposed Mkomazi Park Tanzania.' Unpublished postgraduate diploma dissertation. College of African Wildlife Management, Mweka.

Achebe, C. 1964. *Arrow of God.* Heinemann Educational, London.

Adams, J.S. & McShane, T.O. 1992. *The Myth of Wild Africa. Conservation without Illusion.* University of California Press, Berkeley.

Adams, W.M. 1990. *Green Development. Environment and Sustainability in the Third World.* Routledge, London.

——1996. *Future Nature: A Vision for Conservation.* Earthscan, London.

——& Hulme, D. 2001a. 'Conservation & community. Changing narratives, policies & practices in African conservation.' In D. Hulme and M. Murphree (eds) *African Wildlife & Livelihoods. The Promise & Performance of Community Conservation.* James Currey, Oxford and Heinemann, Portsmouth, NH.

——& Hulme, D. 2001b. 'If community conservation is the answer in Africa, what is the question?' *Oryx* **35**: 1–8.

Alexander, J. & McGregor, J. 2000. 'Wildlife and politics: CAMPFIRE in Zimbabwe.' *Development & Change* **31**: 605–27.

Altieri, M.A. 1993. 'Ethnoscience and biodiversity: Key elements in the design of sustainable pest management systems for small farmers in developing countries.' *Agriculture, Ecosystems & Environment* **46**: 257–72.

——1999. 'The ecological role of biodiversity in agroecosystems.' *Agriculture, Ecosystems & Environment* **74**: 19–31.

Ament, J. & Gillett, J. 1975. 'The vascular plants of Meru National Park, Kenya.' *J. East African Nat. Hist. Soc. & Nat. Mus.* **154**: 11–34.

Anderson, C.A. 1959. 'Handbook on range management – Near East – Southeast Asia.' Compiled by Int'l Coop. Admin., Washington, DC and Catholic Press, Beirut.

Anderson, D.M. 1984. 'Depression, Dust Bowl, demography and drought: The colonial state and soil conservation in East Africa in the 1930s.' *African Affairs* **83**: 321–43.

——1988. 'Cultivating pastoralists: Ecology & economy of the Il Chamus of Baringo, 1840–1980.' In D. Johnson & D.M. Anderson (eds) *The Ecology of Survival. Case Studies from Northeast African History.* Westview Press, Boulder, CO.

——& Broch-Due, V. (eds) 1999. *The Poor are Not Us. Poverty & Pastoralism in Eastern Africa.* James Currey, Oxford and Ohio University Press, Athens, OH.

——& Grove, R. 1987. 'Introduction: The scramble for Eden: past present and future in African conservation.' In D. Anderson and R. Grove (eds) *Conservation in Africa. People, Policies and Practice.* Cambridge University Press, Cambridge.

——& Johnson, D.H. 1988. 'Introduction: Ecology and society in northeast African history.' In D. Johnson & D.M. Anderson (eds) *The Ecology of Survival. Case Studies from Northeast African History.* Westview Press, Boulder, CO.

Anderson, G.D. 1967. 'A reconnaissance survey of the land use potential of Mkomazi Game Reserve and an appraisal of factors affecting present and potential land use and productivity in its environs.' Unpublished report to the Ministry of Agriculture and Co-operatives.

Anon. 1865. 'Notes on a journey to Kilima-ndjaro, made in the company of the Baron Von der Decken. By the late Richard Thornton, Geologist to the Expedition; compiled from the journals of the author.' *Journal of the Royal Geographical Society* **35**: 15–21.

Anstey, D. 1958. 'Mkomazi Game Reserve.' *Tanganyika Notes & Records* **50**: 68–70.

Arhem, K. 1986. 'Pastoralism under pressure: The Ngorongoro Maasai.' In J. Boesen, K. Havnevik, J. Koponen, and R. Odgaard (eds) *Tanzania: Crisis and Struggle for Survival.* Africana Publishing Company, New York.

Baker, P.R. 1967. 'Environmental influences on cattle marketing in Karamoja.' Occasional Paper no. 5. Department of Geography, Makerere University College, Kampala.

Barret, C.S. & Arcese, P. 1995. 'Are Integrated Conservation-Development Projects (ICDPs) sustainable? On the conservation of large mammals in Sub-Saharan Africa.' *World Development* **23**: 1073–84.

Barry Turner, J. 1967 'Annual progress report.' Unpublished report to Canadian University Students Overseas.

Baumann, O. 1890. *In Deutsch-Ostafrika. Während des Aufstandes. Resie der Dr Hans Meyer'schen Expedition in Usambara.* Eduard Hölzel, Olmütz.

——1891. *Usambara und seine Nachbargebiete.* Dietrich Reimer, Berlin. Page numbers refer to a manuscript copy of a translation made by M.A. Godfredsen.

Baxter, P.T.W. & Hogg, R. (eds) 1990. *Property, Poverty & People: Changing Rights in Property & Problems of Pastoral Development.* Manchester University Press, Manchester.

Bayart, J-F. 1993. *The State in Africa. The Politics of the Belly.* Longman, Harlow.

Behnke, R.H. 1985. 'Measuring the benefits of subsistence versus commercial livestock production in Africa.' *Agricultural Systems* **162**: 109–35.

——& Scoones, I. 1993. 'Rethinking range ecology: Implications for rangeland management in Africa.' In R.H. Behnke, I. Scoones and

C. Kerven (eds) *Range Ecology at Disequilibrium. New models of Natural Variability and Pastoral Adaptation in African Savannas.* Overseas Development Institute, London.

——, Scoones, I. & Kerven, C. 1993. *Range Ecology at Disequilibrium. New Models of Natural Variability and Pastoral Adaptation in African Savannas.* Overseas Development Institute, London.

Beidelman, T.O. 1960. 'The Baraguyu.' *Tanganyika Notes & Records* **54**: 245–78.

Beinart, W. 1989. 'Introduction: The politics of colonial conservation.' *Journal of Southern African Studies* **15**: 143–62.

Bekure, S., de Leeuw, P.N., Grandin, B.E. & Neate, P.J.H. 1991. *Maasai Herding. An Analysis of the Livestock Production System of Maasai Pastoralists in Eastern Kajiado District, Kenya.'* ILCA, Nairobi.

Bell, R.H.V. 1987. 'Conservation with a human face: Conflict and reconciliation in African land use planning.' In D.M. Anderson & R. Grove (eds) *Conservation in Africa. People, Policies and Practice.* Cambridge University Press, Cambridge.

Belsky, A.J. 1987. 'Revegetation of natural and human caused disturbances in the Serengeti National Park, Tanzania.' *Vegetatio* **70**: 51–9.

Berkes, F. 1989. *Common Property Resources. Ecology and Community-Based Sustainable Development.* Belhaven Press, London.

Berntsen, J. 1976. 'The Maasai and their neighbours: Variables of interaction.' *African Economic History* **2**: 1–11.

——1979a. 'Economic variations among Maa-speaking peoples.' In B.A. Ogot (ed.) *Ecology and History in East Africa.* Kenya Literature Bureau: Nairobi. *Hadith* 7.

——1979b. 'Pastoralism, raiding and prophets: Maasailand in the nineteenth century.' Unpublished Ph.D. thesis. University of Wisconsin.

——1980. 'The enemy is us: Eponymy in the historiography of the Maasai'. *History in Africa* **7**: 1–21.

Blaikie, P. & Jeanrenaud, X. 1997. 'Biodiversity and human welfare.' In K.B. Ghimire & M.P. Pimbert (eds) *Social Change and Conservation. Environmental Politics and Impacts of National Parks and Protected Areas.* Earthscan, London.

Bollig, M. & Göbel, B. 1997. 'Risk, uncertainty and pastoralism: An introduction.' *Nomadic Peoples* **NS1**: 5–21.

Bonfiglioli, A.M. 1992. 'Pastoralists at a crossroads. Survival and development issues in African pastoralism.' UNICEF/UNSO Project for Nomadic Pastoralists in Africa.

Bonner, R. 1993. *At the Hand of Man. Peril and Hope for Africa's Wildlife.* Butler & Tanner, Frome.

Bonté, P. & Galaty, J.G. 1991. 'Introduction.' In J.G. Galaty & P. Bonté (eds) *Herders, Warriors and Traders. Pastoralism in Africa.* Westview Press, Boulder, CO.

Braithwaite, R. 1996. 'Biodiversity and fire in the savanna landscape'. In O. Solbrig, E. Medina & J. Silva (eds) *Biodiversity and Savanna Ecosystem Processes. Ecological Studies* vol **121**: 121–42.

Bravman, B. 1998. *Making Ethnic Ways. Communities and their Transformations in Taita, Kenya, 1800–1950.* Heinemann, Portsmouth, NH & James Currey, Oxford.

Broch-Due, V. 1990. '"Livestock speak louder than sweet words": Changing property rights and gender relations among the Turkana.' In P.T.W. Baxter and R. Hogg (eds) *Property, Poverty and People: Changing Rights in Property and Problems of Pastoral Development.* University of Manchester Press, Manchester.

Brockington, D. 1998. 'Land loss and livelihoods. The effects of eviction on pastoralists moved from the Mkomazi Game Reserve, Tanzania.' Unpublished Ph.D. thesis, University College London.

——1999. 'Conservation displacement and livelihoods. The consequences of the eviction for pastoralists moved from the Mkomazi Game Reserve, Tanzania.' *Nomadic Peoples* (NS) **3**: 74–96.

——2000. 'Pastoralism on the margins. The decline and dispersal of herding on the Umba Nyika from 1800 to 1919.' *Azania.* **35**: 1–19.

——2001a. 'Communal property and degradation narratives. Debating the Sukuma immigration into Rukwa region, Tanzania' *Cahiers d'Afrique.* **20**: 1–22.

——2001b. 'Women's income and livelihood strategies of dispossessed pastoralists. The case of Mkomazi Game Reserve' *Human Ecology.* **29**: 307–38.

——& Homewood, K.M. 1996. 'Received wisdom, science, & pastoralists: debates concerning Mkomazi Game Reserve, Tanzania.' In M. Leach and R. Mearns (eds) *The Lie of the Land.* James Currey, Oxford and Heinemann, Portsmouth, NH, for the International African Institute.

——& Homewood, K.M. 1999. 'Pastoralism around Mkomazi: The interaction of conservation and development.' In M. Coe, N. McWilliam, G. Stone and M. Packer (eds) *Mkomazi: The Ecology, Biodiversity and Conservation of a Tanzanian Savanna.* Royal Geographical Society (with the Institute of British Geographers), London.

——& Homewood, K.M. 2001. 'Degradation debates and data deficiencies. The case of the Mkomazi Game Reserve, Tanzania.' *Africa* **71**: 449–80.

Bromley, D.W. & Cernea, M.M. 1989. *The Management of Common Property Resources. Some conceptual and operational fallacies.* World Bank Discussion Papers **57**. The World Bank, Washington, DC.

Brookfield, H. & Stocking, M. 1999. 'Agrodiversity: definition, description and design.' *Global Environmental Change* **9**: 77–80.

Brosius, J.P., Tsing, A.L. & Zerner, C. 1998. 'Representing communities: Histories and politics of community-based natural resources management.' *Society and Natural Resources* **11**: 157–68.

Brown, K. 1998. 'The political ecology of biodiversity, conservation and development in Nepal's Terai: Confused meanings, means and ends.' *Ecological Economics* **24**: 73–87.

Bryceson, D.F. 1999. 'African rural labour, income diversification and livelihood approaches: A long term development perspective.' *Review of African Political Economy* **80**: 171–89.

——& Jamal, V. 1997. *Farewell to Farms. De-agrarianisation and Employment in Africa.* Ashgate, Aldershot.

Buhl, S. & Homewood, K. 2000. Milk selling among Fulani women in northern Burkina Faso.' In D. Hodgson (ed.) *Rethinking Pastoralism in Africa: Gender, Culture and the Myth of the Patriarchal Pastoralist.* James Currey, Oxford and Ohio University Press, Athens, OH.

Campbell, D. 1993. 'Land as ours, land as mine: economic, political and ecological marginalisation in Kajiado District.' In T. Spear and R. Waller (eds) *Being Maasai. Ethnicity and Identity in East Africa.* James Currey, London.

Canney, S. 2001. 'Satellite mapping of vegetation change: human impact in an East African semi-arid Savanna.' Unpublished D.phil thesis, University of Oxford.

Chabal, P. & Daloz, J-P. 1999. *Africa Works. Disorder as Political Instrument.* James Currey, Oxford and Indiana University Press and Indianapolis Bloomington, IN, for the International African Institute.

Charnley, S. 1994. 'Cattle, commons and culture: The political ecology of environmental change on a Tanzanian rangeland.' Unpublished Ph.D. dissertation, Stanford University.

Chidzero, B.T.G. 1961. *Tanganyika and International Trusteeship.* Oxford University Press, Oxford.

Child, B. 1996. 'The practice and principles of community-based wildlife management in Zimbabwe: The CAMPFIRE programme.' *Biodiversity and Conservation* **5**: 369–98.

Child, G. 1996. 'The role of community-based wild resource management in Zimbabwe.' *Biodiversity and Conservation* **5**: 355–67.

CHL 1996. 'United Republic of Tanzania, integrated tourism master plan 2nd Tourism Planning Workshop.' CHL Consulting Group, Dublin.

Clements, F.E. 1916. 'Plant succession: An analysis of the development of vegetation.' *Carnegie Institute Publications* **242**: 1–512.

Cobb, S. 1980. 'Tsavo. The first thirty years.' *Swara* **3**: 12–17.

Coe, M. 1990. 'The conservation and management of semi-arid rangelands and their animal resources.' In A.S. Goudie (ed.) *Techniques for Desert Reclamation.* John Wiley, Chichester.

——1995. 'A preliminary report on the field research of the Mkomazi Research Programme'. *Mkomazi Research Programme: Progress report, July 1995.* Royal Geographical Society, London.

——1999. 'Introduction.' In M. Coe, N. McWilliam, G. Stone and M. Packer (eds) *Mkomazi: The Ecology, Biodiversity and Conservation of a*

Tanzanian Savanna. Royal Geographical Society (with the Institute of British Geographers), London.

——& Collins, N.M. (eds) 1986. *Kora: An Ecological Inventory of the Kora National Reserve, Kenya.* National Museums of Kenya/Royal Geographical Society, London.

——& McWilliam, N., Stone, G. & Packer, M. (eds) 1999. *Mkomazi: The Ecology, Biodiversity and Conservation of a Tanzanian Savanna.* Royal Geographical Society (with the Institute of British Geographers), London.

——, Vollesen, K., Abdallah, R. and Mboya, E.I. 1999. 'The Flora of Mkomazi and its regional context.' In M. Coe, N. McWilliam, G. Stone and M. Packer (eds) *Mkomazi: The Ecology, Biodiversity and Conservation of a Tanzanian Savanna.* Royal Geographical Society (with the Institute of British Geographers), London.

——& Ndolanga, M.A. 1994. 'Scientific report for Mkomazi Ecological Research Programme 1994–6.' *Mkomazi Ecological Research Programme.* Royal Geographical Society, London.

Cohen, A.P. 1993. 'Segmentary knowledge: a Whalsay sketch.' In M. Hobart (ed.) *An Anthropological Critique of Development. The Growth of Ignorance.* Routledge, London.

Colchester, M. 1998. 'Who will garrison the fortress? A reply to Spinage.' *Oryx* **32**: 245–48.

Collett, D. 1987. 'Pastoralists and wildlife: image and reality in Kenya Maasailand.' In D. Anderson and R. Grove (eds) *Conservation in Africa. People, Policies and Practice.* Cambridge University Press, Cambridge.

Conte, C. 1996. 'Nature reorganised. Ecological history in the plateau forests of the West Usambara Mountains, 1850–1935.' In G. Maddox, J.L. Giblin and I.N. Kimambo (eds) *Custodians of the Land. Ecology and Culture in the History of Tanzania.* James Currey, London.

Dahl, G. 1979. *Suffering Grass. Subsistence and Society of Waso Borana.* Stockholm Studies in Anthropology. Department of Social Anthropology, University of Stockholm.

——& Hjort, A. 1976. *Having Herds. Pastoral Herd Growth and Household Economy.* Studies in Social Anthropology. Department of Social Anthropology, University of Stockholm.

Davies, S. 1996. *Adaptable Livelihoods: Coping with Food Insecurity in the Malian Sahel.* Wiley, Chichester.

Davis, S.D., Heywood, V. & Hamilton, A. 1994 *Centres of Plant Diversity. A Guide and Strategy for their Conservation.* Volume 1: *Europe and Africa.* IUCN, Cambridge.

De Leeuw, P.N. & Wilson, R.T. 1987. 'Comparative productivity of indigenous cattle under traditional management in sub-Saharan Africa.' *Quarterly Journal of International Agriculture* **26**: 377–90.

De Souza, M. & de Leeuw, P.N. 1984. 'Smallstock use of reserved grazing areas on Merushi Group Ranch.' Proceedings, CSRP Workshop on Small Ruminants, Nairobi.

Deihl, C. 1985. 'Wildlife and the Maasai. The Story of East African Parks.' *Cultural Survival Quarterly* **9**: 37–40.

Dietz, T. 1987. *Pastoralists in Dire Straits. Survival Strategies and External Interventions in a Semi-Arid Region at the Kenya/Uganda Border: Western Pokot, 1900–1986.* Nederlandse Geografische Studies **49**. Instituut voor Sociale Geografie, Universiteit van Amsterdam.

——1993. 'The state, the market, and the decline of pastoralism: Challenging some myths, with evidence from Western Pokot in Kenya/Uganda.' In J. Markakis (ed.) *Conflict and the Decline of Pastoralism in the Horn of Africa.* Macmillan Press, Basingstoke.

——1997. *Entitlements to Natural Resources: Contours of Political Environmental Geography.* International Books: Utrecht.

Dorobo Tours & Safaris Ltd & Olivers Camp. 1994. 'Potential models for community-based conservation among pastoral communities adjacent to protected areas in northern Tanzania.' In N. Leader Williams, J.A. Kayera, & G.L. Overton (eds). *Community Based Conservations in Tanzania.* Planning and Assessment for Wildlife Management, Department of Wildlife, Dar es Salaam.

Dublin, H. 1995 'Vegetation dynamics in the Serengeti–Mara ecosystem: The role of elephants, fire and other factors.' In A. Sinclair & P. Arcese (eds) *Serengeti II: Dynamics, Management and Conservation of an Ecosystem.* Chicago University Press, Chicago, IL.

Duffy, R. 2000. *Killing for Conservation. Wildlife policy in Zimbabwe.* James Currey, Oxford and Indiana University Press, Bloomington, IN, for the International African Institute.

Dyson-Hudson, N. 1980. 'Strategies of resource exploitation among East African savanna pastoralists.' In D.R. Harris (ed.) *Human Ecology in Savanna Environments.* Academic Press, London.

——& Dyson-Hudson, N. 1969. 'Subsistence herding in Uganda.' *Scientific American* **220**: 76–89.

Ekemode, G.O. 1973. 'German rule in north-east Tanzania, 1885–1914.' Unpublished Ph.D. thesis, SOAS, University of London.

Ellis, J.E. and Swift, D.M. 1988. 'Stability of African pastoral systems: Alternate paradigms and implications for development.' *Journal of Range Management* **41**: 450–59.

——, Coughenour, M.B. & Swift, D.M. 1993. 'Climate variability, ecosystem stability and the implications for range and live-stock development.' In R.H. Behnke, I. Scoones and C. Kerven (eds) *Range Ecology at Disequilibrium. New Models of Natural Variability and Pastoral Adaptation in African Savannas.* Overseas Development Institute, London.

Eltringham, S.K. 1984. *Wildlife Resources and Economic Development.* John Wiley, New York.

——1994. 'Can wildlife pay its way?' *Oryx* **28**: 163–8.

——1997. Letter to the editor. *Tanzanian Affairs* **58**: 30.

Emerton, L. 1999a. 'Balancing the opportunity costs of wildlife conservation for communities around Lake Mburo National Park, Uganda.' *Evaluating Eden Series*, Discussion Paper **5**. IIED, London.

——1999b. 'Mount Kenya: The economics of community conservation.' *Evaluating Eden Series*, Discussion Paper **4**. IIED, London.

——2001. 'The nature of benefits and the benefits of nature. Why wildlife conservation has not economically benefitted communities in Africa.' In D. Hulme & M. Murphree (eds) *African Wildlife & Livelihoods. The Promise & Performance of Community Conservation.* James Currey, Oxford and Heinemann, Portsmouth, NH.

——& Mfunda, I. 1999. 'Making wildlife economically viable for communities living around the Western Serengeti, Tanzania.' *Evaluating Eden Series,* Discussion Paper **1**. IIED, London.

Enghoff, M. 1990. 'Wildlife conservation, ecological strategies and pastoral communities. A contribution to the understanding of parks and people in East Africa.' *Nomadic Peoples* **25–7**: 93–107.

Ensminger, J. 1992. *Making a Market. The Institutional Transformation of an African Society.* Cambridge University Press, Cambridge.

Evangelou, P. 1984. *Livestock Development in Kenya's Maasailand. Pastoralist Transition to a Market Economy.* Westview Press, Boulder, CO.

Fairhead, J. & Leach, M. 1996. 'Enriching the landscape: Social history and the management of transition ecology in the forest–savanna mosaic of the Republic of Guinea.' *Africa* **66**: 14–36.

——1996. *Misreading the African Landscape: Society and Ecology in a Forest–Savanna Mosaic.* Cambridge University Press, Cambridge.

Farler, J.P. 1882. 'Native routes in East Africa from Pangani to the Masai country and the Victoria Nyaza.' *Proceedings of the Royal Geographical Society* NS **4**: 730–53.

Feierman, S. 1974. *The Shambaa Kingdom. A History.* University of Wisconsin Press, Madison, WI.

Fendall, C.P. 1921. *The East African Force 1915–1919. An Unofficial Record of its Creation and Fighting Career; Together with some Account of the Civil and Military Administrative Conditions in East Africa before and during that Period.* H.F. and G. Witherby, London.

Ferguson, J. 1990. *The Anti-politics Machine. 'Development', Depoliticization, and Bureaucratic Power in Lesotho.* University of Minnesota Press, Minneapolis, MN.

Fisher, W.F. 1997. 'Doing good? The politics and anti-politics of NGO practices.' *Annual Review of Anthropology* **26**: 439–64.

Fitzjohn, T. 1993. 'The Mkomazi Project. Field Director's Report.' In unpublished document, 'The Mkomazi Project. Field Director and Trustee's Report of the Friends of Mkomazi Visit, October 1993'. Produced by GAWPT, UK.

Fleisher, M.L. 1997. 'Kuria cattle raiding: a case study in the capitalist transformation of an East African sociocultural institution.' Unpublished Ph.D. thesis, Michigan University.

Fosbrooke, H.A. 1948. 'An administrative survey of the Masai social system.' *Tanganyika Notes & Records* **26**: 1–50.

——1992. 'Eviction of pastoralists from Mkomazi Game Reserve.' Interim Report to IIED, London.

Fratkin, E. 1991. *Surviving Drought and Development: Ariaal Pastoralists of Northern Kenya*. Westview Press, Boulder, CO.

——1997. 'Pastoralism: Governance and development issues.' *Annual Review of Anthropology* **26**: 235–61.

——& Roth, E.A. 1990. 'Drought and differentiation among Ariaal pastoralists of Kenya.' *Human Ecology* **18**: 385–401.

——, Nathan, M.A. & Roth, E.A. 1999. 'Health consequences of pastoral sedentarization among Rendille of Northern Kenya.' In D.M. Anderson & V. Broch-Due (eds) *The Poor are Not Us. Poverty & Pastoralism in Eastern Africa*. James Currey, Oxford and Ohio University Press, Athens, OH.

——& Smith, K. 1995. 'Women's changing economic roles with pastoral sedentarisation: Varying strategies in alternate Rendille communities.' *Human Ecology* **23**: 433–454.

Friedman, M. 1962. *Capitalism and Freedom*. University of Chicago Press, Chicago, IL.

Frontera, A.E. 1978. *Persistence and Change: A History of Taveta*. Crossroads Press, Waltham.

Fujimura, J.F. 1992. 'Crafting science: Standardized packages, boundary objects, and "translation".' In A. Pickering (ed.) *Science as Practice and Culture*. University of Chicago Press, Chicago, IL.

Galaty, J.G. 1980. 'The Maasai Group-Ranch: politics and development in an African pastoral society.' In P. Salzman (ed.) *When Nomads Settle. Processes of Sedentarisation as Adaption and Response*. Praeger, New York.

——1982. 'Being "Maasai"; being "people-of-cattle": Ethnic shifters in East Africa.' *American Ethnologist* **9**: 1–20.

——1991. 'Pastoral orbits and deadly jousts: Factors in the Maasai expansion.' In J.G. Galaty and P. Bonté (eds) *Herders, Warriors and Traders. Pastoralism in Africa*. Westview Press, Boulder, CO.

——1993. 'Maasai expansion and the new East African pastoralism.' In T. Spear and R. Waller (eds) *Being Maasai*. James Currey, London.

——& Bonté, P. 1991. 'The current realities of African pastoralists.' In J.G. Galaty and P. Bonté (eds) *Herders, Warriors and Traders. Pastoralism in Africa*. Westview Press, Boulder, CO.

——& Munei, K.O. 1999. 'Maasai land, law and dispossession.' *Cultural Survival Quarterly* **22**: 68–71.

——, Hjort af Ornas, A., Lane, C. & Ndagala, D. 1994. 'Introduction.' *Nomadic Peoples* **34–5**: 7–21.

Ghimire, K.B. & Pimbert, M.P. 1997. 'Social change and conservation: An overview of issues and concepts.' In K.B. Ghimire & M.P. Pimbert (eds) *Social Change and Conservation. Environmental Politics and Impacts of National Parks and Protected Areas.* Earthscan, London.

Giblin, J.L. 1990a. 'Trypanomiasis control in African history: An evaded issue?'*Journal of African History* **32**: 59–80.

——1990b. 'East Coast Fever in socio-historical context: a case study from Tanzania.' *International Journal of African Historical Studies* **23**: 401–21.

——1992. *The Politics of Environmental Control in Northeastern Tanzania, 1840–1940.* University of Pennsylvania Press, Philadelphia.

Gibson, C.C. 1999. *Politicians and Poachers. The Political Economy of Wildlife Policy in Africa.* Cambridge University Press, Cambridge.

——& Marks, S.A. 1995. 'Transforming rural hunters into conservationists: An assessment of community-based wildlife management programmes in Africa.' *World Development* **23**: 941–57.

Gillett, J. 1983. 'The vascular plants of the Kora Research Area in East Central Africa.' Cited in M. Coe (ed.) *The Flora and Fauna of the Kora National Reserve*, Nat. Mus. Kenya & Royal Geographical Society, London. mimeo.

Godwin, J. 1995. 'Tanzania embraces fugitive hunter.' *Express*, March 26–29.

Graham, A. 1973. *The Gardeners of Eden.* Allen & Unwin, Hemel Hempstead.

Graham, O. 1989. 'A land divided: The impact of ranching on a pastoral society.' *The Ecologist* **19**: 184–5.

Grainger, A. 1999. 'Constraints on modelling the deforestation and degradation of open woodlands.' *Global Ecology and Biogeography Letters* **8**: 179–90.

Grandin, B.E. 1988. 'Wealth and pastoral dairy production: A case study from Maasailand.' *Human Ecology* **16**: 1–21.

——, de Leeuw, P.N. & Lembuya, P. 1989. 'Drought, resource distribution, and mobility in two Maasai Group Ranches, southeastern Kajiado District.' In T.E. Downing, W.W. Gitu, W. Kangethe and C.M. Kamau (eds) *Coping with Drought in Kenya: National and Local Strategies.* Lynne Rienner, Boulder, CO.

Gray, A. 1996. 'Indigenous resistance to involuntary relocation.' In C. McDowell (ed.) *Understanding Impoverishment. The Consequences of Development-induced Displacement.* Berghan Books, Oxford.

Greenway, P.J. 1969. 'A check list of plants recorded in Tsavo National Park East.' *J.E. Afr. Nat. Hist Soc. and Nat. Mus.* **27(3)**: 162–209.

Guillain, M. [n.d.]. *Documents sur l'histoire, la géographie at le commerce de l'Afrique Orientale. Relation du voyage d'exploration à la*

côte orientale d'Afrique exécuté pendant les années 1846, 1847 et 1848.
Bouchard-Huzard, Paris.

Gulliver, P. 1961. 'Land shortage, social change and social conflict in East Africa.' *Journal of Conflict Resolution* 5: 16–26.

Guyer, J.I. 1986. 'Intra-household processes and farming systems research: Perspectives from anthropology.' In J.L. Moock (ed.) *Understanding Africa's Rural Households and Farming Systems.* Westview Press, Boulder, CO.

——& Richards, P. 1996. 'The invention of biodiversity: Social perspectives on the management of biological variety in Africa.' *Africa* **66**: 1–13.

Hackel, J.D. 1999. 'Community conservation and the future of Africa's wildlife.' *Conservation Biology* 13: 726–34.

Håkansson, N.T. 1995. 'Irrigation, population pressure, and exchange in precolonial Pare, Tanzania.' *Research in Economic Anthropology* **16**: 292–323.

Hardin, G. 1968. 'The tragedy of the commons.' *Science* **162**: 1243–8.

Harpers Bazaar. April 1993. 'Going wild. On safari in Tanzania.'

Harris, D.R. (ed.) 1980. *Human Ecology in Savanna Environments.* Academic Press, London.

Harris, L.D. 1970. 'Some structural and functional attributes of a semi-arid East African ecosystem.' Unpublished Ph.D. thesis. Colorado State University.

Hartley, D. 1997. 'Community wildlife management: A review of the ODA's experience in Tanzania.' Unpublished report to the Overseas Development Administration, London.

Hartley, J. 1986 *A Guide to Lakes Baringo and Bogoria.* Evans Bros, Nairobi.

Havenik, K.J. 1993. *Tanzania. The Limits to Development from Above.* Motala Grafiska AB, Motala.

Hay, M.J. 1976. 'Luo women and economic change during the colonial period.' In N.J. Hafkin and E.G. Bay (eds) *Women in Africa. Studies in Social and Economic Change.* Stanford University Press, Stanford, CA.

Hemmingway, P., Cormack, A. & Robinette, L. 1966. 'Appraisal of range condition on the Kalimawe Controlled Area.' Tanga Regional Archives, File TA4, Box 12 G1.

Herskovits, M.J. 1926. 'The cattle complex in East Africa.' *American Anthropologist* **28**: 230–72; 361–80; 494–528; 633–64.

Hingston, R.W.G. 1931. 'Proposed British national parks for Africa.' *The Geographical Journal* 77: 401–28.

Hobart, M. 1996. 'Ethnography as practice, or the unimportance of penguins.' *Europœa* **11**: 3–36.

Hodgson, D. 1995. 'The politics of gender, ethnicity and "development". Images, intervention and the reconfiguration of Maasai identities in Tanzania, 1916–1993. Unpublished Ph.D. thesis. University of Michigan.

———2000. 'Taking stock: State control, ethnic identity and pastoralist development in Tanganyika, 1948–58.' *Journal of African History* **41**: 55–78.

Hoffman, M., Bond, W.J. and Stock, W.D. 1995. 'Desertification of the eastern Karoo, South Africa: Conflicting paleoecological, historical and soil isotopic evidence.' *Environmental Monitoring and Assessment* **37(1-3)**: 159–77.

Hogg, R. 1980. 'Pastoralism and impoverishment: The case of the Isiolo Boran of northern Kenya.' *Disasters* **4**: 299–310.

———1986. 'The new pastoralism: poverty and dependency in northern Kenya.' *Africa* **56**: 319–33.

———1992. 'Should pastoralism continue as a way of life?' *Disasters* **16**: 131–6.

Homewood, K.M. 1992. 'Development and the ecology of Maasai pastoralist food and nutrition.' *Ecology of Food and Nutrition* **29**: 61–80.

———1994. 'Pastoralists, environment and development in East African Rangelands.' In B. Zaba and J. Clarke (eds) *Environment and Population Change*. Ordina Editions, Liège.

———1995. 'Development, demarcation and ecological outcomes in Maasailand.' *Africa* **65**: 331–50.

———& Brockington, D. 1999. 'Biodiversity, conservation and development.' Paper accepted by *Global Ecology and Biogeography Letters*.

———& Lewis, J. 1987. 'Impact of drought on pastoral livestock in Baringo, Kenya, 1983–85.' *Journal of Applied Ecology* **24**: 615–31.

———& Rodgers, W.A. 1991. *Maasailand Ecology. Pastoralist Development and Wildlife Conservation in Ngorongoro, Tanzania*. Cambridge University Press, Cambridge.

———, Kiwasila, H. & Brockington, D. 1997. 'Conservation with development? The case of Mkomazi, Tanzania.' Report submitted to the Department for International Development, London.

———, Lambin, E.F., Coast T., Kariuki, A., Kikula, I., Kivelia, J., Said, M., Serneels, S. & Thompson, M., (forthcoming) 'Long term changes in African savanna wildlife and land cover: Pastoralists, population or policies?'. Paper submitted to *Proc. Nat. Acad. Sci.*

———, Rodgers, W.A. & Arhem, K. 1987. 'Ecology of pastoralism in the Ngorongoro Conservation Area, Tanzania.' *Journal of Agricultural Science*. **108**: 47–72.

Horowitz, M., & Little, P. 1987. 'African pastoralism and poverty: Some implications for drought and famine.' In M. Glantz (ed.) *Drought and Hunger in Africa*. Cambridge University Press, Cambridge.

House-Midamba, B. 1995. 'Kikuyu market women traders and the struggle for economic empowerment in Kenya.' In B. House-Midamba and F.K. Ekechi (eds) *African Market Women and Economic Power. The Role of Women in African Economic Development*. Greenwood Press, Westport, CT.

Howard, P.C., Viskanic, P., Davenport, T.R.B., Kigenyi, F., Baltzer, M., Dickinson, C.J., Lwanga, J., Matthews, R.A. & Balmford, A. 1998. 'Complementarity and the use of indicator groups for reserve selection in Uganda.' *Nature* **394**: 472–5.

Huish, S.A., Ole, Kuwai J. & Campbell, K.L.I. 1993. *Wildlife Census Mkomazi 1991.* Tanzania Wildlife Conservation Monitoring, Arusha.

Hulme, D. & Murphree, M. 1999. 'Communities, wildlife and the new conservation in Africa.' *Journal of International Development* **11**: 277–85.

——& Murphree, M. 2001a. *African Wildlife & Livelihoods. The Promise & Performance of Community Conservation.* James Currey, Oxford and Heinemann, Portsmouth, NH.

——& Murphree, M. 2001b. 'Community conservation in Africa. An introduction.' In D. Hulme & M. Murphree (eds) *African Wildlife & Livelihoods. The Promise & Performance of Community Conservation.* James Currey, Oxford and Heinemann, Portsmouth, NH.

——& Murphree, M. 2001c. 'Community conservation as policy. Promise & performance.' In D. Hulme and M. Murphree (eds) *African Wildlife & Livelihoods. The Promise & Performance of Community Conservation.* James Currey, Oxford and Heinemann, Portsmouth, NH.

Hurskainen, A. 1984. *Cattle and Culture: The Structure of a Pastoral Parakuyo Society.* The Finnish Oriental Society, Helsinki.

Huston, M.A. 1994. *Biological Diversity: The Coexistence of Species on Changing Landscapes.* Cambridge University Press, Cambridge.

Huxley, E. 1935. *White Man's Country. Lord Delamere and the Making of Kenya. Volume One 1870–1914.* Chatto & Windus, London.

Ibeun, J.S. 1976. 'A management plan proposal for Mkomazi Game Reserve.' Thesis submitted for Diploma in Wildlife Management, College of African Wildlife Management, Mweka.

Igoe, J. 2000. 'Ethnicity, civil society, and the Tanzanian pastoral NGO movement: The continuities and discontinuities of liberalized development.' Unpublished Ph.D. thesis, Boston University, Department of Anthropology.

——forthcoming a. 'Scaling up civil society: Donor money, NGOs, and Tanzania's pastoral land tenure movement.'

——forthcoming b. 'Ecology, ethnicity, and globalization: A theoretically eclectic analysis of community conservation and NGOs in Tanzania.'

——forthcoming c. 'Becoming indigenous people: NGOs and globalization of identity politics in two East African herding societies.'

——& Brockington, D. 1999. 'Pastoral land tenure and community conservation in East African rangelands: A case study from northeastern Tanzania.' *Pastoral Land Tenure Series* **11**. IIED, London.

IIED 1994 *Whose Eden? An Overview of Community Approaches to Wildlife Management.* International Institute for Environment and Development, London.

ILCA 1981. 'Introduction to East African Range Livestock Systems Study/Kenya'. International Livestock Centre for Africa (ILCA/Kenya Working Document 23, Nairobi.

Iliffe, J. 1969. *Tanganyika under German Rule, 1905–1912*. Cambridge University Press, Cambridge.

——1979. *A Modern History of Tanganyika*. Cambridge University Press, Cambridge.

Illius, A. & O'Connor, T. 1999. 'On the relevance of non equilibrium concepts to arid and semi-arid grazing systems.' *Ecological Applications* **9**: 798–813.

Inamdar, A. 1995. 'Wildlife census, Mkomazi, April 1994. An interim report on results of an aerial census of the Mkomazi Game Reserve.' WWF Regional Office, Eastern Africa.

——1996. 'The ecological consequences of elephant depletion.' Unpublished Ph.D. thesis, University of Cambridge.

Jackman, B. 1999 'The lion man of Cockfosters.' *The Saturday Telegraph*, 18 April: 3.

Jacobs, A. 1965. 'The traditional political organisation of the pastoral Masai.' Unpublished D. Phil thesis, Oxford University.

Johnston, H.H. 1886. *The Kilima-ndjaro expedition*. Kegan & Trench, London.

Johnston, L. 1997. 'Barred from the animals' kingdom.' *The Observer*, 6 April.

Juma, I.H. & Mchome, S.E. 1994. 'Legal opinion. Forceful evictions of pastoralists from Mkomazi Game Reserve.' Unpublished document.

Kabuye, C.H.S., Mungai, G.M. & Mutangah, J.G. 1986. 'Flora of Kora National Reserve.' In M. Coe, & N.M. Collins, (eds) *Kora: An Ecological Inventory Study of the Kora National Reserve, Kenya*. Royal Geographical Society, London.

Kandeh, H.B.S. & Richards, P. 1996. 'Rural people as conservationists: Querying neo-Malthusian assumptions about biodiversity in Sierra Leone.' *Africa* **66**: 90–103.

Kangwana, K. 2001. 'Can Community Conservation strategies meet the conservation agenda?' In D. Hulme and M. Murphree (eds) *African Wildlife & Livelihoods. The Promise & Performance of Community Conservation*. James Currey, Oxford and Heinemann, Portsmouth, NH.

Kelsall, T. 1998. 'Donors, NGOs, and the State: The creation of a public sphere in Tanzania.' Paper presented at the ASA African Globalization Conference, University of Central Lancashire.

Kenyatta, J. 1953 (1938). *Facing Mount Kenya. The Tribal Life of the Kikuyu*. Secker & Warburg, London.

Kerven, C. 1992. *Customary Commerce: A Historical Reassessment of Pastoral Livestock Marketing in Africa*. ODI Agricultural Occasional Paper **15**. Overseas Development Institute, London.

Kilewe, A.M. & Thomas, D.B. 1992. *Land Degradation in Kenya: A Framework for Policy and Planning.* Commonwealth Secretariat, London.

Kimambo, I. 1969. *A Political History of the Pare of Tanzania, c. 1500–1900.* Heineman Educational Books & East African Publishing House, Nairobi.

——1991. *Penetration and Protest in Tanzania.* James Currey, London; Heinemann, Nairobi; Ohio University Press, Athens, OH.

——1996. 'Environmental control and hunger in the mountains and plains of northeastern Tanzania.' In G. Maddox, J. Giblin and I.N. Kimambo (eds) *Custodians of the Land. Ecology & Culture in the History of Tanzania.* James Currey, London.

Kipuri, N. & Nangoro, B. N. Ole 1996. 'Community benefits through wildlife resources.' Evaluation report for TANAPA's Community Conservation Service Programme.

Kiss, A. (ed.) 1990 *Living with Wildlife. Wildlife Resource Management with Local Participation in Africa.* World Bank Technical Paper **130** (Africa Technical Department Series). The World Bank, Washington, DC.

Kiwasila, H. 1997. 'Not just a Maasai Garden of Eden.' *The Observer,* letters. 13 April.

——& Homewood, K. 1999. 'Natural resource use by reserve-adjacent farming communities.' In M. Coe, N. McWilliam, G. Stone & M. Packer (eds) *Mkomazi: The Ecology, Biodiversity and Conservation of a Tanzanian Savanna.* Royal Geographical Society (with the Institute of British Geographers), London.

Kjaerby, F. 1979. *The Development of Agro-pastoralism Among the Barabaig in Hanang District.* Bureau of Resource Assessment and Land Use Planning Research Paper **56**, University of Dar es Salaam.

Kjekshus, H. 1996 [1977]. *Ecology Control & Economic Development in East African History.* James Currey, London.

Knight, M.H. & Morkel, P. 1994. 'Assessment of the proposed Mkomazi rhino sanctuary. Mkomazi Game Reserve, Tanzania.' Unpublished report to the IUCN African Rhino Specialist Group.

Knowles, J.N. & Collett, D.P. 1989. 'Nature as myth, symbol and action: Notes towards a historical understanding of development and conservation in Kenyan Maasailand.' *Africa* **59**: 433–60.

Koch, E. 1997. 'On the bicornis of a dilemma.' *Out There, Ecofile:* 107–9.

Koenig, O. 1954. *Pori Tupu.* Michael Joseph, London.

Korten, D. 1980. 'Community organisation and rural development: A learning process approach.' *Public Administration Review* **40**: 480–511.

Kramer, R., Schaik, C. von, & Johnson, J. 1997 *Last Stand. Protected Areas and the Defense of Tropical Biodiversity.* Oxford University Press, New York.

Krapf, J.L. 1854. *Vocabulary of the Engútuk Eloikõb*. Lu. Fried. Fues, Tübingen.

——1860. *Travels, Researches and Missionary Labours during Eighteen Years of Residence in Eastern Africa*. Trübner and Co., London.

Kruger, O. & McGavin, G. 1997. 'The insect fauna of Acacia species in Mkomazi Game Reserve, north east Tanzania.' *Ecological Entomology* **22**: 440–4.

Lack, P.C. 1999. 'Birds of Mkomazi.' In M. Coe, N. McWilliam, G. Stone & M. Packer (eds) *Mkomazi: The Ecology, Biodiversity and Conservation of a Tanzanian Savanna*. Royal Geographical Society (with the Institute of British Geographers), London.

Lal, D. 1995. 'Eco-fundamentalism.' *International Affairs* **71**: 515–28.

Lamprey, R. & Waller, R. 1990. 'The Loita-Mara Region in Historical Times: Patterns of subsistence, settlement and ecological change.' In P. Robertshaw (ed.) *Early Pastoralists of South-western Kenya*. Memoir 11. British Institute in Eastern Africa, Nairobi.

Lane, C. 1996 *Ngorongoro Voices. Indigenous Maasai Residents of the Ngorongoro Conservation Area in Tanzania Give their Views on the Proposed General Management Plan*. Forest Trees and People Programme, Lantbruks University, Sweden.

——& Moorehead, R. 1995. 'New directions in range land and resource tenure and policy.' In I. Scoones (ed.) *Living with Uncertainty. New Directions in Pastoral Development in Africa*. IT Publication, London.

Leach, M. & Mearns, R. (eds) 1996. *The Lie of the Land*. James Currey, Oxford and Heinemann, Portsmouth, NH, for the International African Institute.

Le Roy, A. [n.d.] *Au Kilima Ndjaro. Histoire de la formation d'une mission catholique en Afrique orientale*. Les éditions de l'oeuvre d'auteil, Paris.

Lemenye, J. 1955. 'The life of Justin: An African autobiography. Part 1.' *Tanganyika Notes & Records* **41**: 30–56.

Leuthold, W. 1977. 'Changes in tree population in Tsavo East National Park, Kenya.' *E. Afr. Wildl. J.* **15**: 61–9.

——1996. 'Recovery of woody vegetation in Tsavo National Park, Kenya 1970–1994.' *African Journal of Ecology* **34**: 101–12.

Liang, L., Stocking, M., Brookfield, H. & Jansky, L. 2001. 'Biodiversity conservation through agrodiversity.' *Global Environmental Change* **11**: 97–101.

Lindsay, W.K. 1987. 'Integrating parks and pastoralists: some lessons from Amboseli.' In D. Anderson and R. Grove (eds) *Conservation in Africa. People, Policies and Practice*. Cambridge University Press, Cambridge.

Little, P.D. 1985. 'Absentee herd owners and part time pastoralists. The political economy of resources use in Northern Kenya.' *Human Ecology* **13**: 131–51.

——1994 'The link between local participation and improved conservation: A review of issues and experiences.' In D. Western and R.M.

Wright (eds) *Natural Connections. Perspectives in Community-based Conservation.* Island Press, Washington, DC.

———1996. 'Pastoralism, biodiversity, and the shaping of savanna landscapes in East Africa.' *Africa* **66**: 37–51.

Lobulu, B. 1999. 'Dispossession and land tenure in Tanzania. What hope from the courts?' *Cultural Survival Quarterly* **22**: 64–7.

Lonsdale, J. 1992. 'The Conquest State of Kenya, 1895–1905.' In J. Lonsdale & B. Berman (eds) *Unhappy Valley. Conflict in Kenya and Africa. Book One: State and Class.* James Currey, London.

Luanda, N.N. 1986. 'European commercial farming and its impact on the Meru and Arusha peoples of Tanzania, 1920–55.' Unpublished Ph.D.thesis, University of Cambridge.

Mace, R. 1991. 'Overgrazing overstated.' *Nature* **349**: 280–1.

———& Houston, A. 1989. 'Pastoralist strategies for survival in unpredictable environments: A model of herd composition that maximises household viability.' *Agricultural Systems* **31**: 185–204.

Mackenzie, A.F.D. 1998. *Land Ecology and Resistance in Kenya, 1880–1952.* Edinburgh University Press for the International African Institute, London.

Mackenzie, J.M. 1988. *The Empire of Nature. Hunting, Conservation and British Imperialism.* Manchester University Press, Manchester.

Mackenzie, W. 1973a. 'Conflicts and obstacles in livestock development in Tanzania.' Economic Research Bureau Paper **73.1**. University of Dar es Salaam.

———1973b. 'The livestock economy of Tanzania.' Economic Research Bureau Paper **73.5**. University of Dar es Salaam.

———1977. 'The livestock economy of Tanzania. A study of the beef industry.' Economic Research Bureau Monograph Series **4**. University of Dar es Salaam.

Maddox, G.H. 1991. 'Famine, impoverishment and the creation of a labour reserve in Central Tanzania.' *Disasters* **15**: 35–42.

Maghimbi, S. 1994. 'The movement of peasant farmers from the mountains of the North Pare to the Plains.' Unpublished paper, Department of Sociology and Anthropology, University of Dar es Salaam.

Mangubuli, M. J. J. 1991. 'Mkomazi Game Reserve – A Recovered Pearl.' *Kakakuona* **4**: 11–13.

Marks, S.A. 1984. *The Imperial Lion: Human Dimensions of Wildlife Management in Central Africa.* Westview Press, Boulder, CO.

Marris, P. & Somerset, A. 1971. *African Businessmen. A Study of Entrepreneurship and Development in Kenya.* Routledge & Kegan Paul, London.

Martin, R.B. 1978. 'Project Windfall (Wildlife Industry's New Development for All [in the Sebungwe]).' Project Document submitted and approved by the Department of National Parks and Wildlife Management, Zimbabwe.

——1999. 'The rule of law and African game, and social change and conservation misrepresentation – a reply to Spinage.' *Oryx* **33**: 90–4.

Mbano, B. 1999. 'The status and future of Mkomazi Game Reserve.' In M. Coe, N. McWilliam, G. Stone and M. Packer (eds) *Mkomazi: The Ecology, Biodiversity and Conservation of a Tanzanian Savanna.* Royal Geographical Society (with the Institute of British Geographers), London.

McCabe, J.T. 1997. 'Risk and uncertainty among the Maasai of the Ngorongoro Conservation Area in Tanzania.' *Nomadic Peoples* **NS1**: 54–65.

——Perkin, S. & Sholfield, C. 1992. 'Can conservation and development be coupled among pastoral people? An examination of the Maasai of the Ngorongoro Conservation Area, Tanzania.' *Human Organisation* **51**: 353–66.

McCann, J.C. 1999. *Green Land, Brown Land, Black Land. An Environmental History of Africa.* Heinemann, Portsmouth, NH and James Currey, Oxford.

McWilliam, N. & Packer, M. 1999. 'Climate: variability and importance.' In M. Coe, N. McWilliam, G. Stone and M. Packer (eds) *Mkomazi: The Ecology, Biodiversity and Conservation of a Tanzanian Savanna.* Royal Geographical Society (with the Institute of British Geographers), London.

Mduma, S.R. 1988a. 'Mkomazi Game Reserve: Dangers and recommended measures for its survival, Part I.' *Miombo* **1**: 17–19.

——1988b. 'Mkomazi Game Reserve: Dangers and recommended measures for its survival, Part II.' *Miombo* **2**: 4–5.

Meadows, S.J. & White, J.M. 1979. 'Structure of the herd and determinants of the offtake rates in Kajiado District, Kenya.' ODI *Pastoral Development Network* **7d**. Overseas Development Institute, London.

Menaut, J. 1983. 'The vegetation of African savannas.' *Tropical Savannas: Ecosystems of the World* Vol. 13 (ed. by F. Bourlière) pp. 109–50. Elsevier, Amsterdam.

Meyer, H. 1891. *Across East African Glaciers. An Account of the First Ascent of Kilimanjaro.* Translated from the German by E.H.S. Calder. George Philip, London.

Miombo Editorial. 1960. 'What do we mean by community participation?' *Miombo Technical Supplement* No 1. **Sept. 1996**: 2.

Mishra, H.R. 1982. 'Balancing human needs and conservation in Nepal Royal Chitwan National Park.' *Ambio* **11**: 246–51.

MNRT 1997. *The Mkomazi/Umba Game Reserves General Management Plan, Draft.* Wildlife Division, Ministry of Natural Resources and Tourism, Dar es Salaam.

Monson, J. 1998. 'Relocating Maji-Maji: The politics of alliance and authority in the Southern Highlands of Tanzania, 1870–1918.' *Journal of African History* **39**: 95–120.

Moore, S.F. 1986. *Social Facts and Fabrications. 'Customary' Law on Kilimanjaro 1880–1890.* Cambridge University Press, Cambridge.

Mosse, D. 1997. 'The symbolic making of a common property resource: History, ecology and locality in a tank-irrigated landscape in South India.' *Development and Change* **28**: 467–504.

Murombedzi, J.C. 1999. 'Devolution and stewardship in Zimbabwe's CAMPFIRE programme.' *Journal of International Development* **11**: 287–93.

Murphree, M.W. 1996. 'Approaches to community participation.' In ODA-produced *African Wildlife Policy Consultation, Final Report.* Jay Printers, London.

——2001. 'Community-based conservation – the new myth?' Paper presented at the conference on 'African Wildlife Management in the New Millennium', College of African Wildlife Management, Mweka.

Mustaffa, K. 1997. *Eviction of Pastoralists from the Mkomazi Game Reserve in Tanzania: An Historical Review.* Pastoral Land Tenure Series **8**, International Institute for Environment and Development, London.

Mvula, B.M.S. 1978. 'Interaction between livestock and game animals in Mkomazi Game Reserve, Tanzania.' Thesis submitted for Diploma in Wildlife Management, College of African Wildlife Management, Mweka.

Neumann, R.P. 1991. 'The social origins of natural resource conflict in Arusha National Park, Tanzania.' Unpublished Ph.D. thesis, Department of Geography, University of California, Berkeley.

——1995a. 'Local challenges to global agendas: Conservation, economic liberalization and the pastoralists' rights movement in Tanzania.' *Antipode* **27**: 363–82.

——1995b. 'Ways of seeing Africa: Colonial recasting of African society and landscape in Serengeti National Park.' *Ecumene* **2**: 149–169.

——1997. 'Primitive ideas: Protected area buffer zones and the politics of land in Africa.' *Development and Change* **28**: 559–582.

——1998. *Imposing Wilderness. Struggles over Livelihood and Nature Preservation in Africa.* University of California Press, Berkeley.

New, C. 1873. *Life, Wanderings and Labours in Eastern Africa. With an Account of the First Successful Ascent of the Equatorial Snow Mountain, Kilima Njaro and Remarks upon East African Slavery.* Hodder & Stoughton, London.

Newland, R.N. 1908. 'Review of the cattle trade in British East Africa.' *The Agricultural Journal of British East Africa* **1**: 263–8.

Newmark, W.D. & Hough, J.L. 2000. 'Conserving wildlife in Africa: Integrated conservation and development projects and beyond.' *Bioscience* **50**: 584–92.

Norton-Griffiths, M. 1996. 'Property rights and the marginal wildebeest: An economic analysis of wildlife conservation options in Kenya.' *Biodiversity and Conservation* **5**: 1557–77.

Noss, A.J. 1997. 'Challenges to nature conservation with community development in central African forests.' *Oryx* **31**: 180–8.

Nyerges, A. 1996. 'Ethnography in the reconstruction of African land use histories: A Sierra Leone example.' *Africa* **66**: 122–44.

O'Riordan, T. 2000. 'Environmental Science on the move.' In T. O'Riordan (ed.) *Environmental Science for Environmental Management*. Prentice Hall, Harlow.

Oates, J.F. 1995. 'The dangers of conservation by rural development: A case study from the forests of Nigeria'. *Oryx* **29**: 115–22.

Ogot, B.A 1968. 'The role of the pastoralist and the agriculturalist in African History.' In T.O. Ranger (ed.) *Emerging Themes of African History. Proceedings of the International Congress of African Historians, Dar es Salaam October 1965*. East African Publishing House, Nairobi.

Oliver, P. 1994. 'Oliver's Camp and community conservation.' Paper presented to the Planning and Assessment for Wildlife Management (PAWM) unit workshop 'Tanzanian Community Conservation'. Dar es Salaam.

Oliver-Smith, A. 1996. 'Fighting for a place: The policy implications of resistance to development-indiced settlement.' In C. McDowell (ed.) *Understanding Impoverishment. The Consequences of Development-induced Displacement*. Berghahn Books, Oxford.

Olthof, W. 1995. 'Wildlife resources and local development: Experiences from Zimbabwe's CAMPFIRE Programme.' In J.P.M. Van den Breemer, C.A. Drijver & L.B. Venema (eds) *Local Resource Management in Africa*. John Wiley, Chichester.

Onesmo-Zacharia, M. 1990. 'Land use conflicts in semi-arid areas: An approach to sustainable management of wildlife resources. Mkomazi Game Reserve Case Study.' Unpublished M.Sc. thesis, Agricultural University of Norway.

Ostrom, E., Burger J., Field, C.B., Norgaard, R.B. & Policansky, D. 1999. 'Revisiting the commons: Local lessons, global challenges.' *Science* **284**: 278–82.

Ostrom, E. 1990. *Governing the Commons. The Evolution of Institutions for Collective Action*. Cambridge University Press, Cambridge.

Parker, I.S.C. & Archer, A.L. 1970. 'The status of elephant, other wildlife and cattle in MGR with management recommendations.' A Wildlife Services Ltd report to the Tanzanian Government.

Parker, K.W. 1951. 'A method for measuring trend in range condition on national forest ranges.' US Forest Service, Washington, DC, mimeo.

Peacock, C.P. 1987. 'Herd movement on a Maasai group ranch in relation to traditional organisation and livestock development.' *Agricultural Administration and Extension* **27**: 61–74.

Peden, D.G. 1984. *Livestock and Wildlife Inventories by District in Kenya, 1977–1983*. KREMU, Nairobi.

Pellew, R. 1983. 'The impacts of elephant, giraffe and fire on the *Acacia* woodlands of the Serengeti.' *Afr. J. Ecol.* **21**: 41–74.

Peluso, N.L. 1993. 'Coercing conservation? The politics of state resource control.' *Global Environmental Change* **June** 199–217.

Perlov, D.C. 1987. 'Trading for influence: The social and cultural economics of livestock marketing among the highland Samburu of northern Kenya.' Unpublished Ph.D. thesis, University of California, Los Angeles.

Péron, X. 1995. *L'occidentalisation des Maasai du Kenya. Privatisation foncière et destruction sociale.* Editions L'Harmattan, Paris.

Pielou, E.C. 1975. *Ecological Diversity.* Wiley, New York.

Pimbert, M.P. & Pretty, J.N. 1996. 'Parks, people and professionals: putting "participation" into protected area management.' In B.K. Ghimire & M.P. Pimbert (eds) *Social Change and Conservation.* Earthscan Publications Limited, London.

Potkanski, T. 1997. 'Pastoral concepts, herding patterns and management of natural resources among the Ngorongoro and Salei Maasai of Tanzania.' *Pastoral Land Tenure Series,* **Monograph 2**. International Institute for Environment and Development, London.

Pratt, D.J. and Gwynne, M.D. 1977. *Rangeland Management and Ecology in East Africa.* Hodder & Stoughton, London.

Prendergast, J.R., Wood, S.N., Lawton, J.H. & Eversham, B.C. 1993. 'Correcting for variation in recording effort in analyses of diversity hotspots.' *Biodiversity Letters* **1**: 39–53.

Prins, H.H.T. 1992. 'The pastoral road to extinction: Competition between wildlife and traditional pastoralism in East Africa'. *Environmental Conservation* **19**: 117–23.

Proctor, J.D. 1998. 'The social construction of nature: Relativist accusations, pragmatist and critical realist responses.' *Annals of the Association of American Geographers* **88**: 352–76.

Raikes, P.L. 1981. *Livestock Development and Policy in East Africa.* Scandanavian Institute of African Studies, Uppsala.

Ribot, J. 1998. 'Theorising access: Forest profits along Senegal's charcoal commodity chain.' *Development and Change* **29**: 307–41.

Rigby, P. 1985. *Persistent Pastoralists. Nomadic Societies in Transition.* Zed Books, London.

Robinette, W. Leslie & Gilbert, V.C. 1968. 'Appraisal of range conditions for livestock in Umba River Area adjacent to Mkomazi Game Reserve.' TNA, File G1/7.

Roe, E. 1991. 'Development narratives, or making the best of blueprint development.' *World Development* **19**: 287–300.

Rogers, P., Brockington, D., Kiwasila, H. & Homewood, K. 1999. 'Environmental awareness and conflict genesis: People versus parks in Mkomazi Game Reserve.' In T. Granfelt (ed.) *Managing the Globalised Environment.* Intermediate Technology Publications, London.

Roth, E.A. 1996. 'Traditional pastoral strategies in a modern world: An example from northern Kenya.' *Human Organisation* **55**: 219–24.

Russell-Smith, A., Davies, J., McGavin, G. & Kruger, O. 1997 *Invertebrate biodiversity of the Mkomazi Game Reserve, Tanzania.* Final technical report for the Darwin Initiative Funded project. Royal Geographical Society, London.

Rutten, M.M.E.M. 1992. *Selling Wealth to Buy Poverty. The Process of the Individualisation of Landownership among the Maasai Pastoralists of Kajiado District, Kenya, 1890–1990.* Nijmegen Studies in Development and Cultural Change **10**. Verlag Breitenbach Publishers, Saarbrucken and Fort Lauderdale, FL.

Sandford, S. 1983. *Management of Pastoral Development in the Third World.* Wiley, Chichester.

Schama, S. 1996. *Landscape and Memory.* Fontana Press, London.

Scoones, I. 1995. *Living with Uncertainty. New Directions in Pastoral Development in Africa.* IT Publications, London.

Scott, J.C. 1985. *Weapons of the Weak. Everyday Forms of Peasant Resistance.* Yale University Press, New Haven, CT

Sen, A. 1988. 'Property and hunger.' *Economics and Philosophy* **4**: 57–68.

Shaw-Taylor, L. forthcoming. 'The Hammond–Neeson thesis revisited: Did agricultural labourers have common pasture rights?'

Shepherd, G. 1992. *Managing Africa's Dry Forests: A Review of Indigenous Methods.* Agricultural Occasional Paper **14**. Overseas Development Institute, London.

Shivji, I.G. 1995. 'Problems of land tenure in Tanzania. A review and appraisal of the report of the Presidential Commission of Enquiry into Land Matters.' Paper prepared for the IIED and presented at the Land Policy Workshop held at Arusha 15 – 19 Jan. 1995.

——& Kapinga, W.B. 1998. *Maasai Rights in Ngorongoro, Tanzania.* International Institute for Environment and Development, London and Hakiardhi, Dar es Salaam.

Sikana, P., Kerven, C. & Behnke, R.H. 1993. 'From subsistence to specialised commodity production: commercialisation and pastoral dairying in Africa.' *Pastoral Development Network Paper* **43d**. Overseas Development Institute, London.

Simons, H. & Nicolasen, T. 1994. 'Outreach programme for the Mkomazi Game Reserve.' In N. Leader Williams, J. A. Kayera, & G. L. Overton (eds). *Community-based Conservation in Tanzania: Planning and Assessment for Wildlife Management.* Department of Wildlife, Dar es Salaam.

Sinclair, A.R.E. & Fryxell, J.M. 1985. 'The Sahel of Africa: Ecology of a disaster,' *Canadian Journal of Zoology* **63**: 987–94.

Smith, C.S. 1894. 'The Anglo-German boundary in East Equatorial Africa. Proceedings of the British Commission 1892.' *The Geographical Journal* **4**: 424–435.

Smith, D.M. 2000. *Moral Geographies. Ethics in a World of Difference.* Edinburgh University Press, Edinburgh.

Sobania, N. 1988a. 'Fisherman herders: Subsistence, survival and cultural change in northern Kenya.' *Journal of African History* **29**: 41–56.

——1988b. 'Pastoral migration and colonial policy: A case study from northern Kenya.' In D. Johnson & D.M. Anderson (eds) *The Ecology of Survival. Case Studies from Northeast African History.* Westview Press, Boulder, CO.

——1990. 'Social relationships as an aspect of property rights: Northern Kenya in the pre-colonial and colonial periods.' In P.T.W. Baxter & R. Hogg (eds) *Property, Poverty and People: Changing Rights in Property and Problems of Pastoral Development.* Manchester University Press, Manchester.

——1993. 'Defeat and dispersal. The Laikipiak and their neighbours at the end of the nineteenth century.' In T. Spear and R. Waller (eds) *Being Maasai. Ethnicity and Identity in East Africa.* James Currey, London.

Sommer, G. & Vossen, R. 1993. 'Dialects, sectiolects, or simply lects?' In T. Spear and R. Waller (eds) *Being Maasai. Ethnicity and identity in East Africa.* James Currey, London.

Songorwa, A.N. 1999. 'Community-based wildlife management (CWM) in Tanzania: Are communities interested?' *World Development* **27**: 2061–79.

Southgate, C. & Hulme, D. 1996. 'Land, water and local governance in Kajiado: A district overview.' *Rural Resources, Rural Livelihoods Working Paper Series*, **Paper 3**. Institute for Development Policy and Management, University of Manchester, Manchester.

Spear, T. 1993a. 'Being "Maasai" but not "People of Cattle". Arusha Agricultural Maasai in the Nineteenth Century.' In T. Spear and R. Waller (eds) *Being Maasai. Ethnicity and Identity in East Africa.* James Currey, London.

——1993b. 'Introduction.' In T. Spear and R. Waller (eds) *Being Maasai. Ethnicity and Identity in East Africa.* James Currey, London.

Spear, T. & Waller, R. (eds) 1993. *Being Maasai. Ethnicity & Identity in East Africa.* James Currey, London.

——1997. *Mountain Farmers.* Mkuki na Nyota, Dar es Salaam; James Currey, Oxford; University of California Press, Berkeley, CA.

Spencer, P. 1973. *Nomads in Alliance: Symbiosis and Growth among the Rendille and Samburu of Kenya.* Oxford University Press, London.

——1988. *The Maasai of Matapato. A Study of Rituals of Rebellion.* Manchester University Press for the International African Institute, London.

Spinage, C. 1998. 'Social change and conservation misrepresentation in Africa.' *Oryx* **32**: 265–76.

Spinage, C. 1999. 'A reply to Colchester.' *Oryx* **33**: 5–8.

Star, S.L. & Griesemer, J.R. 1989. 'Institutional ecology, "translations", and boundary objects: Amateurs and professionals in Berkeley's Museum of Vertebrate Zoology, 1907–39.' *Social Studies of Science* **19**: 387–420.

Stattersfield, A.J., Crosby, M.J., Long, A.J. & Wedge, D.C. 1998 *Endemic Bird Areas of the World. Priorities for Biodiversity Conservation.* Birdlife Conservation Series **7**, Birdlife International. Cambridge.

Steinhart, E.I. 1989. 'Hunters, poachers and gamekeepers: Towards a social history of hunting in colonial Kenya.' *Journal of African History* **30**: 247–64.

Struhsaker, T. 1998. 'A biologist's perspective on the role of sustainable harvest in conservation.' *Conservation Biology* **12**: 930–2.

Strum, S.C. 1994. 'Lessons learned.' In D. Western and R.M. Wright (eds) *Natural Connections. Perspectives in Community-based Conservation.* Island Press, Washington, DC.

Sullivan, S. 1996. 'Towards a non-equlibrium ecology: Perspectives from an arid land.' *Journal of Biogeography* **23**: 1–5.

——1998. 'People, plants and practice in Namibian drylands. Socio-political and ecological dimensions of resource-use by Damara farmers in north-west Namibia.' Unpublished PhD thesis, University of London.

——1999 'The impacts of people and livestock on topographically diverse open wood-and-shrublands in arid north-west Namibia.' *Global Ecology and Biogeography Letters* **8**: 257–77.

——2000. 'Getting the science right, or introducing science in the first place? Local "facts", global discourse – "desertification" in north-west Namibia.' In P. Stott & S. Sullivan (eds) *Political Ecology.* Arnold, London.

——& Rohde, R. (forthcoming) 'Non-equilibrium grazing systems: A response to Illius and O'Connor.' *Journal of Biogeography.*

Sutton, J.E.G. 1993. 'Becoming Maasailand.' In T. Spear and R. Waller (eds) *Being Maasai. Ethnicity and Identity in East Africa.* James Currey, London.

Talle, A. 1988. *Women at Loss. Changes in Maasai Pastoralism and their Effects on Gender Relations.* Stockholm Studies in Social Anthropology **19**. Department of Social Anthropology, University of Stockholm.

Tenga, R. 1999. 'Legitimizing dispossession. The Tanzanian High Court's decision on the eviction of Maasai pastoralists from the Mkomazi Game Reserve.' *Cultural Survival Quarterly* **22**: 60–3.

The Times 1997. *Spotlight on Africa.* 25 April.

Thompson, E.P. 1977. *Whigs and Hunters: The Origin of the Black Act.* Penguin, Harmondsworth.

Thomson, J. 1885. Reprinted 1968. *Through Maasailand.* Sampson Low, Marston, Searle & Rivington, London.

Thornton, R.K.R. (ed.) 1997. *John Clare.* J.M. Dent, London.

Tiffen, M., Mortimore, M. & Gichuki, F. 1993. *More People, Less Erosion. Environmental Recovery in Kenya.* Wiley, Chichester.

Turnbull, C.M. 1973. *The Mountain People.* Jonathon Cape, London.

Turner, M. 1998a. 'Long term effects of daily grazing orbits on nutrient availability in Sahelian West Africa I. Gradients in the chemical composition of rangeland soils and vegetation.' *Journal of Biogeography* **25**: 669–82.

——1998b. 'Long term effects of daily grazing orbits on nutrient availability in Sahelian West Africa II. Effects of a phosphorus gradient on spatial patterns of annual grassland production.' *Journal of Biogeography* **25**: 683–94.

——1999. 'Spatial and temporal scaling of grazing impact on the species composition and productivity of Sahelian annual grasslands.' *Journal of Arid Environments* **41** : 277–97.

Turton, D. 1977. 'Response to drought: The Mursi of southwestern Ethiopia.' *Disasters* **1**: 275–87.

——1984. 'Mursi response to drought: Some lessons for relief and rehabilitation.' *Production Pastorale et Société* **15**: 9–18.

——1985. 'Mursi response to drought: Some lessons for relief and rehabilitation.' *African Affairs* **84**: 331–46.

——1987. 'The Mursi and National Park development in the Lower Omo Valley.' In D. Anderson and R. Grove (eds) *Conservation in Africa. People, Policies and Practice.* Cambridge University Press, Cambridge.

——1988. 'Looking for a cool place: The Mursi, 1890s-1980s.' In D. Johnson & D.M. Anderson (eds) *The Ecology of Survival. Case Studies from Northeast African History.* Westview Press, Boulder, CO.

——1995. 'Pastoral livelihoods in danger. Cattle disease, drought, and wildlife conservation in Mursiland, South-Western Ethiopia.' Oxfam Working Paper. Oxfam, Oxford.

——1996. 'Migrants and Refugees. A Mursi Case Study.' In T. Allen (ed.) *In Search of Cool Ground. War, Flight and Homecoming in Northeast Africa.* James Currey, London.

——& Turton, P. 1984. 'Spontaneous resettlement after drought: An Ethiopian case.' *Disasters* **8**: 178–189.

United Republic of Tanzania. 1991. *Report of the Commission of Inquiry into Land Matters. Vol. I. Land Policy and Land Tenure Structure.* United Republic of Tanzania, Dar es Salaam.

United Republic of Tanzania. 1993. *Report of the Commission of Inquiry into Land Matters. Vol. II. Selected Land Disputes and Recommendations.* United Republic of Tanzania, Dar es Salaam.

Von Hohnel, L. 1894. *Discovery of Lakes Rudolf and Stefanie. A Narrative of Count Sammual Teleki's Exploring and Hunting Expedition in Eastern Equatorial Africa in 1887–1888.* Translated by N. Bell. Longmans, Green, London.

Von Lettow-Vorbeck. 1920. *My Reminiscences of East Africa.* Hurst & Blackett, London.

Wainwight, C. & Wehrmeyer, W. 1998. 'Success in integrating conservation and development? A study from Zambia.' *World Development* **26**: 933–44.

Wakefield, T. 1870. 'Routes of native caravans from the coast to the interior of Eastern Africa, chiefly from information given by Sadi Bin

Ahedi, a native of a district near Gazi, in Udigo, a little north of Zanzibar.' *Journal of the Royal Geographical Society* **40**: 303–39.

Waller, R. 1976. 'The Maasai and the British, 1895–1905: The origins of an alliance.' *Journal of African History* **17**: 529–53.

——1979. 'The lords of East Africa. The Maasai in the mid-nineteenth century, 1840–85.' Unpublished Ph.D. thesis, University of Cambridge.

——1984. 'Interaction and identity on the periphery: The Trans-Mara Maasai.' *International Journal of African Historical Studies* **17**: 243–84.

——1985a. 'Ecology, migration and expansion in East Africa.' *African Affairs* **84**: 347–70.

——1985b. 'Economic and social relations in the Central Rift Valley: The Maa-speakers and their neighbours in the Nineteenth Century.' In A. Ogot (ed.) *Kenya in the Nineteenth Century*. Bookwise, Nairobi.

——1986. 'Research on Maasai history.' Unpublished report to the Economic & Social Research Council, London.

——1988. '*Emutai*: Crisis and response in Maasailand, 1883–1902.' In D. Johnson & D.M. Anderson (eds) *The Ecology of Survival. Case Studies from Northeast African History*. Westview Press, Boulder, CO.

——1993. 'Acceptees and aliens: Kikuyu settlement in Maasailand.' In T. Spear & R. Waller (eds) *Being Maasai. Ethnicity and Identity in East Africa*. James Currey, London.

——& Homewood, K.M. 1997. 'Elders and experts: Contesting veterinary knowledge in a pastoral community.' In A. Cunningham and B. Andrews (eds) *Western Medicine as Contested Knowledge*. Manchester University Press, Manchester.

—& Sobania, N. 1994. 'Pastoralism in historical perspective.' In E. Fratkin, K.A. Galvin and E.A. Roth (eds) *African Pastoralists Systems, An Integrated Approach*. Lynne Rienner, Boulder, CO and London.

Watson, R.M. 1991. 'Mkomazi – restoring Africa.' *Swara* **14**: 14–6.

Watson, R.M., Parker, I.S.C & Allan, T. 1969. 'A census of elephant and other large mammals in the Mkomazi region of northern Tanzania and southern Kenya.' *E. Afr. Wildl. J.* **7**: 11–26.

Watts, M. 1991. 'Entitlements or empowerment? Famine and starvation in Africa.' *Review of African Political Economy* **51**: 9–26.

Wells, M., Brandon, K. & Hannah, L. 1992 *People and Parks: Linking Protected Area Management with Local Communities*. The World Bank, Washington, D.C.

West, P.C. & Brechin, S.R. 1991. *Resident Peoples and National Parks*. University of Arizona Press, Tuscon, AZ.

Western, D. 1982. 'The environment and ecology of pastoralists in arid savannas.' *Development & Change* **13**: 183–211.

——1994. 'Ecosystem conservation and rural development: The case of Amboseli.' In D. Western & R.M. Wright (eds) *Natural Connections:*

Perspectives in Community-based Conservation. Island Press, Washington, DC.

——& Finch, V. 1986. 'Cattle and pastoralism: Survival and production in arid lands.' *Human Ecology* **14**: 77–94.

——& Pearl, M., Pimm, S.L., Walker, D., Atkinson, I. & Woodruff, D. 1989. 'An agenda for conservation action'. In D. Western & M.C. Pearl (eds) *Conservation for the Twenty-first Century.* Oxford University Press, Oxford & New York.

——& Ssemakula, J. 1981. 'The future of savanna ecosystems.' *Afr. J. Ecol.* **19**: 7–19.

——& van Praet, C. 1973. 'Cyclical changes in the habitat and climate of an East African ecosystem.' *Nature* **241**: 104–6.

——& Wright, R.M. 1994. 'The Background to Community-based Conservation.' In D. Western and R.M. Wright (eds) *Natural Connections: Perspectives in Community-based Conservation.* Island Press, Washington, DC.

Westoby, M., Walker, B.H. & Noy-Mier, I. 1989. 'Opportunistic management for rangelands not at equilibrium.' *Journal of Rangeland Management.* **42**: 266–74.

White, F. 1983. *The Vegetation of Africa. A Descriptive Memoir to Accompany the UNESCO-AETFAT-UNSO Vegetation Map of Africa.* UNESCO, Paris.

White, J.M. & Meadows, S.J. 1981. *Evaluation of the Contribution of Group and Individual Ranches in Kajiado District, Kenya, to Economic Development and Pastoral Production Strategies.* Ministry of Livestock and Development, Nairobi.

Wijngaarden, W. van. 1985. *Elephants – Trees – Grass – Grazers.* ITC Publication **4**, Dept of Natural Resources, Surveys and Rural Development of the International Institute for Aerospace Survey and Earth Sciences, ITC, Enschede, Netherlands.

Wildlife Conservation and Management Department. 1988. 'Tsavo Elephant Count, 1988.' Wildlife Conservation and Monitoring Department, Ministry of Tourism and Wildlife, Government of Kenya.

Wildlife Sector Review Task Force. 1995. *A Review of the Wildlife Sector in Tanzania. Volume 1: Assessment of the Current Situation.* Ministry of Tourism, Natural Resources and the Environment, Dar es Salaam.

Williams, J., Arlott, N. & Fennessy, R. 1981. *National Parks of East Africa.* Collins Field Guide. Harper Collins, London.

Willis, J. 1992. 'The makings of a tribe: Bondei identities and histories.' *Journal of African History* **33**: 191–208.

Willoughby, J.C. 1889. *East Africa and its Big Game. The Narrative of a Sporting Trip from Zanzibar to the Borders of the Maasai.* Green & Co., London.

Wøien, H. & Lama, L. 1999. 'Market commerce as wildlife protector? Commercial initiatives in community conservation in Tanzania's northern rangelands.' *Pastoral Land Tenure Series* **12**. International Institute for Environment and Development, London.

World Commission on the Environment and Development (WCED) 1997. *Our Common Future*. Oxford University Press, Oxford.

Young, R. 1962. *Through Maasailand with Joseph Thomson*. Northwestern University Press, Evanston, IL.

Zaal, F. & Dietz, T. 1999. 'Of markets, meat, maize and milk. Pastoral commoditization in Kenya.' In D. Anderson and V. Broch-Due (eds). *The Poor are Not Us. Poverty & Pastoralism in Eastern Africa.* James Currey, Oxford and Ohio University Press, Athens, OH.

Zaba, B. 1985. *Measurement of Emigration using Indirect Techniques. Manual for the Collection and Analysis of Data on Residence of Relatives*. Ordina Editions, Liège.

Zwanenberg, R.M.A. van with King, A. 1975. *An Economic History of Kenya and Uganda 1800–1970*. Macmillan Press, London.

INDEX